HOW EDUCATIONAL IDEOLOGIES ARE SHAPING GLOBAL SOCIETY

Intergovernmental Organizations, NGOs, and the Decline of the Nation-State

Sociocultural, Political, and Historical Studies in Education
Joel Spring, Editor

HOW EDUCATIONAL IDEOLOGIES ARE SHAPING GLOBAL SOCIETY

Intergovernmental Organizations, NGOs, and the Decline of the Nation-State

Joel Spring
Queens College
City University of New York

(HAR)
LC
1090
S67
2004

 LAWRENCE ERLBAUM ASSOCIATES, PUBLISHERS
2004   Mahwah, New Jersey   London

Copyright © 2004 by Lawrence Erlbaum Associates, Inc.
All rights reserved. No part of this book may be reproduced in any form, by photostat, microform, retrieval system, or any other means, without prior written permission of the publisher.

Lawrence Erlbaum Associates, Inc., Publishers
10 Industrial Avenue
Mahwah, New Jersey 07430

Cover design by Kathryn Houghtaling Lacey

Library of Congress Cataloging-in-Publication Data

Spring, Joel H.
How educational ideologies are shaping global society : intergovernmental organizations, NGOs, and the decline of the nation-state / Joel Spring.
    p. cm. — (Sociocultural, political, and historical studies in education)
Includes bibliographical references and index.
ISBN 0-8058-4915-7 (cloth : alk. paper)
ISBN 0-8058-4916-5 (pbk. : alk. paper)
1. International education. 2. Education and state. 3. Nationalism and education. 4. Intergovernmental cooperation.
I. Title. II. Series.

LC1090.S67 2004
370.116—dc22
                                               2004041155
                                                    CIP

Books published by Lawrence Erlbaum Associates are printed on acid-free paper, and their bindings are chosen for strength and durability.

Printed in the United States of America
10 9 8 7 6 5 4 3 2 1

Contents

Preface

Similar forms of schooling are appearing around the globe as the nation-state slowly erodes under the power of a growing global civil society. Traditional forms of nationalist education attempt to mold loyal and patriotic citizens who are emotionally attached to symbols of the state. However, the pressures of globalization are forcing nation–states to reconsider these nationalist educational goals. These changes are fueled by a clash between the free market and consumer-based ideas of neoliberals and human rights and environmental educators. Neoliberals assume that the good society is based on economic growth and consumerism and that it can be achieved through competition in a free global market. In this framework, students are educated for the needs of the workplace and the insecurities of a global market, which includes mass migrations of workers. Throughout this book, I quote Michael Hardt and Antonio Negri's statement, *"A specter haunts the world and it is the specter of migration."*[1] A result of the mass migration of world labor is a call for multicultural education to stabilize an international workforce. In addition, the mass migration of labor is undercutting the traditional cultural unity of the nation state. Neoliberal educational policies are attempting to prepare workers for both a multicultural workplace and the destabilizing effects of mass migration.

In contrast to neoliberals, human rights educators are more concerned with the education of activist global citizens. Inherent in human rights doctrines is a collective responsibility to ensure the rights of all people. Therefore, human rights educators tend to reject the economic individualism of the free market for a socially responsible person who works to ensure that all people have the right to shelter, health care, education, and a living wage. By teaching students to protect the rights of others, human rights educators are contributing to the growth of a global civil society that shares a common set of ethical standards.

Today, environmentalists are the most radical educators because they reject the industrial and consumerist paradigm that has dominated most economic thought, including capitalism and communism. Central to environmental education is the concept of the biosphere and Deep Ecology. The biosphere paradigm prepares students to see a world where there is a close interrelationship and dependence between all animal and plant species, and the land, water, and air. Rather than the good society being measured by economic growth and the consumption of products, the biosphere paradigm envisions a good society based on the quality of the environment and the equality of animal and plant species. Two key terms among environmental educators are *sustainable development* and *sustainable consumption*. Similar to human rights educators, environmental teachers are contributing to the growth of a global civil society that might share common ethical standards.

OVERVIEW

In chapter 1, I use Singapore as an example of a strong nation-state changing its nationalist school system to educate a patriotic worker-citizen trained for participation in a global economy. As nation-states adapt their schools to global requirements other nongovernmental organizations are spreading global educational ideologies. In chapter 2, I use the example of the World Bank to discuss the spread of a neoliberal educational ideology that emphasizes training workers for a competitive global free market. In chapter 3, I discuss the worldwide network of human rights and peace educators who are teaching a global set of ethics. Environmentalism, as I discuss in chapters 4 and 5, is aiding the effort by educators to create a common set of standards for global behavior. In chapter 6, I examine the educational implications of the argument that what is occurring is a global struggle between civilizations rather than an evolution to a peaceful global civil society. In this last chapter, after a discussion of the idea of a clash of civilizations, and religious and language differences in a global society, I affirm my belief in the truly radical nature of environmental education.

ACKNOWLEDGMENTS

I would like to thank the following for their help in conceptualizing this book: Timothy Reagan, University of Connecticut, and Terence G. Wiley, Arizona State University.

Nationalist Education in the Age of Globalization: Global Workers Carrying Their Nations in Their Hearts

Strong nation-states, such as Singapore and the United States, are adjusting their educational systems to prepare workers for a global economy. However, these governments still want their educational systems to stress loyalty to the nation-state and to teach citizenship within the framework of the needs of government. This is in sharp contrast to other educational trends which advocate citizenship as a function of a global civil society. The current goal of strong nation-states is embodied in the Singapore government's goal of educating global workers who carry their nation in their hearts.

In this chapter, I examine the relationship of education to the nation-state within the context of a globalizing economic and political system. Along with providing background on the relationship between schooling and the nation-state, I focus on Singapore as a contemporary example of the attempt to retain a strong sense of nation while participating in the global economy.

By nation-state, I mean a territory with fixed geographic boundaries where the citizens are united in recognition of a central governing body which claims to represent the will of the people. The unification of the people is dependent on the common experience of school attendance with its accompanying rituals of nation building. Singapore is a recent nation-state. It was conceived as part of the globalizing project of the British empire in the 19th century as a crossroad for transportation and the warehousing of goods. After becoming an independent nation in 1966, it is now a center of global economics. Its recent birth provides a good example of the role of schooling in uniting a people and creating a sense of nationhood. Singapore exemplifies the spread of Western models of the nation and of schooling.

WESTERN MODELS OF THE NATION-STATE AND SCHOOLING

For better or worse, Western models of the nation-state and schooling now dominate global discussions of education. Consequently, it is these models that first must be examined before considering how to achieve a form of education that is beneficial to all of humanity. The establishment of the Western-style nation-state, which included the creation of national school systems, occurred at the same time that Western colonialism engulfed the world from the 18th through the 20th centuries. Western colonial powers transported their schools across the oceans. In order to combat the spread of European colonialism, Japan adopted the Western educational model in the 19th century as part of its attempt to strengthen its nation-state to resist Western imperialism. In turn, Japan transported its model to other Asian nations as it extended its empire. Consequently, Western models overwhelmed indigenous educational models in Australia, Asia, Africa, and the Americas. Islam remained a major alternative, but even many of its leaders studied in Western universities. Also, indigenous groups continued to resist by protecting and, in some cases, restoring traditional educational methods.

The Western model of schooling involves mass compulsory education funded by the government and serving the needs of the nation. In this model, the content of education is determined by public interests and needs as opposed to purely individual, religious, or cultural concerns. Education takes place in a specified building where children are separated from other adults except for adult teachers and school administrators. This creates a separate society of children with its own rituals and customs. In classrooms, students are taught using standardized methods and according to a standardized curriculum. The major source of instruction is the textbook, specifically written for classroom use, which reflects the requirements of a standardized curriculum. Separating children from the community and placing them in a controlled environment provides the opportunity to mold entire generations to serve political and economic interests.

These separated communities of children are the incubators of the modern nation-state. Western-style schooling is now so universally accepted that few can imagine alternative models. However, with globalization, the desire for free movement of goods, money, and workers is reducing the importance of the nation-building aspects of Western education.

Schooling supports the political needs of the nation-state through educating and disciplining a loyal, patriotic citizenry imbued with nationalism and acceptant of the legitimacy of the state. A public school system strengthens a nation-state by culturally unifying sometimes multicultural and multilingual populations existing within its territorial boundaries. Citizens must be convinced of the validity of the state's territorial boundaries because they are politically constructed and might not reflect any meaningful geographical division. Also, a nation-state depends on citizens believing in the legitimacy of its government's organization and actions. Consequently, public school systems serve the nation-state by creating a shared experience as students; developing a sense of nationhood and a common culture through teaching a national history and literature; instilling emotional loyalty to the nation-state through patriotic exercises, flag salutes, and nationalistic rhetoric and song; and educating a citizenry that accepts the legitimacy of the government and their own political role within the system. Also, the nation-state is built on a particular economic system which requires public schools to teach a commitment to maintaining that economic arrangement and training to fit into the economic infrastructure. In summary, the nation-state uses education to prepare a disciplined citizen and worker.

The 1973 Syrian Constitution highlights the influence of the Western utilization of education to support the nation-state. The early leaders of Arab nationalism, who influenced the content of the Syrian Constitution, studied in Germany where they encountered the ideas of national socialism. For instance, Sati' al-Husri argued that national education was key to building Arab nationalism. Born into a Syrian family in Yemen in 1882, he studied education in Paris, Switzerland, and Belgium. Attracted to German romantic notions of nationalism, Al-Husri argued that history was the consciousness of a nation while language was its soul. During World War I, he was appointed Ottoman Director of Education in Syria. Eventually, he became chair of Arab Nationalism at the Institute for Advanced Arab Studies. His writings became compulsory readings in nationalist school systems throughout the Arab world. His ideas are included in many of the constitutions of the Arab world. He believed national education was the key to revitalizing the Arab world and awakening the oppressed people of the Islamic world. He argued that the teaching of history should emphasize the "glorious past in order to provide a basis for the national awakening."[1] He wrote, "The struggle for the national awakening requires much more effort and hardship to spread belief in the nation, and all available means must be used to strengthen this belief."[2]

The following articles from the 1973 Syrian Constitution reflect Sati' al-Husri's influence on Arab nationalism, and in turn, Western influence on the role of education in supporting the nation-state.

Article 21 [Goals] The educational and cultural system aims at creating a socialist nationalist Arab generation which is scientifically minded and attached
to its history and land, proud of its heritage, and filled with the spirit of struggle to achieve its nation's objectives of unity, freedom, and socialism, and to
serve humanity and its progress.

Article 22 [Progress] The educational system has to guarantee the people's
continuous progress and adapt itself to the ever-developing social, economic,
and cultural requirements of the people.

Article 23 [Socialist Education, Arts, Sports] The nationalist socialist education is the basis for building the unified socialist Arab society. It seeks to
strengthen moral values, to achieve the higher ideals of the Arab nation, to develop the society, and to serve the causes of humanity. The state undertakes to
encourage and to protect this education.[3]

The Syrian Constitutions provides one of many examples of the use of
schools to promote the cause of the nation-state. In this context, schools
are to educate Syrians who are "scientifically minded and attached to its
history and land, proud of its heritage, and filled with the spirit of struggle
to achieve its nation's objectives ... [and build a] a unified socialist Arab society."

To understand education's role in the pursuit of these goals, one must
realize that Syria is an entity imagined and invented by human beings. Consequently, its citizens must be taught to believe in the existence of a culture
defined by the territorial boundaries of the nation and by a common history. The acceptance of this common culture and history makes it possible
for citizens to imagine and feel a relationship to other citizens. It is the basis
for achieving a "unified socialist society."

Prior to the development of public schools and newspapers, people in
separate communities shared few common experiences and had little opportunity to imagine themselves part of a nation and having common
bonds with others. With the spread of newspapers and schools in the 19th
century, people were connected by shared news events, a reading of common school books, and instruction in national history and literature. These
common experiences provided the intellectual material for people to imagine the existence of common bonds between peoples within the territorial
limits of a nation-state.

Architects of the nation-state recognized the importance of galvanizing the
population into an imagined whole. Jean Jacques Rousseau is one important
example of an 18th-century political theorist who considered mass education
essential to the development of the nation-state. In his 1772 *Considerations on
the Government of Poland* he stated, "It is education that should put the national
stamp on men's minds and give the direction to their opinions and tastes which
will make them patriots.... National education is the privilege of free men who
share common interests and are united under law."[4]

According to Rousseau, education helps develop the "popular sovereignty" and "general will" as the foundation of the nation-state. Neither of these concepts has a concrete existence. Each is purely imaginary and presumes that a group of people sharing a common territory are collectively more than their individual lives. The imagined and intangible qualities of "popular sovereignty" and "general will" are highlighted in his educational treatise *Emile* (1762). While this book is devoted to the education of a single individual, Emile, Rousseau argued that individual freedom can only be achieved through the general will.

The relationship between education, freedom, and the general will is discussed in the final stage of Rousseau's plan for Emile's education. Rousseau sends his student on a tour of other countries, in part, to examine different types of governments. Rousseau explains that the nation-state is formed by a social contract among individuals. In forming a social contract, according to Rousseau, individuals merge into an organic whole. It is this imagined organic whole that forms the popular sovereignty and exerts the general will. Rousseau stated that the social contract

> produces a moral and collective body, consisting of as many members as there are votes in the Assembly. This public personality is usually called the *body politic*, which is called by its members the *State* when it is passive, and the *Sovereign* when it is active, and a *Power* when compared with its equals. With regard to the members themselves, collectively they are known as the *nation*, and individually as *citizens*....[5]

Within this political construct, the nation is an amalgam of *citizens* whose public personality is the *body politic*. This is the almost mystical language of the nation-state which is governed by abstract entities such as the *public* and *popular sovereignty*. The *public* and the *body politic* are continually reconstituted as territorial boundaries expand and contract, and people migrate in and out of the nation. During this process, the person and the nation become inseparable. In reference to Emile's education, Rousseau writes, "Individuals having only submitted themselves to the sovereign, and the sovereign power being only the general will, we shall see that every man in obeying the sovereign only obeys himself, how much freer are we under the social pact than in the state of nature."[6] Within this paradigm, citizens gain their freedom through the collective being of the nation.

Similar to religion, people have to be taught to believe in the existence of the *public*, *popular sovereignty*, the *body politic*, and the *nation*. If fact, the very existence of these abstractions requires people to imagine them and to believe in them. They do not exist outside individual minds. Referring to the fully educated Emile, Rousseau stated, "The public good, which to others is a mere pretext, is a real motive for him [Emile]. He learns to fight against himself and to prevail, to sacrifice his own interest to the common weal."[7]

While Emile describes the education of an individual, Rousseau in other writings applied these concepts to the mass schooling of citizens for the nation-state. In his 1755 article, "Political Economy," Rousseau argued that national education should submerge the identity of students into the collective identity of the nation-state. In this manner, individual will cannot be separated from the *general will*. He argued, "If from infancy children are led to think of their personal interests as completely bound up with the interests of the state and never to regard their own existence as having any meaning apart from it, they will come in time to identify themselves in some measure with the grand Whole and become conscious members of their country."[8]

Education, Rousseau argued, must be a function of the nation-state and the "subject matter, sequence and character of their [the students'] studies should be regulated by law."[9] Public schooling must replace private and parental forms of education. "Public education, regulated by the state," Rousseau maintained, "under magistrates appointed by the supreme authority, is an essential condition of popular government."[10] He warned that education should not be left to "ignorance and prejudice of fathers" because the "matter is of far greater concern to the state than to the fathers. The state abides, the family passes."[11]

In *Considerations on the Government of Poland*, Rousseau argued that creation of a national identity is essential to survival of the state. Through education, games, festivals, and ceremonies, Poles need to develop an identity that separates them from the *others* or *foreigners*. He applied this same argument to all nations. This national identity, he argued, can be achieved by having students study national history and literature, and the lives of national figures whose biographies have transformed them into mythical heroes. Of course, these are invented and imagined national histories, literatures, and mythical heroes. Also, geography should be taught so that the student can image the territorial borders of the nation-state. In his prescription for inculcating into the student an allegiance to a national identity, Rousseau anticipated standard parts of nationalistic forms of education.

> When he is learning to read I would have him read about his own country, At ten he should be acquainted with all its products: at twelve with all its provinces, roadways and towns. At fifteen he should know all its history: as sixteen all its laws. There should not be a noble deed or distinguished man in all Poland but are so enshrined in heart and memory that he can give instant account of them.[12]

Rousseau's educational dictates can be found in the example of the Syrian Constitution and all forms of education for the nation-state. The goal of Syrian schools is to teach the students to imagine themselves as part of the *public* or *body politic* that constitutes the nation. As stated in the Constitution, students learn to submit their will to the nation and to sacrifice themselves for the public good. The student is "filled with the spirit of struggle to achieve its nation's objectives of unity, freedom, and socialism." Similar to Rousseau's argument, the student gains her/his "freedom" through obeying the will of the nation. Obedience to the nation is construed as the same thing as obedience to the self.

NATIONAL SCHOOLING AND THE SECULAR RELIGION OF THE STATE

As noted historian George Mosse wrote regarding early ideas about the nation-state, "The nation ... was now said to be based upon the people themselves, on their general will .... The worship of the people thus became the worship of the nation, and the new politics sought to express this unity through the creation of a political style which became, in reality, a secularized religion."[13] An important aspect of the secularized religion of the nation-state is the use of symbols to represent the intangible entities of the *people* and *nation*. Since the 19th century, the flag has a central symbolic representation. Mosse wrote, "The concept of the general will lend itself to the creation of myths and their symbols. The new politics attempted to draw the people into active participation in the national mystique through rites and festivals, myths and symbols which gave a concrete expression to the general will."[14]

The ritualistic flag ceremony and singing of the national anthem are shown in the contemporary Chinese movie *Not One Less*. Focusing on the need to improve rural education, the film shows the mayor and the teacher outside a mud-walled, one-room schoolhouse organizing the children for the flag ceremony. The children start to sing the national anthem, but the mayor interrupts by calling for the display of the national flag. A student runs into the school room for the flag, and then several students raise it slowly up a pole. The students stand at attention with their right arms raised in a salute and sing,

> Rise up!
> We are no man's slave,
> Together we will build a great new wall ....
> Together we have one goal!

The nation-state, or more specifically the Emperor state, was born in Japan with the introduction of Western-style mass schooling in the 19th century. Mass education provided the opportunity for transferring the population's loyalties from the family and clan to the nation-state. Concerned with the moral effects of education, the Japanese government issued the 1879 *Imperial Rescript: The Great Principles of Education* which lamented,

"Although we set out to take in the best features of the West and bring in new things … this procedure had a serious defect: It reduced benevolence, justice, loyalty and filial piety to a secondary position."[15] The document called for a stress on moral education, which includes worship of the nation-state as embodied in the emperor. Concerning the Imperial Rescript, Teruhisa Horio wrote, "It was a masterful formulation of the moral base created to mandate the switch in people's loyalties from family and clan to Emperor and nation …. Thus the Emperor-State was created and education made into one of its more important structural functions."[16]

In place of the flag salute, students and teachers in early Japanese schools were required to bow to the portrait of the Emperor. The national school system was a crucial factor in the operation of the Emperor-State. The Emperor was the source of the national morality to be taught through schools. By making the Emperor the foundation of the new national morality, educational leaders believed they were compensating for the ability of Western nations to use Christianity to demand moral obedience. In other words, the school ritual of bowing became a religious ritual honoring the nation-state. The ancient belief in "a single line of Emperors from time immemorial" merged with the belief in an "essential national polity."[17]

Twentieth-century totalitarian states, such as Germany, the Soviet Union, and Italy, represent the most extreme examples of the usage of schools to promote the worship of the people and the nation. School rituals—including flag salutes, the singing of national anthems, the hanging of the leader's picture on the wall in front of the class, the study of national history, assemblies devoted to national songs and pledges, and student marches—all served to promote the secularized religion of the nation-state.

Totalitarian countries seek total control by going beyond the school into the family to promote worship of the nation. The great Soviet educator Anton Makarenko stated, "The decisive factor in successful family upbringing lies in the constant active and conscious fulfillment by parents of their civic duty towards Soviet society. In those cases where this duty is really felt by parents, where it forms the basis of their daily lives, there it necessarily guides the family's work of upbringing too."[18] Makarenko worried about the good citizens who did not realize that they should translate their civic duties into the process of childrearing. For Makarenko, the same methods that made the good citizen should be used to make the good child. In this manner, the child's personality would become inseparable from the *people* of the Soviet *nation*.

The religious nature of the U.S. Pledge of Allegiance highlights the sacred qualities associated with the ideas of the *people*, the *body politic*, the *popular sovereignty*, the *general will*, and the *nation*. The U.S. government made explicit the mystical qualities of the nation-state by including the word *God* in its Pledge of Allegiance. Chanted in classrooms by schoolchildren around the country, the U.S. Pledge of Allegiance imbues students with the godlike and mystical qualities of the state. Originally, the U.S. Pledge of Allegiance was introduced in 1890s without the word *God*. The goal was to develop in immigrant school children an emotional attachment to the American nation-state. It was to give them a sense that they were part of the collective enterprise and spirit of the state. The original pledge was written in 1892 by socialist Francis Bellamy who wanted to include the word *equality* as a method for pushing his personal political agenda. However, school superintendents at the time objected to the word *equality* because they opposed political equality for women and African Americans. Standing before the U.S. flag with their hands raised in various positions (after the 1940s, the right hand placed over the heart became the favored position), schoolchildren across the country school chanted in unison: "I pledge allegiance to my Flag and to the Republic for which it stands, one nation, indivisible, with liberty and justice for all." Worrying that immigrant children might confuse the phrase "my flag" with allegiance to the flag of the country from which they had immigrated, the American Legion and the Daughters of the American Revolution insisted that "my flag" become "the flag of the United States."[19]

In the context of globalization, one can understand the concerns of the American Legion and the Daughters of the American Revolution. Immigrant schoolchildren can easily become confused as they move from one nation-state to another, with each nation claiming their loyalties and trying to educate them into believing that their personalities are inseparable from the body politic of the nation. From this perspective, immigration involves a painful bodily and mental separation to be followed by a merger of self into the body politic of another nation. The public schools provide the means for political rebirth and healing.

In the 1950s, the Pledge of Allegiance underwent another transformation that raised the U.S. nationalism to new religious heights. In 1954, it was recommended that the phrase "under God" be added to the Pledge. The new Pledge referred to "one nation, under God." Congressional legislation supporting the change declared that the goal was to "acknowledge the dependence of our people and our Government upon ... the Creator ... [and] deny the atheistic and materialistic concept of communism."[20] For similar reasons, Congress in 1955 added the words "In God We Trust" to all paper money.

The deification of the nation-state continued into the 21st century after attempts were made to remove "one nation, under God" from the Pledge of Allegiance. In reaction to these attempts, U.S. Supreme Court Justice Antonin Scalia claimed that people were going overboard in trying to keep God out of government. As main speaker at the January 12, 2003 Religious Freedom Day celebration, Scalia declared, according to *The New York Times*, that "the framers [of the U.S. Constitution] had not intended for God to be stripped from public life. 'That is contrary to our whole tradition,' he said, mentioning as examples the words 'in God we trust' that appear on currency, presidential Thanksgiving proclamations, Congressional chaplains and tax exemption for places of worship."[21]

The deification of the nation-state is exemplified in U.S. President George W. Bush's 2003 State of the Union Address. Bush referred to the nation's "calling," a term which refers to the Christian concept of a personal religious mission. The speech personifies the nation and gives it a collective calling linked to imperial expansion: "As *our nation moves* troops and builds alliances to make our world safer, we must also remember *our calling as a blessed country is to make this world better* [emphasis added]."[22] Throughout the speech, the nation is treated as a living being capable of receiving religious blessings and guidance: "May he guide us now, and may God continue to bless the United States of America .... We do not know—we do not claim to know all the ways of Providence, yet we can trust in them, placing our confidence in the loving God behind all of life and all of history. May he guide us now, and may God continue to bless the United States of America."[23]

In summary, public schools are an essential ingredient in the birth of the nation-state. They are necessary for creating a common experience that gives individuals membership in the *people* and *nation*. I cannot overemphasize the importance of this common experience, particularly before the advent of mass media. In the shared experience of schooling, students engage in the rituals of statehood through flag salutes, anthems, nationalist songs, and marches. Performed in groups, these state rituals link the individual to the idea of a collective *people*. The intangible ideas of the *public*, the *popular sovereignty*, the *body politic* and the *nation* become realities in the imagination and emotions of the student. Obedience to the rules of the school is preparation for obedience to the rules of the state. The school disciplines the student into accepting the discipline of the state.

The teaching of national histories and literature convince the student that the territorial boundaries of the state are the real territorial boundaries of the *people*. The student is taught that they are separate and different from those living outside the borders of their nation-state. Students are taught to think of those living within the territorial boundaries of their state as their *people* while all those outside the state's boundaries are the *others* or *foreigners*. Thinking and feeling that one belongs to a nation's *people* interferes with thinking that one belongs to humanity. By dividing the world into separate *peoples*, rather than one humanity, schools contribute to war, racism, and other forms of inhuman and unjust actions.

THE NATION-STATE AND GLOBALIZATION

The nation-state is being weakened, as I discuss in detail throughout this book, by global regulatory organizations, global mass media, and the global flow of populations. Intergovernmental and nongovernmental organizations are increasingly playing a role in establishing and enforcing global laws and regulating economic transactions. These organizations are advocating a variety of educational causes ranging from schooling for human capital development to education for the protection of human rights. These differing ideologies are receiving support from a number of global organizations and economic trends. For instance, specific educational ideologies are being advanced by international organizations, such as the World Bank, the Organization for Economic Cooperation and Development (OECD), and the United Nations Educational, Scientific and Cultural Organization (UNESCO); and nongovernment organizations (NGOs), such as human rights education groups. In addition, educational policies are reaching across the traditional borders of the nation-state with the growth of regional trading blocs, such as the European Union, Mercosur, North American Free Trade Agreement (NAFTA), the African Union, and the Asia-Pacific Economic Cooperation (APEC).

Mass media are transmitting a culture which blurs the lines between national cultures. Of course, national cultures are artifacts of the nation-state. Public schools are essential instruments for organizing and disseminating national cultures. Mass media undercut the role of the school in creating and maintaining national cultures by destroying the boundaries between national cultures and creating hybrid world cultures. A tendency toward cultural uniformity is being aided by multinational publishers of textbooks, tests, and software.

The mass migration of the world's peoples is undermining people's sense of location within a particular nation-state. Also, mass migration is forcing school systems to deal with issues of multiculturalism and multilingualism. As Michael Hardt and Antonio Negri stress in their book *Empire*, "Today the mobility of labor power and migratory movements is extraordinarily diffuse and difficult to grasp. Even the most significant population movements of modernity (including the black and white Atlantic migrations) constitute lilliputian events with respect to the enormous population transfers of our times. *A specter haunts the world and it is the specter of migration.*"[24]

What will be the political and economic functions of schools as the forces of globalization slowly erode the strength of the nation-state? To answer this question, I have examined the relationship between Western schooling and the growth of the nation-state. Next I examine the current status of national education in Singapore.

GLOBALIZATION AND THE NATION-STATE: SINGAPORE

Singapore provides a good example of the effort to maintain a strong nation-state while its economy relies on global trade and financial operations.

Its school system utilizes what have become traditional methods of nationalist education to try to make its citizens' personal identities inseparable from that of the nation-state and to submerge individual wills into the collective will of the *people* and *nation*. And, because of its historical development, it exemplifies the multicultural and multilingual issues resulting from the global movement of populations. Central issues for Singapore's government are educational rights related to language and culture.

In *Education and the Rise of the Global Economy*, I described Singapore's educational system as a model of human capital development.[25] Today, Singapore's leaders remain committed to strengthening their nation-state and using education to promote economic growth. It was originally founded as a center for trade in 1819 by Thomas Stamford Raffles who took possession of the island (originally called *Singhapura*, meaning 'Lion City') for the British East India Company. With a population of only 3.2 million and covering an area roughly 3.5 times the size of the capital of the United States, Washington, D.C., Singapore remains a center of globalization. The World Economic Forum classifies Singapore, along with Hong Kong, Switzerland, and Luxembourg, as "entrepot economies" relying on trade and financial services. What this means is that unlike Asian countries such as Japan and Korea which have developed their own national industries, Singapore's economic growth depends on multinational corporations. As a consequence, Singapore is the second busiest port in the world, and it is often called the Switzerland of Asia.[26]

Singapore's government relies on the schools to maintain a strong nation-state. In 1997 Singapore's Ministry of Education declared, "The mission of the Education Service is to mold the future of the nation, by molding the people who will determine the future of the nation."[27] In the same year, Minister of Education Teo Chee Hean stated, "We will strengthen National Education to ensure the next generation remains resilient and cohesive."[28] Similar to the leadership of other nation-states, the Deputy Prime Minister Lee Hsien Loong stressed the importance of teaching Singapore's history as a method of creating social cohesion. After bemoaning the lack of knowledge of Singapore's history among students and the younger generation, he declared, "This ignorance [of history] will hinder our effort to develop a shared sense of nationhood. We will not acquire the right instincts to bond together as one nation, or maintain the will to survive and prosper in an uncertain world."[29] In general, Lee argued, "National Education aims to develop national cohesion, the instinct for survival and confidence in our future."[30] In keeping with the idea that citizens of nation-states must feel one with the *people*, Lee argued, "you must yourselves feel passionately for the country, and understand instinctively our collective interests and what we stand for."[31]

NATIONALISM AND MULTICULTURALISM:
UNITY THROUGH DIVERSITY

Key to the development of the nation-state is invention of a national culture. An obstacle to building a sense of national culture is Singapore's multicultural and multiracial population. Typical of the mass migration of peoples under the process of globalization, the British brought workers from China, India, and Malaysia. Racial harmony has been a major problem in Singapore as evidenced by the annual recognition of Racial Harmony Day on the 21st of July to mark violent race riots that occurred in 1964.

Singapore's educational efforts are an attempt to balance concerns about cultural and language rights with the desire to create national unity. A result is that national culture is based, in part, on the idea that the nation accepts diversity. Therefore, one element of unity is the recognition of the ability of diverse cultures and languages to exist side by side while becoming the *people* and *nation*. This is what is meant by *unity through diversity*.

As indicated in Table 1.1, national unity is challenged by differences in ethnic background, religion, and language. Differences in religion indicate the potential for explosive cultural confrontations with 51% of the total population being Buddhist/Taoist followed by Islamic (14.9%), Christian (14.6%) and Hindu (4.0%). Even within ethnic groups, there is potential for religious conflict given that 55.4% of the ethnic Indian population is Hindu and 25.6% is Islamic (see Table 1.1). This difference could result in violent religious clashes similar to conflicts in India between Hindus and Moslems. Adding fuel to potential conflicts is the fact that economic status differs between ethnic groups. The average monthly income for ethnic Chinese (S$3,237) and for ethnic Indians (S$3,093) is about 50% more than the average monthly income of ethnic Malays (S$2,040).[32]

Ethnic Malays have the strongest potential for disrupting the national unity. Their status is similar to that of other indigenous populations, such as Native Americans, whose lands were expropriated by colonialists. In creating Singapore, the British simply took over Malay lands. Also, Malays are a homogenous religious group with 99.6% of its population being Islamic. Similar to other indigenous groups around the world, they occupy the lowest rung on the income scale. Given their economic position and the fact that Islam does not recognize the legitimacy of Buddhism and Hinduism as religions, Malays have reasons for resenting the overwhelming economic dominance of the ethnic Chinese population.

In its efforts to build unity through diversity, Singapore, in its 1995 Constitution, provides for special protection of ethnic Malays along with the protection of other racial and religious minorities.

TABLE 1.1

**Ethnic Composition, Religion, and Language Spoken at Home
of Singapore's Residents According to the 2000 Census**

	Chinese	*Malay*	*Indians*	*Others*
Percentage of Singapore's Residents	76.8%	13.9%	7.9%	1.4%
Religion (aged 15 and over) within each ethnic group	Christian 16.5% Buddhism/ Taoism 64.4% Islam 0.2 % Hinduism 0.0%	Christian 0.3% Buddhism/ Taoism 0.1% Islam 99.6 % Hinduism 0.0%	Christian 12.1% Budhism/ Taoism 0.7% Islam 25.6 % Hinduism 55.4%	Christian 53.3% Budhism/ Taoism 13.9% Islam 22.3 % Hinduism 1.1%
Language Most Frequently Spoken At Home (aged 5 years and over)	English 23.9% Mandarin 45.1% Chinese Dialects 30.7% Malay 0.3% Tamil 0.0%	English 7.9% Mandarin 0.1% Chinese Dialects 0.1% Malay 91.6% Tamil 0.1%	English 35.6% Mandarin 0.1% Chinese Dialects 0.1% Malay 11.6% Tamil 42.9%	English 68.5% Mandarin 4.4% Chinese Dialects 3.2% Malay 15.6% Tamil 0.2%

Source: "Key Indicators of the Resident Population," *http://www.singstat.gov.sg/keystats/ people.html#demo.*

Article 152 Minorities and Special Position of Malays

(1) It shall be the responsibility of the Government constantly to care for the interests of the racial and religious minorities in Singapore.

(2) The Government shall exercise its functions in such manner as to recognize the special position of the Malays, who are the indigenous people of Singapore, and accordingly it shall be the responsibility of the Government to protect, safeguard, support, foster and promote their political, educational, religious, economic, social and cultural interests and the Malay language.[33]

Also, the educational rights section of the 1995 Constitution recognizes religious diversity in education. Article 16, "Rights in Respect of Education," provides for public support of schools privately operated by a religious group. Section 2 of Article 16 states, "Every religious group has the right to establish and maintain institutions for the education of children and provide therein instruction in its own religion, and there shall be no discrimination on the ground only of religion in any law relating to such institutions or in the administration of any such law." Governmental financial support of these religious schools is guaranteed in Section 1 of Article 16: "There shall be no discrimination against any citizens of Singapore on the grounds only of religion, race, descent or place of birth ... in providing out of the funds of a public authority financial aid for the maintenance or education of pupils or students in any educational institution (whether or not maintained by a public authority and whether within or outside Singapore)."[34]

In keeping with its Constitutional requirement to constantly "care for the interests of the racial and religious minorities in Singapore," the government supports the use of multiple languages in the schools. The most widely used language in the home for the total population is Mandarin (35.%), followed by Chinese dialects (23.8%), English (23%), Malay (14.1%), and Tamil 3.2%.[35] Four languages (Mandarin, English, Malay, and Tamil) are utilized in the primary schools. However, English has become the favored language because of its importance in the globalized economy. Students are currently placed in ability tracks in the fourth year of primary school according to their abilities in English, a mother tongue (Mandarin, Malay, or Tamil), and mathematics. In each of the three ability tracks, the students continue studying their mother tongue and English. More time is spent teaching English than teaching the mother tongue. According to the official curriculum guide, "33% of the curriculum time will be spent on English, 27% on the mother tongue."[36]

NATIONALIST EDUCATION: IDENTITY, ICONS, AND HEROES

Unity through recognition of diversity in religion, language, and ethnicity is only one aspect of the Singaporean government's effort to invent a national culture. Also, the nation's role in the global economy influences governmental approaches to educating students for the *people* and the *nation*. First, there is the fact that Singapore's very existence resulted from global trade, and its population is a product of the global migration of workers. Second, government leaders urge Singaporeans to retain an identity with Singapore while participating directly in a global economy.

Singapore's National Day celebration of its 1966 founding as an independent nation-state exemplifies the effort to balance global forces with nationalism and unite its polyglot population. National Day celebrations use educational and symbolic methods to immerse the individual into the collective spirit of the *people* and *nation*. The National Day school curriculum uses methods that follow in the tradition of Rousseau's proposals for Poland. Students are taught to imagine themselves as Singaporeans who are different from *others* or *foreigners*. Significantly, students are prepared for a sense of *nation* within a globalized economy populated by transient workers. Wherever they might be physically located, their emotions and imaginations are trained to retain their identity as Singaporeans and to remain loyal to their *people* and *nation*. This process educates a nationalist for employment anywhere in the world.

Singapore's Ministry of Education dictates that National Day school activities are designed to train student imaginations so that they can retain their identity as Singaporeans while joining the migratory laborers of the global economy. In one activity, the teacher is instructed to divide the class into small groups and to present each group with the following scenario: "Imagine your parents have been posted to a foreign country. You are now a new pupil studying in a secondary school abroad. Singapore's National Day is coming very soon. How would you celebrate National Day?"[37] Students are asked to discuss this scenario in their small groups and then present their conclusions to the rest of the class. The teacher is instructed to highlight the following aspects of belonging to a unique people and nation within a globalized economy.

1. Wherever one is, it is important to remember one's family, friends and country
2. When people are outside Singapore they feel more Singaporean
3. Celebrating National Day is an expression of one's sense of belonging and loyalty to Singapore[38]

Another classroom activity exemplifies George Mosse's argument that the new secular religion of the *people* and *nation* requires their expression in visible and tangible symbols. Mosse contended, "[The] permanent symbol helped to condition the population to the new politics [of the *people* and *nation*]: not only holy flames, flags, and songs but, above all national monuments in stone and mortar. The national monument as a means of self-expression served to anchor the national myths and symbols in the consciousness of the people."[39] Illustrating Mosse's statement, the lesson, "Made in Singapore," states its purpose as allowing "pupils to express their pride for the nation through their choice of a national landmark/icon/feature."[40] Students are asked "to guess landmarks, icons or other national features found on a Singapore $10 note and a fifty-cent coin" and then to explain the "reasons why these landmarks, icons or national features were chosen to be used for our currency."[41] Next, students' imaginations are engaged in thinking about "landmarks, icons or national features which they think best depicts Singapore and its people" for use on postage stamps and on national currency. The lesson's outcome is supposed to give students "pride for the place they call home—the place that they grew up in, people with familiar faces, and surrounded by their family friends and neighbors."[42]

Utilizing national heroes that sacrifice themselves for the good of the *people* is commonplace in most nationalist forms of education. Heroes allow students to imagine themselves as making the same sacrifices for the *people* and *nation*. A National Day lesson called "I can make a difference" builds on the theme of heroic personal sacrifice to the *nation*. The lesson utilizes three important historical figures in Singapore's development who have gained mythic status: Tan Tock Seng, Lieutenant Adnan, and Narayanan Pillai. Tan was a successful ethnic Chinese merchant who gave his money to the poor and founded the still-existing Tan Tock Seng hospital. Lieutenant Adnan played a major role in the resistance movement during Japan's occupation of Singapore during World War II. Narayan Pillai was Singapore's first building contractor and an Indian merchant who played a key part in the establishment of modern Singapore. Narayan Pillai is also known as the founder of Sri Mariamman Temple, the oldest Hindu temple in Singapore.

The teacher is instructed to pass out written summaries of their "deeds and contributions to their fellow men." The teacher is told to "get pupils to discuss how these pioneers made a difference in the lives of the their fellow men" and "have pupils discuss how they too can care for their fellow citizens and get them to reflect on how they can make a difference."[43] In concluding the lesson, the teacher is instructed to "summarize the discussion and highlight that

- one does not have to sacrifice oneself or be wealthy to be able to make a difference
- each of us has a role to play and must give of our best
- underlying all of this is the important message that we are each a part of Singapore.[44]

It is important to note that two of these three national heroes are merchants. Schools in most nation-states mythologize military and political leaders for use as national heroes. These seem like logical choices, given the central role of global economics in creating and defining Singapore. Also, students can imagine themselves as heroic businesspeople working for the good of the Singaporean economy. Merchants as national heroes contribute, as I explain in the next section, to a sense of nationalism that is economic in content.

The suggested activities for Nation Day are complemented by the 2003 "Desired Outcomes of Education," issued by Singapore's Ministry of Education. These education outcomes specifically deal with citizenship training for the nation-state. The opening caption of the document declares:

The Singaporean—an Individual, a Citizen Education does two things: it develops the individual and educates the citizen.[45]

In language that stresses the requirement of schools to prepare the individual for sacrifice to the *people* and *nation*, the document states, "An educated person is also someone who is responsible to his community and country." Also, the document stresses that individual identity should be made inseparable from that of the *people* and *nation* and that the role of the school is to assist the student in imagining the territorial boundaries of Singapore as a *nation*.

> It is society at large which gives us a sense of identity and purpose, security and confidence. In turn, we have obligations and responsibilities to the community. Therefore, our schools will teach our children to identify Singapore as our home; a home to live in, strive to improve, and defend.[46]

The actual outcomes section of the document highlight the effort to relate nationalism to Singapore's role in the global economy.

Outcome of the Education
Students should:

- be morally upright, be culturally rooted yet understanding and respecting differences, be responsible to family, community and country
- believe in our principles of multi-racialism and meritocracy, appreciate the national constraints but see the opportunities
- be constituents of a gracious society
- be willing to strive, take pride in work, value working with others
- be able to think, reason and deal confidently with the future, have courage and conviction in facing adversity
- be able to seek, process and apply knowledge
- be innovative—have a spirit of continual improvement, a lifelong habit of learning and an enterprising spirit in undertakings
- think global, but be rooted to Singapore[47]

An official 2003 publication by Singapore's central coordinating agency for National Education has the descriptive title *Engaging Hearts & Minds*. This publication stresses the importance of building a nationalistic spirit in an age of globalization. It asserts, "In this age of globalization, Singaporeans have become much more mobile .... Amidst all of this, the value of National Education lies in what it sets out to achieve: Building common ground. Connecting the past, present and future. Preparing us for our future."[48] An important question asked in *Engaging Hearts & Minds*: "Isn't National Education just government propaganda?"[49] This is a question that could be raised about all forms of nationalistic education. Interestingly, the government's response does not deny the charge of propaganda but urges educators to avoid the appearance of conveying propaganda to students. The publication states, "The image of 'government propaganda' is something National Education practitioners have to grapple with. To overcome this image, it is important for practitioners to truly understand what National Education is about. It is also important to understand how to convey National Education subtly, creatively and effectively."[50] A tour guide for students visiting Singapore's historical sites warns, "The youth view National Education as propaganda and they immediately put an invisible shield around themselves." "But," she claims, "when we bring them out to a site, they see for themselves that it's not propaganda I tell them, 'You can choose to believe me, you can choose not to believe me, but you've seen it for yourself. You are Singaporeans—you need to know."[51]

There is an admitted militaristic aspect to nationalist education in Singapore. Reflecting the title *Engaging Hearts & Minds*, the publication states, "More than the mind, National Education is about engaging the heart–so that reluctant soldiers transform themselves into committed soldiers."[52] Commander Bernard Tan of Singapore's 7th Infantry Battalion reports, "My commanders and I integrate National Education into our men's daily activities."[53]

Of course, economic growth remains central to National Education. In answer to the question, "How can we ensure Singapore's economic competitiveness?," *Engaging Hearts & Minds* provides the answer, "National Education is an opportunity to discuss economic challenges facing Singapore and to get Singaporeans to consider what they can do as individuals to contribute to the economic success of the whole nation."[54]

ECONOMIC NATIONALISM: PRIDE, SELF-SACRIFICE, AND PROVIDING A SAFE HAVEN

Singapore's merchant heroes highlight the role of economics in inventing Singapore as a nation-state. Singaporeans are proud of the high standard of living provided by their economy. Their identity as a people is dependent on Singapore's role in the global economy. Economic pride is indirectly touched on by newspaper columnist Chua Lee Hoong in his column in *The Straits Times* titled, "This National Day, celebrate the joy of work."[55] Bemoaning the loss of jobs from companies moving from Singapore to other countries with lower wages, Chua exhorts Singaporeans to follow the model of citizens who are willing to do their own work rather than hiring foreign workers or are willing to take jobs at low wages. In one example, a man eschews the hiring of foreign workers to improve his house and takes on the job himself. In another, a women loses her job but takes a lower paying job at a McDonald's. Chua relates, "The other day, she proudly showed me her pay. It wasn't much, but it had restored her sense of self-worth. McDonald's is one enlightened employer."[56] Chua concludes, "If more workers were like them, I dare say no one need ever remain unemployed in Singapore. Old jobs may go, but where there's a will, a new one can always be found."[57]

Chua's article speaks directly to the pride Singaporeans have in their high standard of living. They are proud that they can import low-paid workers, primarily from Bangladesh, to do menial tasks, such as cleaning hotel rooms, streets, and construction laborers. Their nation has given their citizens economic advantages in the global market.

Schools emphasize the contribution of a strong work ethic to the economic well-being of the *nation*. Singapore's educational system fosters emotional attachments to work and to Singapore's financial achievements. Singapore's leaders hope that graduates will instinctively think about how they can improve Singapore's economy. In 1997, while praising Japan's emphasis on dedication to working for the group and the nation, Singapore's Deputy Prime Minister Lee Hsien Loong called for a nationalist education to motivate citizens to work for the good of the country. He felt that ignorance of the nation's history was hampering feelings of economic community. "This ignorance," he stated, "will hinder our effort to develop a shared sense of nationhood. We will not acquire the right instincts to bond together as one nation, or maintain the will to survive and prosper in an uncertain world."[58]

The 1997 mission statement of the Singapore's Ministry of Education, "Molding the Future of Our Nation," stresses a work ethic, " Every child must learn to take pride in his work, to do his best and excel in whatever he does, and to value and respect honest work," and links that work ethic to helping the nation: "Education equips us with the skills and knowledge, as well as the right values and attitudes to assure the livelihood of the individual and the country's survival and success. We must learn to be self-reliant, yet able to work closely with others; individually competitive, yet with a strong social conscience."[59]

Prime Minister Goh Chok Tong's projects an image of a corporate society where a worker's imagination and thinking are devoted to economic improvement. "We want to have an environment," he contends, "where workers and students are all the time *thinking of how to improve* [emphasis added]. Such a national attitude is a must for Singapore to sustain its prosperity."[60]

Singapore's economic nationalism also includes maintaining a close relationship between economic and educational planning. In 1966, Prime Minister Lee Kuan Yee called for the concentration of government expenditures on areas that would spark economic growth. "For instance," he said, "take education, expenditure on this is a necessity. In a highly urbanized society, our future lies in a well-educated population, trained in the many disciplines and techniques of a modern industrial society."[61] In the 1990s, the Singapore government organized schools for the education of workers for an information technology industry. The dream was to make Singapore the center for development of software and new information technology.

In 2003, Professor Allan Luke of Australia's Queensland University was hired by the Singapore government to reform the educational system so that it produced more creative workers. Government leaders believed that educational changes were necessary to ensure Singapore's position in the global economy. According to Luke, Singapore's political leaders assured him that they remained committed to the maintenance of a strong nation-state because of their small size and hostile neighbors. However, they felt that the rigidity of instructional methods in their schools was limiting the ability of schools to educate workers who were creative and independent thinkers which, in turn, was causing the economy to suffer.[62]

There is, of course, another reason why Singapore's government would want to educate a citizenry dedicated to the good of the *people* and *nation*, and obedient to the state's laws. A strong nation with obedient citizens is a secure home for international corporations. The behavior of international corporations justifies this conclusion. In the early 21st century, Singapore's leaders shifted their planning from information technology to biotechnology. In 2003, Singapore opened Biopolis, a biomedical research park, as a community of research scientists. In addition to Biopolis, the Tuas Biomedical Park was opened to house biomedical manufacturing. At the opening ceremonies of Biopolis, Minister Lim Swee Say announced, "So far, global leaders including GlaxoSmithKline, Meerck, Pfizer, Schering Plough, Aventis, Wyeth, Siemens, Baxter and Becton Dickinson have selected Singapore as a base for global manufacturing."[63] Also, Singapore's government is promoting the genetic engineering of agricultural crops, particularly for Asian markets. For this purpose, the government opened the Agri-Bio Park and the Lim Chu Kang Agrotechnology Park.

In summary, Singapore's economic nationalism embraces three elements. The first is pride in the high standard of living provided by the economy. The second involves teaching people to think of the value of their work for the good of the nation. And third, educating an obedient citizenry who will provide a safe haven for multinational corporations.

CULTURAL DIVERSITY AND ECONOMIC NATIONALISM

However, economic concerns to "think global, but be rooted to Singapore" can conflict with the nationalist goal of unity through diversity as it did in Singapore's Prime Minister Goh Chok Tong's 2002 National Day Rally Speech. In the speech, Goh asked, "How do we make progress in this tougher world environment?" After referring frequently to the rapid growth of China's economy, Goh stated, "we must find ways to ride on China's growth. In this regard, I urge Chinese Singaporeans to encourage their children to work hard at learning the Chinese language. As China grows, the economic value of the Chinese language will increase."[64] As part of the effort by Singapore to exploit China's economic growth, Goh argued that the educational system must emphasize Chinese culture and language.

In the context of Goh's speech, "to think global" means emphasizing Chinese language and culture, educating some Singaporeans for fluency in the two major languages of globalization, Mandarin and English. Goh urged:

> We should aim to have most young Chinese Singaporeans speak social Mandarin fluently, and hopefully read Chinese newspapers as well ... we should encourage more students to pursue Chinese and China-related studies at university. Our universities will intensify their China-related programs. We must produce in every cohort a group of bilingual Chinese elite ... proficient in the Chinese language. They should be knowledgeable about Chinese history and culture, and have a good understanding of contemporary China .... Key to developing the next generation of Chinese elite is having enough good Chinese language teachers. They will determine whether we succeed in transmitting the Chinese language and culture to our young.[65]

Goh's speech should be considered against the background of Singapore's multicultural and multilinguistic national culture. It is this national culture that is supposedly going to keep the global-thinking Singaporean "rooted to Singapore." Goh alluded to this in the closing of his speech: "However, as we do more to promote Chinese culture and language, it is important not to forget our multi-racial society."[66]

The reaction to Goh's speech provides evidence of the delicate balance between economic nationalism and the goal of unity through diversity. Goh's speech promoted the economic and cultural interests of the already dominant ethnic Chinese. Other ethnic groups immediately responded to this bias. The *Straits Times* reported a feedback session on the speech where Singaporean Indians felt that they were "left out" and "neglected" by the Prime Minister in what they considered the "most prominent speech of the year."[67] One reason for feeling neglected was the lack of a Tamil translation of the speech on the government Web site while translations were made available in English, Malay, and Chinese. Ethnic Indians complained that while Goh emphasized improving instruction in Chinese, he failed to mention improving instruction in Tamil or Malay. In addition, they expressed concern that the Prime Minister did not mention aid to Indian students from poor families even though he talked about a $10 million Education Trust Fund for Malays.

Regarding the Prime Minister's apparent favoritism of ethnic Chinese, the newspaper reported, "One man said his wife and her mother, when watching the rally on TV, commented that they should 'pack up and go back to India'."[68] One woman "brought up a conversation she had with a 12-year-old, who saw the education system as favoring Chinese students."[69] Others stated that "as leader of the land, he should have given fair play to all the races when addressing what is popularly seen as a State of the Union address. Otherwise, it may send the wrong signal, they noted."[70]

Ethnic Chinese were upset because the Prime Minister emphasized economic rather than cultural reasons for learning Chinese. The *Straits Times* reported that ethnic Chinese worried that if the Chinese language were promoted purely for economic reasons, then interest might decline if the Chinese economy faltered. One man asked, "So if Russia's economy were to rise up next, would we have to abandon Chinese and go learn Russian instead?"[71] Some criticized Goh's call for cultivating a Chinese elite: "Why not raise standards across the board, they suggested."[72] However, the article did report that some supported economic rather than cultural reasons because cultural arguments might cause problems between ethnic groups. "It's neutral and can be promoted to the entire nation. It can also be accepted by most people. If you use cultural reasons, it may be too sensitive," stated the chair of the meeting, Seng Han Thong.[73]

THREE PARTS OF NATIONAL EDUCATION: UNITY THROUGH DIVERSITY; IDENTITY, ICONS, AND HEROES; AND ECONOMIC NATIONALISM

The National Heritage Tours planned by Singapore's Ministry of Education are a brilliant nationalist educational plan designed to give students a national identity and to allow them to imagine the *people* and *nation* in tangible symbols of history and statehood. The Tours encompass all three aspects of nationalist education described in this chapter, namely unity through diversity, national icons and heroes, and economic nationalism. The Ministry of Education expects all students to go on these tours with paid licenced heritage tour guides or retired teachers. In other words, the National Heritage Tours are an important part of the education of all Singaporean students. The Ministry of Education's guidelines prescribes, "In the pupils' ten years of formal education, they would be expected to go on at least three heritage tours—one while in their primary school and two in their secondary school."[74] In the context of education for the nation-state, the Ministry's guidelines emphasize that "These tours would help to reinforce and consolidate what they have learnt in the classroom and *strengthen their feelings for and attachments to Singapore* [emphasis added]."[75]

The tour for primary students fosters the idea of unity through diversity. The tour for lower secondary students focuses on political and military icons. And lastly, the tour for upper secondary students promotes the country's economic history. Taken together, the National Heritage Tours provides a culminating experience in the educational efforts to a *people* and a *nation*.

The National Heritage Tour for primary students promotes unity through diversity by taking students to ethnic historical sites. The tours' objectives emphasize pride in Singapore's identity as a multicultural society. The objectives are given in the Ministry's guidelines as:

1. Understand and appreciate the rich cultural and historical heritage of our people
2. Foster a sense of pride in the rich diversity of our heritage
3. Share a common bond which will hold our society together as a people and as a nation[76]

Objectives 2 and 3 are important because pride in a diverse heritage is linked to sharing a common bond as "a *people* and as a *nation* [emphasis added]."

Primary school students visit three ethnic districts which were protected in 1989 as historical conservation areas. The Kampong Glam area is described as, "Traditionally a Malay residential area with ethnic-based activities, it contains mainly two-storey shophouses of the Early and Transitional Shophouse Styles." Kreta Ayer (Chinatown) "contains mainly two- and three-storey shophouses of Transitional, Late and Art Deco Shophouse Styles." And Little India "is recognized as the hub of Indian community life in Singapore. It contains mainly two-storey shophouses of the Early, Transitional, Late and Art Deco Shophouse Styles."[77]

On the tour of these ethnic areas, according to the official Ministry of Education bulletin, the

> world of their [students'] great-grandparents and our pioneers will come alive. Some of their customs and traditions will be familiar, but what about the culture and festivities of other, different ethnic groups? Why is 'Little India' so called, and why is it situated around Serangoon Road? Who decided that Chinatown should be where it is? Why are there so many different temples? Who live in Kampong Glam? The pupils will discover the answers to these and other questions on the tours.[78]

Lower secondary students are taken to the political and military sites at Fort Canning, the Civic District, and World War II battlefield locations.

These are what historian Mosse referred to as the "national monuments in stone and mortar" that give tangible evidence of the existence of a *nation*. This tour, according to the Minister of Education, "will take them [lower secondary pupils] to sites that will help them appreciate our past, understand our present and think about our future."[79]

The visit to Fort Canning Hill brings students face-to-face with the country's British imperial founding. Prior to British expropriation of the land, it was a port ruled by a dynasty of five generations of maharajahs. They built their palaces at the summit of Fort Canning Hill. The area was sacked and burned by Portugese colonialists in 1614. After Stamford Raffles' arrival in 1819, the hill became known as "Government Hill." Fort Canning was built in 1861 and named after Viscount George Canning, then Governor-General and First Viceroy of India. Students visit Fort Canning Center, a former military barrack restored in the 1970s.[80]

At Fort Canning, students see a tangible symbol of what makes their identity different from that of the residents of the surrounding country of Malaysia. Fort Canning symbolizes prior English rule and traditions which gives a particular flavor to Singaporean life. The monument also symbolizes Singapore's birth in the context of globalization. It is a physical icon of a Singaporean nationalism that requires citizens to "think global, but be rooted to Singapore."

The Civic District Tour confronts students with buildings that embody the administrative apparatus of the nation. They are the historic and current symbols of the *nation*. According to the government's official description of the area, it "is home to a valuable collection of architecturally and historically significant buildings such as the Supreme Court, Raffles Hotel, National Museum, former Hill Street Police Station and the Singapore Art Museum (former Saint Joseph's Institution)."[81] Singapore's government has made a conscious effort to merge the past into the present in these symbols of nationhood. "The main objective of the Civic District Master Plan," states the official plan for the area, "is to reinforce this important and historical part of the city through adaptive re-use of the older and distinctive buildings, and the sensitive introduction of new developments."[82]

Military history and heroes have traditionally served to teach self-sacrifice and unite nations around a glorious past. The most important part of Singapore's military history was Japanese conquest and control during World War II. A memorial at Beach Road Camp remembers the estimated 2000 officers and men of the Singapore Volunteer Corps (SVC) who were killed in WWII. A visit to this site completes the tour of the bricks and mortars of nationhood.

The National Heritage Tour for upper level secondary students focuses on economic history. This tour combines economic nationalism with an introduction to the process of creating historical symbols to build nationalism. The Ministry of Education's guidelines state that through the history of economic development, students will "see the conscious efforts that have been made to conserve and preserve old buildings so that our heritage will not be forgotten."[83] The main part of the tour is described this way:

> Pupils will discover the vibrant history and economic importance of the Singapore River and the changes that have taken place over the years. At the Urban Redevelopment Authority, pupils will understand and appreciate the importance of mapping out a vision for the long-term physical development of land-scarce Singapore. The vision is translated into a Concept Plan that affects business, housing, recreation and leisure, the environment and transport. Pupils will see this deliberate planning when they go on the three heritage tours of the Singapore River, the Central Business District (CBD) and the Museum Precinct and its Vicinity.[84]

Intended to be a culminating experience in nationalistic education, the National Heritage Tours are similar to Rousseau's educational plans for Emile and Poland. Through contact with physical representations of the an invented *nation*, students' identities and emotions are linked to pride in being Singaporean. What Singapore's government adds to this nationalistic mix is economic nationalism, which is given concrete meaning in the upper secondary level tour.

CONCLUSION: "THINK GLOBAL, BUT BE ROOTED TO SINGAPORE"

Singapore exemplifies one educational ideology bound up in the process of globalization. First, this educational ideology supports traditional forms of nationalist education to maintain a strong nation-state. The goal is for Singaporeans to retain an identity and remain loyal to their nation-state and its economic system wherever they are in the world. In this manner, territorial boundaries are removed from immersion of self in the *people* and *nation*.

Second, Singapore's government has resolved the issue of multiculturalism and multilingualism by giving cultural and educational support to its major ethnic communities. The government provides support for multiple languages and cultures in the school system. At the same time, it emphasizes the global language of English. Nationalism is predicated on the idea of unity through diversity.

Third, economic planning is integrated into educational planning. School curricula are adapted to changing economic needs as reflected in the development of information technology and biotechnology. Schools attempt to educate students to think of their work as a contribution to the national economy. Also, the education of obedient citizens provides a feeling to leaders of multinational corporations that Singapore will be a safe haven for economic activities.

Singapore provides one educational ideology for a global society where boundaries between national cultures are disintegrating and populations are migrating from region to region. Throughout this book, I continually compare differing educational ideologies, including that of Singapore, as a means for evaluating the future direction of the world's educational systems.

Schooling Workers for a Global Free Market: The World Bank

"Education is at the heart of the World Bank's mission to reduce global poverty," declares the Bank's report, *Education and Development*. The report continues with the impressive claim, "The World Bank is the largest single external financer of education."[1] As the largest financer, the World Bank is able to exert influence over educational policy by specifying the terms of loans to nations and private organizations. Also, its debt collection policies can influence national education budgets.

The World Bank is at the heart of a globalization process which is breaking down the boundaries of the nation-state. Inherent in the World Bank's activities is an ideology that encompasses a particular view of an ideal world order and system of schooling. This vision is applied to all global regions and it is embodied in most, if not all, World Bank plans. If implemented, it would create a uniform global political and economic order. However, the World Bank's activities are under constant scrutiny by a global community composed of international intergovernmental organizations and non-governmental organizations (NGOs). Intergovernmental organizations, such as the United Nations, are composed of representatives of nation-states. NGOs, as defined by John Boli and George Thomas, are voluntary organizations "that make rules, set standards, propagate principles, and broadly represent humanity." They represent humanity in the sense that members of an organization, such as human rights and environmental groups, believe their values should be universally applied.[2]

The internet is a powerful technological tool utilized by the World Bank, NGOs, and intergovernmental organizations to link members and spread information around the world. Human rights, environmental, and other organizations use the Internet to sound global alarms about what they consider to be impending crises. Besides global linkages, the Internet is now a major player in global educational projects. This is exemplified by the United Nations "cyberschoolbus" Web site, which provides school lessons and curricula on human rights, the functioning of the United Nations, and related issues.[3] The World Bank calls Information and Communications Technologies one of its important educational tools. Referring to the Bank-supported project, The African National University, World Bank officials state, "The digital age has sought to accelerate the pace of development by reaching some of the rural poor."[4]

THE GLOBAL COMMUNITY, THE WORLD BANK, AND THE CIVIL SOCIETY

As the largest global investor in education, the World Bank is an intergovernmental organization that works with other global organizations. Founded as an intergovernmental financial organization in 1947 to rebuild Europe, it is now owned by more than 184 member countries. Its shareholders are the member countries. The bank lends money for educational projects to global NGOs, such as, according to their pamphlet "Early Child Development: The First Step to Education for All," the Barnard van Leer Foundation, Aga Khan Foundation, Save the Children, Christian Children's Fund, Open Society Institute, World Vision, and SmithKline Beecham.[5]

In addition, the World Bank uses educational standards established by other intergovernmental organizations. According to the World Bank's report, "Education Sector Strategy," "Specific international targets have been agreed on for universal primary education, adult literacy and gender parity in basic education within the Education for All initiative and the OECD's Development Assistance Committee (DAC) goals."[6] Education for All initiative resulted from a 1990 world conference in Jomtien, Thailand, sponsored by the United Nations Educational, Scientific and Cultural Organization (UNESCO), the United Nations Children's Fund (UNICEF), the United Nations Development Program (NDP), and the World Bank. The meeting was attended and the initiative was supported by 155 nations and 150 NGOs.[7] The other source of educational standards, the Organization for Economic Cooperation and Development (OECD), similar to the World Bank, originated as part of European reconstruction following World War II. Originally called the Organization for European Economic Cooperation, it changed its name and extended its global reach in 1961. I discuss Education For All and OECD later in the book.[8] For now, I am just concerned with placing the work of the World Bank in the tangled web of the global community.

Historically, according to Akira Iriye's *Global Community: The Role of International Organizations in the Making of the Contemporary World*, the World Bank is part of a global community that has been evolving since the 19th century.[9] Iriye contends that traditional histories of international relations primarily focus on national governments and diplomacy. What is missing from this historical perspective, he asserts, is the growth of a global community composed of a tangled web of interrelationships between intergovernmental organizations and NGOs. Since the 19th century, the network of NGOs has formed a *global civil society* which sometimes supplants and competes with the actions of nation-states.

The World Bank officially defines "the term *civil society* organizations or *CSOs* to refer to the wide array of non-governmental and not-for-profit organizations that have a presence in public life, expressing the interests and values of their members or others, based on ethical, cultural, political, scientific, religious or philanthropic considerations."[10] The World Bank recognizes the importance of the global civil society and on its Web site declares:

> The emergence and growth of Civil Society over the past two decades has been one of the most significant trends in international development. The World Bank recognizes that civil society plays an especially critical role in helping to amplify the voices of the poorest people in the decisions that affect their lives, improve development effectiveness and sustainability, and hold governments and policymakers publicly accountable. The purpose of this web site is to provide Civil Society Organizations (CSOs) with information, links, and materials on the World Bank's evolving relationship with civil society in Washington and throughout the world.[11]

A more activist definition of civil society was made by World Bank 2003 Presidential Fellow Lecture, Kumi Naidoo, who is Secretary General and CEO of Civicus: World Alliance for Citizen Participation. In his World Bank lecture, Naidoo asserted that "civil society burst onto the public stage at the Earth Summit in 1992 .... [it] was the first major conference where 'civil society' became a prominent player in the global level. Since the Earth Summit, civil society has come into its own as an important political, social and economic actor."[12] According to Civicus publications, the declaration of the Earth Summit "used the term [civil society] for the first time in an official international document connected to development."[13]

Civicus, the organization represented by Naidoo, defines its mission as "strengthening citizen action and civil society throughout the world ... [and creating a] worldwide community of informed, inspired, committed citizens engaged in confronting the challenges facing humanity."[14] In Naidoo's definition of civil society, he includes NGOs, trade unions, religious groups, networks, and individual activists. Civil society, he argues, mediates between the family, the nation-state, and the international economic market. Through its actions, the civil society is promoting an activist form of democracy. "We must resist," he said, "the notion that elections equal democracy, that a victory at the ballot box is a blank check to rule without any interface and dialogue with citizens between elections. To reduce democracy to the singular act of voting once every four or five years is clearly an error."[15] An active civil society will make elected officials accountable to the public.

The development of the Internet has been a primary means for maintaining the new global civic society. The *Civicus World: Newsletter of CIVICUS: World Alliance for Citizen Participation* states, "The current explosion of advocacy activities among CSOs has been fueled by ... the advent of new information technologies such as the Internet which have provided powerful, new opportunities to advocates to disseminate information and mobilize support national and internationally."[16] In addition, highly visible world conferences such as the 1992 Rio Earth Summit and the 1995 Beijing UN Conference on Women helped operationalist relations between NGOs.

The members of the global civil society should be distinguished from the *people* of the nation-state. I use Michael Hardt and Antonio Negri's term the *multitude* to refer to the population of the global civil society. In distinguishing the multitude from the people, they wrote, "The modern conception of the people is in fact a product of the nation-state .... Whereas the multitude is an inconclusive constituent relation, the people is a constituted synthesis that is prepared for sovereignty. The people provides a single will and action that is independent of and often in conflict with the various wills and actions of the multitude. Every nation must make the multitude into a people."[17]

In his history of the global community, Iriye divided the organizations of global civil society by their functions, such as humanitarian relief, cultural exchange, peace and disarmament, developmental assistance, human rights, and environmentalism.[18] Other nongovernmental organizations could be included, such as multinational corporations and religious organizations. Intertwined with global civil society are intergovernmental organizations such as the World Bank. Together, these form the basic structure of Iriye's *global community*.

The *global community*, which includes intergovernmental organizations, the global civil society, and multinational corporations, is a complex web in which the demarcations between the parts are fuzzy. The complexity of interrelationships results from the historical evolution of the global community. For instance, Iriye used the International Red Cross as an example of the overlapping lines between nations and NGOs. In 1864, the Swiss government convened an international conference of government leaders to write a treaty that would ensure better treatment of those wounded in war. However, prior private efforts had already created the Red Cross headquarters in Geneva. The representatives of governments attending the conference signed a treaty supporting the Red Cross. The intergovernmental treaty contributed to the Red Cross as an NGO humanitarian organization being caught up in international politics. For instance, Japan insisted that Korea, which it had colonized in the early 20th century, not be allowed to ratify the original treaty as a separate nation. The International Red Cross acceded to Japan's wishes and the Korean Red Cross was put under the jurisdiction of the Japanese Red Cross. Iriye concluded, "The line between the state apparatus and a nonstate organization was never clear-cut."[19]

Today, human rights organizations form the largest group of NGOs. Since 1850, 35,000 not-for-profit NGOs appeared on the world stage. While many of these disappeared over time, after World War II the rate dissolutions declined markedly. For instance, in 1969 approximately 134 new NGOs were created whereas only about 20 dissolved.[20] The number of human rights organizations increased from 33 in 1953 to 168 in 1993 and they represent about 26.6% of the total global NGOs. The next largest number of NGOs is environmental with 90 groups in 1993 forming 14.3% of the global number. Environmental NGOs have been the fastest growing with only two groups having existed in 1953. Following environmentalist groups are NGOs concerned with women's rights, whose numbers grew from 10 in 1953 to 61 in 1993. Other NGOs, in descending order of total number of organizations, are concerned with peace, Esperanto, world order, development, ethnic unity/group rights, and international law.[21]

The prominent position in global civil society of human rights, environmental, and women's rights NGOs highlights global efforts to regulate activities of nation-states. All three of these groups express global concerns about violations of their principles by individual nation-states. They claim to represent "world cultural norms."[22] Human rights are, by their very nature, defined as universal. In a similar fashion, women's organizations claim a universal standard for the rights of women. And environmental issues cannot be contained within the boundaries of the nation-states. In *Activists Beyond Borders*, Margaret Keck and Kathryn Sikkink contended, "All of our networks [global NGOs] challenge traditional notions of sovereignty. Most views of sovereignty in international relations focus almost exclusively on … states as the sole determinants of sovereignty."[23] The authors asserted that global NGOs have made the boundaries of sovereignty of the nation-state "fuzzy–and contested."[24]

EDUCATING FOR WORLD CITIZENSHIP IN A GLOBAL CIVIC SOCIETY

World citizenship, according to John Boli, Thomas Loya, and Teresa Loftin, is the result of the growth of NGOs. And, in their analysis, they found that Western nations do not dominate the membership in NGOs.

While in the 19th century international NGOs tended to be concentrated in Western countries, by the 21st century the researchers found NGO participation "in all geographical regions of the world, across all levels of development, for old and new countries, for countries of every dominant religion ...."[25] With regard to Western influence, the authors concluded, "World culture is increasingly global, decreasingly the provenance of the Europeans and Anglo-Americans, who dominated it in its early stages."[26]

From their analysis of international data, the researchers derived a concept of world citizenship. Throughout this book, I refer to their world citizenship concept because of its implications for global education. For instance, how is education for world citizenship different from that of national citizenship? Also, since, at this point in time, world citizenship is limited to only a few, does that imply the development of a global social structure will create a special class of people called *world citizens*?

Boli, Loya, and Loftin identify the following characteristics of people with world citizenship:

1. They know about and have contact with NGOs
2. Their education orients them towards participation in NGOs
3. They are people with higher education and they have the financial resources for travel
4. World citizenship is more probable for people involved in social service activities and voluntary work
5. World citizenship is more probable for people with a weak national identity.[27]

Civicus promotes education for world citizenship in a global civil society which, in turn, impacts organizations like the World Bank. The World Bank, in organizing an internal Civil Society group and inviting Kumi Naidoo to give the 2003 Presidential Fellows Lecture, recognizes this new movement for civic education. Coupled with the concept of world citizenship, this civic education incorporates a variety of concerns, including human rights and environmentalism. I elaborate on this new civic education in the next chapter after considering the educational policies of the World Bank.

THE WORLD BANK AND ANTIGLOBALIZATION

The existence of a global community creates a new arena for conflict different from the violent military action between nations. For instance, the antiglobalization movement has criticized the World Bank for its environmental and economic growth policies. Some of these, the antiglobalization movement claims, hinder educational development in many countries. The antiglobalization movement received world press coverage for protests at

World Bank meetings in 1999 and 2000, and nonviolent protests turned violent at the 1999 World Trade Organization's meeting in Seattle.

The various NGOs associated with antiglobalization are not opposed to the growth of a global civil society. What these groups are opposed to is the type of global society supported by organizations such as the World Bank. Antiglobalization forces are specifically critical of the role of nation-states in destroying the environment and violating human rights. For instance, environmental activist Lynton Caldwell, in his history of the environmentalist movement, *International Environmental Policy*, wrote, "Distinctive among the many forms of human dominion is the nation-state, which has been the characteristic structure for extending human preemption of the earth. It was developed in Europe and accompanied the expansion of European peoples into the Americas, into South Africa and Australia, and across northern Asia to the Pacific Ocean."[28]

Two hundred anti-World Bank organizations belong to the coalition "50 Years Is Enough: U.S. Network for Global Economic Justice."[29] A manifesto of the movement, *Democratizing the Global Economy: The Battle Against the World Bank and the International Monetary Fund*, stresses fundamental differences in approaches between groups like the World Bank and antiglobalization organizations. From the antiglobalization perspective, the globalization effort by organizations like the World Bank emphasize economic growth based on the pursuit of profits and increased consumption of products. "Whereas," *Democratizing the Global Economy* declares, "the core values of the corporate paradigm focus on maximizing profit and increasing the quantity of things a person owns, we challengers focus our core values on the quality of relations among people and between people and the environment."[30] The antiglobalization movement stresses human rights and protection of the environment. They accuse globalization efforts by the World Bank of destroying forests and oceans. Antiglobalization forces want to create "institutional building blocks for a sustainable global economy with no starving children; an economy that leaves the planet for future generations in better condition than it was when we received it."[31]

The 2002 platform of the "U.S. Network for Global Economic Justice" declares:

> We call for the immediate suspension of the policies and practices of the International Monetary Fund (IMF) and World Bank Group which have caused widespread poverty, inequality, and suffering among the world's peoples and damage to the world's environment .... [T]hese institutions are anti-democratic ... and their policies have benefitted international private sector financiers, transnational corporations, and corrupt officials and politicians .... We demand that the World Bank Group immediately cease providing advice and resources to advance the goals associated with corporate globalization, such as privatization and liberalization.[32]

Regarding educational policy, this platform expresses several basic differences between the World Bank and antiglobalization forces. First is the concept of democracy. Implied in the educational policies of the World Bank is support for a form of democracy based on representative forms of government. As stated in their platform, the antiglobalization group considers the World Bank to be antidemocratic. As stated in the antiglobalization manifesto, "We do not mean democracy in its traditionally narrow political sense (electing wealthy men who supposedly represent the rest of us in the halls of government. We mean democracy in the broader sense of citizen sovereignty: people *running their own lives* in all spheres (political, economic, cultural)."[33]

The second issue is privatization. As I explain later, the World Bank supports privatized educational systems, including private schools and charging tuition for government schools. The antiglobalization movement opposes privatizing government services, particularly charging for education and health care. As a result of pressure from antiglobalization forces, testimony of actress Valerie Harper before the U.S. House of Representatives, and Representative Jesse Jackson, Jr. (D-Illinois), the U.S. House of Representatives approved legislation that would stop the World Bank in 2002 from requiring developing countries to charge user fees for access to primary education and health care. As reported by the U.S. Network for Global Economic Justice, "User fees, charges imposed for using a health clinic or attending school, have led to increased illness, suffering and death when people cannot pay for health services, and decreased school enrollments when poor families can no longer afford to send their children to school."[34]

One example of an antiglobalization NGO is Greenpeace, which is dedicated to stopping government actions that might prove destructive to the environment. It has a presence in 40 countries across Europe, the Americas, Asia, and the Pacific. The organization refuses to take donations from governments or corporations and relies on contributions from individual supporters and foundation grants. The organization lists as its major concerns climate change, protecting ancient forests, saving oceans, stopping whaling, genetic engineering, nuclear threats, and toxic chemicals.[35] In preparation for a 1985 protest against French nuclear testing in the South Pacific, Greenpeace sent its four ships, including the largest, the *Rainbow Warrior*, to Auckland, New Zealand. While anchored in the harbor, intelligence agents for the French government blew up the *Rainbow Warrior*, killing one crew member.[36] This was striking evidence of potential conflicts between global civil society and nation-states.

Exemplifying conflicts between intergovernmental organizations and NGOs are Greenpeace activists who hung a 60-foot banner from the World

Bank building in Washington, D.C., protesting the Bank's funding of forest destruction. The Greenpeace organization proclaims, "The World Bank is one of the most powerful financial institutions in the world. Together with its sister organization, the International Monetary Fund (IMF), the World Bank formulates and enforces major economic policy decisions for most poor countries."[37] Greenpeace claims that it has forced the World Bank to attend to issues of environmental destruction. Among those efforts were actions in 1994 regarding deforestation and protests against funding projects that lead to ozone destruction. According to the Greenpeace organization, their efforts have had a positive effect of World Bank decisions. "To its credit," Greenpeace contends, "the World Bank is now leading efforts to understand environmental issues and to talk with advocacy organizations."[38] Greenpeace cited the following evidence of its influence:

> In November 2000, Greenpeace asked World Bank President James Wolfensohn to invest in environmentally sound technologies and clean production, and stop funding large discharge pipes that are putting local populations at risk, such as in Gujurat, India. Along with this pressure from Greenpeace and its thousands of cyberactivists worldwide, Wolfensohn wrote to Greenpeace, announcing a shift in World Bank policy in Gujurat.[39]

Greenpeace actions represent the regulatory effects of the global civil society. Human rights groups exercise the same type of regulatory influence. For instance, the World Bank has published a reference guide on governance and human rights. While the mere listing of organizations does not indicate the degree of influence, it at least indicates an awareness of the work of these associations. Amnesty International and Human Rights Watch are the two organizations that dominate their list of references.[40]

In supporting human rights, World Bank policies are endorsed by the United Nations. In the foreword to the World Bank publication, *Development and Human Rights: The Role of the World Bank*, Mary Robinson, U.N. Commissioner for Human Rights acknowledged the interrelationship between the two organizations. She stated, "The World Bank, through it activities and its renewed commitment to human rights, will play a key role in the promotion of human rights and in the building and strengthening of national human rights capacities in the countries in which it operates."[41] Citing the U.N. Universal Declaration of Human Rights, the World Bank contended that the protection of human rights is necessary for economic development. Also, the Bank argued that economic development supports human rights "through its support of primary education, health care and nutrition, sanitation, housing, and the environment."[42]

Again, exemplifying the interconnections of the global community, the World Bank cited its work with World Wildlife Fund in support of a human right to a clean environment. In 1997, the World Bank and the World Wild-life Fund formed an alliance to "conserve 10 percent of the world's forests by 2000."[43] Both groups feel that their activities can be mutually supporting because "the World Bank is the largest lender to developing countries for forest conservation and management. WWF [World Wildlife Fund] is one of the world's leading conservation organizations."[44] This maze of alliances in the global community spawns contradictory positions. For instance, the U.S. government is an important member of the World Bank while it also refuses to ratify the U.N. Universal Declaration of Human Rights.

THE GLOBAL COMMUNITY AND EDUCATION

The World Bank and the U.N. organizations are one of many groups concerned about education in the global community. I have already pointed out the interrelationship between the World Bank, Education For All Initiative, and OECD. Historically, educational organizations played a significant role in forming the global community. Some organizations engaged in specific projects, such as the Esperanto Clubs formed in 1890 to teach Esperanto and advocate its adoption as the global language. This NGO envisions world peace through the use of a common language. The Esperanto movement has lost ground to English and Mandarin in the struggle over linguistic domination of the world.[45] In 1923, the World Federation of Education Associations was formed linking national educational groups into a global web. As late as 1937, prior to the outbreak of World War II, the organization met in Tokyo.[46]

After World War II, global educational organizations blossomed as part of postwar reconstruction, the Cold War, and the dismantling of colonial empires. As previously discussed, OECD, the World Bank, and the U.N. educational organizations were born from the war's ashes. By the 1970s, these organizations' activities expanded beyond postwar reconstruction to issues of development and eradication of poverty. In the process, they created a framework for the globalization of educational policies.

Also, during the Cold War, both the United States and the Soviet Union tried to win the "hearts and minds" of the world's people through student and faculty exchange programs. Both governments recruited foreign students to attend universities in their countries. And, in turn, both countries sent scholars abroad to teach in foreign universities. While the intention was to win allegiance and support for the policies of both countries, a major effect was to create a global community of scholars.

Linked to the global structures created by postwar reconstruction and the Cold War were the remnants of colonial empires. Many previously colonized countries retained the educational infrastructure established by the colonizers. This led to continuation of intellectual contacts between, for instance, England, France, and Spain and their former colonies. In case of former English colonies, many students continued to study a traditional British curriculum and take school exit examinations similar or identical to those taken in Great Britain. Often, former colonies continued to teach the colonizer's languages and use them as the government's official language, particularly in the former British and French empires. Therefore, former colonial school systems continued to maintain global education linkages.

In the case of Japan, the United States imposed the model of U.S. schools, including governance by local school boards. This was a classic example of a conqueror attempting to use schooling to ensure victory over the minds of the conquered. Japan's 1948 Board of Education Law introduced the U.S. model by creating local school boards with elected members and an appointed superintendent of education.[47] In the 1950s, the United States withdrew its objections to nationalistic forms of education. The result, Japanese scholar Teruhisa Horio argued, "gave rise to the contradiction, still visible in Japanese life today, of a form of patriotism that is subordinated to American global interests."[48]

From the 1970s to the present, educational concerns about development, poverty, and the environment have continued to expand the connections between nation-states, intergovernmental organizations, and NGOs. Oxfam (Oxford Committee for Famine Relief) exemplifies the transition of an NGO focused on social problems arising from World War II to a global organization concerned with education and poverty.[49] Today, Oxfam International is a confederation of 12 organizations working in 100 countries. An avowed goal of the movement is to create a global civic movement to influence the actions of nation-states and other global organizations. Their mission statement describes the organization as "an international group of independent non-governmental organizations dedicated to fighting poverty and related injustice around the world. The Oxfams work together internationally to achieve greater impact by their collective efforts."[50] The call for a global civic movement is made in the organization's *Towards Global Equity, Oxfam International's Strategic Plan for 2001–2004*. The plan opens: "Towards Global Equity offers an invitation to the growing number of individuals, groups and organizations throughout the world who share Oxfam's belief that ending poverty *requires a global citizens' movement for economic and social justice* [emphasis added]."[51]

Oxfam explains its strategy with the simple declaration: "We influence powerful people." "To achieve the maximum impact on poverty," the organization maintains, "Oxfams link up their work on development programs, humanitarian response, lobbying for policy changes at national and global level. Our popular campaigns and communications work is aimed at mobilizing public opinion for change."[52]

The World Bank is one organization that Oxfam tries to influence. For example, Oxfam challenged the World Bank in 1997 to do something about debt relief to poor countries. The organization told World Bank President James Wolfensohn that "the lives of 3.2 million children could be saved over seven years" if poor countries could receive relief on their debt payments to the bank. Oxfam pointed out that payments to the World Bank would financially weaken national school systems. The Oxfam report sent to the World Bank claims that "the glaring gap between social spending and debt repayments" would result in:

> Mozambique—debt repayments are double the combined health and education budgets. A quarter of all children die before the age of five from infectious diseases.

> Ethiopia—debt repayments are four times its annual health budget. Over 100,000 children die of easily preventable and treatable diarrhoea.

> Niger—three times its health budget is spent on paying its debts. Life expectancy in Niger averages only 47 years.[53]

In June 2002, the World Bank and Oxfam joined in asking the ministers of the Group of Seven industrialized countries to provide aid to educate 67 million children in 24 of the poorest nations. They asked the group to "pledge to provide the money to put every kid in school."[54]

At the 2002 annual meeting of the World Bank and the International Monetary Fund, the so-called civil society participants included Oxfam representatives from the Netherlands, America, and Germany. In fact, 5 of the 17 or almost one third of representatives of the "civil society" were from Oxfam.[55]

Exemplifying Oxfam's educational involvement is its funding of the Agency for the Development of Women and Children (ADWAC) and the Association of Farmers, Educators, and Traders (AFET). In Gambia, ADWAC and AFET are educating women in reading, math, and small-business skills. The literacy programs are organized as supportive cooperatives (kafos) with the goal of helping participants gain control of their economic lives including food supplies. The goal is economic independence for women, and the results benefit children's lives. Participants state, "When I get on the bus, I can make sure the driver doesn't cheat me and charge me too much …"; "Now I can make sure I bring the correct health card with me when I take one of my children to the clinic …"; and "The kafos enable women to solve problems together. We learned malaria was caused by mosquitoes, so we went to the village leader and asked that all pot holes and dumping areas be cleared to remove the mosquitoes."[56]

While groups like Oxfam and the World Bank are part of an interconnecting web of educational endeavors, their functions are different.

Oxfam collects money from public and private sources for the direct funding of projects. The World Bank collects money from member nations for the purpose of giving loans for development projects. But their paths do cross in the global civil society and, as Oxfam states, one of its goals is to influence the powerful, including the World Bank. As the largest outside global financier of education, members of the global civil society try to influence its actions.

THE WORLD BANK'S GLOBAL VISION

The World Bank's educational ideology contains a particular vision about how society should be organized. For many people, this vision is just assumed to be a necessary part of the advancement of world societies. It is an image of the good society that is often unquestioned because of its promise of economic abundance for all. This image of the good society is embedded in the World Bank's *Education: The World Bank Education Sector Strategy*.[57]

As envisioned by the World Bank, a good society is one based on the mass production of consumer goods within a global economy. Each region or nation contributes to mass production through factory and agricultural goods. The production of agricultural goods is done on large corporate farms or plantations. Small family agricultural units are replaced by large units with factory-like organization. Workers in these larger units are trained for specialized roles and work in corporate teams. Those who previously worked on family farms either work on corporate agricultural units or move to urban centers. The migration of the population from rural to urban centers follows the pattern that occurred in Western industrialized nations in the 19th and early 20th centuries. Displaced rural workers provide the labor supply for new industrial concerns. In addition, gender equality and low fertility rates free women from the home to increase the supply of labor.

In the late 20th and 21st centuries, the migratory pattern of displacement from small agricultural units to urban industrial centers has become global. Displaced from the land, workers move to urban areas where, if they cannot find work, they join others in the search for work in other countries. Both the transition from rural farms and the global migration of labor require "lifelong learning." New skills have to be constantly learned. In addition, workers must have basic literacy and math proficiency to constantly learn new occupational skills.

What is valued is constant economic growth, which requires a continuous development of new products and increased consumption. There is no definable end to this process. When does a society reach a point when it does not need economic growth? Is there a point of stasis? Or is it an endless cycle of developing new products and creating consumer demand? Of course, from the viewpoint of the World Bank, the problem is that many countries have not reached a high enough level of economic development to participate in the mass consumer society. The role of education is to help them make this leap.

World Bank documents admit that global workers live in a world of constant uncertainty. The stability of rural life and traditional labor patterns are overturned for the supposed good of a global free market. Global living is filled with uncertainty. Factories can freely move from country to country in search of cheap labor. The workers left behind must learn new skills or join the migratory movement of global labor. Where factories settle, traditional patterns are upset, as workers must learn new skills and become socialized in the corporate workplace. Traditional holidays, family celebrations, and work patterns give way to the time schedule of the factory.

Consequently, *Education: The World Bank Education Sector Strategy* declares, "Education is a cornerstone of the World Bank Group's overall mission of helping countries fight poverty."[58] Education is the key to preparing untrained workers for new factory systems and corporate farming. It is the key to socializing rural peasants to corporate workplaces. It is the key to retraining workers whose jobs disappear as a company moves in search of cheaper labor. It is the key to preparing women to enter the workforce.

Also, global markets require the protection of governments from graft and corruption. World Bank authorities believe the best protection of multinational corporations from government extortion is a strong representative government and civil society. Education, particularly of women, is considered important in promoting honest governments that protect the free market and promote free trade.

And, because the World Bank thinks in terms of world markets, it envisions a reduced role for the nation-state in the provision of products and services. The World Bank assumes that what is called a neoliberal approach to government is pervading the globe. The basic assumption of neoliberalism is that government services, such as schools, water and sewer systems, electric power, and so on, can be better provided by private companies and nonprofit organizations. This assumption is based on the unproven idea that corporate bureaucracies are more efficient than government bureaucracies and that the free market is more responsive to public interests than governments. The primary role of government, from the perspective of World Bank leaders, is regulating the market to ensure the free flow of goods. Products and services, such as textbooks, schools, utilities, and other traditional functions, are to be turned over to the private sector. In this manner, government services enter the global market with international corporations.

THE WORLD BANK, EDUCATION, AND INTERNATIONAL
WOMEN'S ORGANIZATIONS

The World Bank's willingness to change local cultures to satisfy its global agenda is exemplified by its ties to international women's organizations. While women's rights can be justified as part of human rights, the implementation of these rights can change local cultures. The World Bank's goal of making women active members of a corporate workforce outside the home has profound implications for traditional family structures and childrearing practices. From the standpoint of the World Bank, the implementation of women's rights and the resulting cultural changes are essential for organizing a global mass market economy.

Consequently, women's issues are an important part of the World Bank's educational work. The involvement in gender issues highlights the role of the World Bank administrators in consciously attempting to change local cultures through development and educational projects. The Bank's plans link cultural changes to economic growth. Concern with gender equality is the direct result of the strong influence of NGOs and intergovernmental organizations representing the concerns of women. Also, the ties between women's organizations and the World Bank represent another aspect of the growing interrelationships in global civil society. However, World Bank efforts to network with NGOs concerned with women's issues might be an attempt by the Bank to organize and control the growing power of the global civil society.

The World Bank's involvement with international women's organizations began in the mid-1970s when women's organizations criticized the World Bank for neglecting gender issues in their development programs. As a result, the Bank appointed one advisor in 1977 on Women in Development. Things rapidly changed after the Bank's president James Wolfensohn attended the 1995 U.N. Conference on Women in Beijing. At the conference, he met with members of the Caucus on Economic Justice and accepted a petition from the Women's Eyes on the Bank Campaign. As a result, the Bank set up an External Gender Consultative Group.[59] Out of this effort was created World Bank Partnerships on Gender Issues. According to the official statement of the Bank, "Partnerships in the area of gender and development help the Bank to understand better the needs of clients, and also facilitate the sharing of information on approaches to integrating gender into development, thereby helping the World Bank to strengthen its work in this area."[60]

In 2002, the Bank issued "Integrating Gender into the World Bank's Work: A Strategy for Action," which laid out the Bank's methods for integrating gender issues into all aspects of its work, including education. The report specifically recognized the influence of meetings with women's groups at the 1995 U.N. Beijing conference. The document maintains,

"Greater attention to gender issues is also required by the commitment of the Bank and its member countries to the goals set forth in the United Nations Millennium Declaration, the Beijing Platform for Action, and the Convention on the Elimination of all Forms of Discrimination Against Women (CEDAW), all of which have a strong gender dimension."[61]

The Bank's strategy plan offers an official "Definition of Gender" that underpins the mainstreaming of gender issues into the arena of education:

> The term gender refers to culturally based expectations of the roles and behaviors of males and females. The term distinguishes the socially constructed from the biologically determined aspects of being male and female. Unlike the biology of sex, gender roles and behaviors can change historically, sometimes relatively quickly, even if aspects of these roles originated in the biological differences between the sexes. Because the religious or cultural traditions that define and justify the distinct roles and expected behaviors of males and females are strongly cherished and socially enforced, change in gender systems often is contested. In some countries, there are groups which seek to impose more stringent divisions between males and females than currently exist, while feminist movements seek to reduce or eradicate these divisions.[62]

An example of this gender definition being applied in practice is the World Bank's sponsored Female Secondary School Assistance Project in Bangladesh. This program attempts to overcome traditional resistance against women receiving an education by providing them with small stipends to attend school and tuition aid. By mainstreaming gender issues into general development plans, the officials of the World Bank contend,

> The benefits of educating girls have reached far beyond increasing individual opportunity. Higher education levels for girls have been shown to alleviate problems such as high birth rates, poor health practices, and high infant mortality. This project is providing continued support to a very effective effort on the part of the Bangladeshi government to enable poor rural girls to improve not only their own lives, but the well-being of the country.[63]

Reflecting the World Bank's primary concern with economic results, chapter 1 of the gender strategy report, "The Business Case for Mainstreaming Gender," provides a justification for support of women's education. Demonstrating its businesslike approach to gender issues, the chapter opens, "Gender equality is an issue of development effectiveness, not just a matter of political correctness or kindness to women."[64] The Bank argues that gender equality is important to development because "when women and men are relatively equal, economies tend to grow faster, the poor move more quickly out of poverty, and the well-being of men, women, and children is enhanced."[65]

The goal of gender equality overrides concerns about protecting cultures. This is an important value judgment made by the World Bank's educational activities. In the previous example of Female Secondary School Assistance Project in Bangladesh, the attempt is to change a culture that has traditionally placed little or no emphasis on the education of women. This creates an ethical dilemma. Should a powerful international banking operation consciously attempt to impose what its members think are "good values" on a culture? Is this a form of cultural imperialism? Or are there universal values, such as gender equality, that should override local values?

Clearly, the administrators of the World Bank believe that there are universal values that should serve as guides for development projects including educational projects. In other words, there are particular cultural values associated with the Bank's concept of economic development. As the strategy document states, "Gender-based division of labor, disparities between males and females in power and resources, and gender biases in rights and entitlements—act to undermine economic growth and reduce the well-being of men, women, and children."[66]

Based on an economic and cultural belief regarding gender equality, the "World Bank Operational Policy 4.20 The Gender Dimension of Development" states,

1. The Bank aims to reduce gender disparities and enhance women's participation in the economic development of their countries by integrating gender considerations in its country assistance program.
2. To this end, the Bank assists its member countries to:
   (a) Design gender-sensitive policies and programs to ensure that overall development efforts are directed to attain impacts that are equitably beneficial for both men and women. The Bank helps governments (i) identify barriers—including men's attitudes—that prevent women from participating in and benefitting from public policies and programs, (ii) assess the costs and benefits of specific actions to remove these barriers, (iii) ensure effective program delivery, and (iv) establish monitoring and evaluation mechanisms to measure progress.[67]

As proof of the importance of gender equality to economic development, the authors of "Integrating Gender into the World Bank's Work" argued that educating women raises family incomes by giving women the skills to enter the labor market. This assertion implies a belief that families should have two wage earners and that the stay-at-home mother hinders economic development. This assertion contains a major cultural value about how family life should be organized. "Educated, healthy women are more able to engage in productive activities, find formal sector employment, and earn higher incomes," the report maintained, "... [therefore] investments in female education and health ... *tend to increase the incomes of families .... These investments also help to increase a country's total economic output* [emphasis added]."[68]

The strategy report gave other important and powerful reasons for supporting women's education. First, there is an intergenerational effect caused by educated women giving more emphasis to the education of their own children. Secondly, educated mothers are better able to protect the health of their own children. Third, the report claimed, "Education—especially female education–slows population growth."[69] Finally, in countries with educated women there tends to be less government corruption.[70]

In summary, the World Bank's mainstreaming of gender issues is now an important part of their educational programs. It represents the Bank's commitment to cultural change as part of economic development. It also illustrates the interplay between organizations in the global society. Similar to gender issues, the overall criterion for funding educational projects is economic growth based on a particular developmental model, and the projects involve cultural change.

EDUCATION AND THE CAUSES OF GLOBAL CHANGE

Reflecting its vision of the good society and the resulting change in gender roles, the World Bank's *Education Sector Strategy* document nests education in what it calls the five "Drivers of Change." The first driver of change is global democratization and the growth of a powerful civil society which requires education for citizen participation. As a goal, global democratization is acceptable to both pro- and antiglobalization forces with organizations such as the World Bank placing more emphasis on representative governments and elections, and antiglobalization groups placing more emphasis on direct action by citizens.

The distinguishing features of the World Bank's approach to education appears in discussions of the other four drivers of change. The second driver of change, the strategy document states, is the growth of market economies or, in other words, the triumph of capitalism over socialist planning. The report states, "Where other (mainly centrally planned) systems used to provide fewer opportunities but more certainty, market systems now reward enterprise, risk-taking, skill, and agility, but offer less security and a constantly changing environment."[71]

The assumption of a market economy leads to an educational prescription to enhance individual skills for economic competition. While not discounting the World Bank's faith in the spread of a market economy, it is important to contrast the Bank's approach with that of other educational theorists. For instance, John Dewey argued that school should teach cooperation and social understanding to ensure the advancement of modern economic systems.[72] In contrast, the World Bank document states, "Education is vital: those who can compete best (with literacy, numeracy, and more advanced skills) have an enormous advantage in this faster paced world economy over their less well prepared counterparts."[73]

The third driver of change is the globalization of markets resulting in employers pursuing the best and least expensive workers by shifting their operations from country to country. This, according to the World Bank, means that workers must constantly adapt to changing labor markets. The prescription is lifelong learning or education for the development of human capital. As a result of globalized markets, the strategy report states,

> Tomorrow's workers will need to be able to engage in lifelong education, learn new things quickly, perform more non-routine tasks and more complex problem solving, take more decisions, understand more about what they are working on, require less supervision, assume more responsibility, and—as vital tools to those ends–have better reading, quantitative, reasoning, and expository skills.[74]

In addition, the fourth driver of change is the information revolution which makes possible the use of distance learning to ensure easy access to lifelong education. Information technology, as the World Bank recognizes, provides the opportunity to bridge the boundaries of the nation-state in the provision of educational services. Not only is the World Bank Web site an important means for spreading information about the Bank's projects, including educational projects, but the Bank also supports online learning projects, as I discuss later, like the African Virtual University. Because online learning can be accessed anywhere in the world, it is a powerful force in creating global unity by ignoring the territorial limits of the nation-state.

The fifth driver of change is certainly the most controversial because it envisions a new role for governments. The strategy report states, "Governments are becoming less the direct producers and providers of goods and services and more the facilitators and regulators of economic activity."[75]

For education, neoliberalism retains government financing but shifts school operations to private companies and nonprofit private schools. Also, governments transfer the production of textbooks and learning materials to private companies. The Bank's report treats these changes as an inevitable part of globalization: "The vital question now is not whether other-than-government roles in education will expand–*they will*—but rather how these developments should be incorporated into countries' overall strategies."[76]

Human capital theory is used to evaluate the effectiveness of education as nested in the five drivers of global change. Human capital theory also contains an assumption that the good society is based on economic growth and mass consumption. The educational goal is teaching subjects and skills that contribute to economic growth. Consequently, the measure of a good education is based on economic outcomes. In human capital theory, the financing of schools is treated as an economic investment that should result in measurable economic growth. "Estimates by Nobel-laureate economists," the strategy report states, "have shown that education is one of the best investments in physical capital. Related analysis has demonstrated that the total *stock of human capital worldwide* has a higher value by far, in terms of its contribution to production, than the stock of physical capital."[77]

In addition to human capital theory, the World Bank's educational plans call for developing "social cohesion" which is a variation on traditional nationalistic education. In this sense, they are moving away from the idea that schools should serve the interests of the nation-state. Education supports social cohesion by transmitting "values, beliefs, and traditions."[78] Social cohesion is built around cultural values. The Bank's strategy report *does not* contain any of the propositions of a nationalistic education that call for individual wills to be submerged in the will of the "nation" or that children should be taught to sacrifice for the good of the "nation."

By emphasizing social cohesion over traditional forms of nationalistic education, the World Bank attempts to align school systems more closely with the needs of world markets. In this context, the power of the nation-state is undermined. The weakening of the nation-state is also suggested in changing the role of government from producer and provider of services to that of regulator. Considered together with human capital theory, these aspects of the Bank's educational policies portent a world where students are educated for global labor markets without strong attachment to a particular nation-state.

Bundled with this vision of schooling is health care. Schools are considered ideal sites for the provision of health services which are considered essential for the development of human capital. "Fortunately," the strategy report states, "schools themselves provide cost-effective means of providing simple, well-tried health services, such as deworming and micronutrient (e.g. iron) supplements to solve the most prevalent immediate problems, as well as promoting health lifestyles and life-long benefits."[79]

Gender issues are also woven into the human capital vision of education. The educational strategy document reiterates the positive effect of education on fertility rates, mortality rates, and intergenerational education. And the report suggests cultural change to improve rates of female enrollment in schools. As the report states, "Many factors contribute to the persistence of the gender gap: traditional values and beliefs about the roles of females and males in the society ... and perceptions about the value of schooling for daughters unlikely to enter the marketplace."[80]

In summary, the World Bank's educational ideology is premised on schools serving the cause of economic growth in a global economy and providing social cohesion. Students are evaluated according to their future usefulness as workers in a modernized industrial society. Social cohesion, in contrast to nationalistic education, is to create a stabilized community where social conflicts do not interfere with economic development. Health and gender equality are important because of their impact on economic development. Schools serve a global economy rather than a nation-state. Consequently, governments are to reduce their role as providers of schooling and transfer these powers to the private sector. The private sector, of course, could be tied to international corporate schooling. Governments become regulators of schools by using evaluation tools that are global in nature, such as those of the OECD and Education for All.

WESTERN EDUCATIONAL CLASSIFICATION

The World Bank's classification of educational development underlines its emphasis on spreading Western forms of education and industrial models around the world. Either consciously or unconsciously its classification scheme parallels the triumphant march of Western industrialism around the world. At the top of the classification scheme are the leading industrial countries followed by former Communist countries. At the bottom of the classification list are former colonies in Latin America, Africa, and Asia.

Missing from the World Bank's classification categories are any suggestions that traditional non-Western forms of education are anything more than obstacles to industrialization. Traditional village educations in Africa and Asia go unmentioned in the classification scheme. The assumption is that the good life depends on Western forms of mass consumer society which, in turn, depend on Western forms of schooling.

The World Bank strategy document divides the world into "mature," "reform," "emergent," and "least developed" educational systems. These classifications parallel degrees of industrial development. Mature systems have "well-developed educational infrastructures, fairly high achievement, but with residual problems of inefficiency and inequity (with gaps between the rich the poor, and between males and females being sometimes severe)."[81] Mature educational systems are those of the most advanced industrial societies, particularly those, according to the World Bank, belonging to OECD. OECD membership highlights the parallel the World Bank is making between "mature" educational systems and industrialization. OECD members include Australia, Austria, Belgium, Canada, Czech Republic, Denmark, Finland, France, Germany, Greece, Hungary, Iceland, Ireland, Italy, Japan, Korea, Luxembourg, Mexico, the Netherlands, New Zealand,

Norway, Poland, Portugal, Slovak Republic, Spain, Sweden, Switzerland, Turkey, United Kingdom, and the United States.[82]

"Reform" educational systems "face serious quality and growth demands but where the education system may appear to be of reasonable quality (but where maintenance of the system is under strong threat and, in some contexts, subject to future collapse)."[83] Former Communist countries are identified as having "reform" educational systems including Russia, Eastern Europe, and many of the countries of the former Soviet Union. These former Soviet countries form the Commonwealth of Independent States (Azerbaijan Republic, Republic of Armenia, Republic of Belarus, Georgia, Republic of Kazakhstan, Kyrghyz Republic, Republic of Moldova, and the Ukraine).[84]

And at the bottom of the classification scheme are "emergent" systems in Latin America, North Africa, and Asia "where education participation rates are high but inequality in access and especially in quality is acute," and "least developed systems" in sub-Saharan Africa and parts of south Asia "where universal education remains the exception rather than the rule, and where long-term interventions will be required to create modern education systems."[85]

THE THREE PILLARS OF A GOOD EDUCATION SYSTEM

What World Bank officials consider the "Three Pillars of a Good Education System" exemplifies its efforts in globalizing Western models of schooling and industrialization. The three pillars are "Quality," "Access," and "Delivery." One of three characteristics of "Quality" is a relevant curriculum which is defined as "competencies to thrive in global economy" along with contribution to social development and "flexible and adaptable to changes."[86] Quality then is a curriculum continually in flux as the needs of the global economy change. There is no suggestion that "relevance" should be tied to the needs of the nation-state or to the concerns that antiglobalization forces have with human rights and environmentalism.

Of course, competencies "to thrive in global economy" could mean a variety of things ranging from empowering people so that they can protect themselves from exploitation from multinational corporations to methods of unionization. However, the World Bank is committed to a global economy based on open markets where people and companies compete to maximize their economic returns. Therefore, thriving in a global economy means labor or entrepreneurial skills that maximize the ability to compete with others. It does not mean avoidance or protection from the global economy. Also, "flexible and adaptable to changes" embraces a world where tradition is replaced by the instability of market economies, and the migration of businesses and people.

It is proposed that the quality of the "teaching and learning process" be determined by a measurement process that links test results, methods of instruction, and a curriculum geared toward job skills required by the global economy. This measurement paradigm assumes that the requirements of the labor market will determine what is taught and how it is taught. In turn, some form of assessment will determine whether or not the school was successful in imparting global work skills. Oddly, since students are being educated for an unstable global economy, the measurement paradigm creates a rigid educational system with little room for thinking outside the world of global competencies. Theoretically, the constant monitoring of student learning should result in continual adjustment of the educational process to ensure efficient instruction in global competencies.

The rigid nature of measurement paradigm is reflected in another pillar of the Bank's good education system, namely "Delivery." Good delivery requires "evaluation" which involves "monitoring and feedback to influence plans." The delivery pillar envisions an educational organization guided by tight planning with objectives tied to results. Clear planning and responsibilities are matched to efficient and effective use of resources to ensure instruction in global competencies. Again, there is no match between the tightly organized school plan and the chaotic and unstable global market for which students are being prepared.

There is an air of unreality about this pillar of good education. World Bank's ideal "delivery" system assumes unemotional, unselfish, and rational bureaucrats developing, executing, and monitoring a plan for teaching global competencies. This might be an unrealistic assumption about human behavior. For instance, the World Bank supports a free market economy which is based on the assumption that people will and should pursue their own self-interests. Often, advertising in the free market assumes an irrational consumer more in tune with their emotions than reason. Based on what is assumed as human behavior in the marketplace, the attempt to tightly plan a school system might fall victim to bureaucratic self-interest, intrigue, and the petty emotions of organizational infighting.

The possible disjuncture between the World Bank's rational organization plan for educational systems and its support of the behaviors encountered in global markets raises the issue of alternative organizational forms for schools. There are traditional forms of education. In small agricultural villages, knowledge is passed on in a variety of different methods from story telling to apprenticeship (I discuss these methods later in the book). Educational organization is based on traditions that have evolved through centuries of human practice. These traditions are molded by real human emotions and experience rather than an artificial master plan that tries to tightly link goals with outcomes.

It is important to understand that I am not making a qualitative judgment that tradition is better than measurement-based planning. What I am stressing is that the very model of planning and schooling used by the World Bank introduces cultural change. It forces local residents to think in terms of measured objectives and outcomes. It forces people to think of what should be learned to meet the needs of global markets and how that learning should be measured by some form of objective assessment. The World Bank's "Delivery" pillar of a good education system is rooted in particular assumptions about human behavior.

The other pillar of a good education system, "Access," depends on many conditions outside the control of the school, such as nutrition, health, parental support, and political leadership interested in education. Conditions within the control of schools are equitable access and school supplies. World Bank funding contributes to ensuring both of these conditions. Regarding equitable access, the World Bank focuses its financial support on the education of women. For instance, girls' education receives the most support in the World Bank's "Summary of International Initiatives." Except for Somalia, in every African country receiving World Bank educational loans, girls' education is a central initiative. The same thing is true in other countries. Regarding girls' education, the strategy report states, "The Bank, with its partners, will target its efforts on improving basic education for girls in the 31 countries where girls' enrollment rates lag significantly behind boys' rates, with special emphasis on 15 countries."[87] Nine of these 15 countries are in Africa while the others are Papua New Guinea, Guatemala, Morocco, Yemen, Nepal, and Pakistan.

As stated previously, the emphasis on girls' education changes traditional cultures and contributes to the destabilization of society. While there is an emphasis on women entering the labor market, there are no suggestions as to what form of family organization will replace traditional households. Certainly within the framework of human rights, equal rights and education should be supported for women. However, one must recognize that this protection of human rights overturns centuries of family traditions regarding childrearing. What is the alternative if women enter the workforce? Will day care be provided in societies barely able to support schools? Will there be unsupervised children growing up in new urban slums?

In summary, the World Bank's "Three Pillars of a Good Education" includes a highly rationalized system of schooling for a world destabilized by world markets and the destruction of traditional family organizations. While students are being prepared in "competencies to thrive in [the] global economy," their parents' worlds are being undermined without any clear idea about what should replace them. The global economy, according to the World Bank, involves another level of uncertainty and instability.

Workers must constantly undergo "lifelong" learning as their lives are made insecure by the constant movement of global capital and corporations. There is nothing in the World Bank's educational plans to prepare people for the psychological trauma of being uprooted and living in a state of economic insecurity.

DRAWING BOTSWANA

To breathe life in this portrayal of the World Bank's "Three Pillars of A Good Education," I describe an illustrated booklet prepared by Amallia Orman for my course in Global Ideologies of Education at Lang College of the New School University. The booklet, *Drawing Botswana: Development, Economics, and Education*, was based on her experience living in the country.[88] The first illustration shows a small African village with huts of mud walls and thatched roofs, chickens, and goats. The caption reads, "In the villages lives are still shared. There are few people that have very much." The next drawing shows a house surrounded by razor wire and an electric fence. "In the city there are rich and poor neighborhoods," the caption states. "The family I stayed with had enough money to refer to people living in poor neighborhoods as 'those people'."

The next illustration depicts the consequences of the global economy driving people from their agricultural villages to urban areas. Portraying an urban slum with children running on the streets and shanties built of cinder blocks, Orman provides the powerful statement, "They lived a village life in the city and became dangerous."

The next two illustrations are devoted to education in which the legacy of British colonialism is reflected in the text accompanying a drawing of an African school boy wearing a polo sweater: "English is the official language and medium of education in both government and private schools. Private schools, started for and still attended by the country's expatriates are 'English medium.' They are considered the better schools." And, of course, English is one of the global languages that the World Bank would consider an important part of repertoire of global skills.

The second school illustrations shows a strip of cloth colored by an African design. The reader is told that a teacher encouraged a native Botswana student to attend a technical school to "make a living 'printing shirts for tourists'."

The next illustrations show the unfolding of a mass consumer society in Botswana. In Garborone, the capital city built over the last 30 years, "almost all of its landmarks and points of navigation are shopping malls." In the next illustration of wheelbarrows and heavy equipment, we are told that wealth from diamond mines and foreign aid allows for "rapid development" and "modernization."

The last four illustrations drive home the results of the destabilizing effects of modernization. A pottery jar is shown next to a plastic bucket while a history text with a chapter titled "Botswana Culture" rests at the bottom of the page. "Some objects of cultural significance have lost their everyday use, but many children, especially in villages, still know how to make or use them. But, in time as their lives and landscape change, they might forget." On the opposing page, a group of white tourists are shown driving away from a thatched house. "Then only tourists would experience the natural heating and cooling of traditional building materials and techniques."

In the last two pages, Orman drives home her point with a statement placed on a chalk board, "If indigenous methods of education, agriculture, community living, and family raising are not incorporated into current 'modernization', the reality of life today as well as long ago may just be another." The statement is completed at the end of a line running from the chalk board to a pile of clay pottery marked, "history lesson." With a drawing of hammer and clocks, the story is completed, "and the school system might function to sustain social class differences, as it does in the U.S."

WORLD BANK STRATEGIES: TRAPPED BY A VISION OF EDUCATION AND DEVELOPMENT

At times, World Bank educational plans are limited by their own Western models of education and industrialization. The Bank professes regional educational strategies to implement its concepts of development and modernization, and it believes it has the economic power to implement these strategies. However, Africa's political, economic, and health factors create almost insurmountable obstacles to Western-style modernization and schooling. Shaking free of European colonialism by the 1960s, sub-Saharan Africa is left with a legacy of nation-states that have been devastated by armed conflict. Most sub-Saharan African nations were created by colonialists for the purpose of exploitation. The end of colonialism has meant political instability. In addition, political instability has contributed to steadily declining economic conditions. Added to these conditions is the HIV/AIDS pandemic.

Considering these conditions, the World Bank's primary educational objective for sub-Saharan Africa seems like wishful thinking. The objective is "increasing the average level of education attainment of the population through broad based investment in basic education, developing the technical and vocational skills of the labor force and preparing selected students for scientific and technological careers."[89] In addition, the Bank claims that while its "lending presents only about 20–25% of external education finance, it has considerable influence on policy discussions and aid priorities."[90]

World Bank authorities admit the difficulty of achieving their educational objective for sub-Saharan Africa. According to their own report, *A Chance to Learn: Knowledge and Finance for Education in Sub-Saharan Africa*, since the 1980s the incidence of poverty and actual numbers of people living in poverty *has increased* in the region. "More than 40 percent of Africans live below the $1 a day poverty line."[91] These are startling figures and on the surface suggest that something is seriously wrong in the development strategies implemented by governments and international organizations.

Poverty is a relative term, particularly if a society is not enmeshed in a cash economy but relies on family farming and hunting. However, poverty, particularly after the destructive impact of European colonialism, can be measured in real human terms in sub-Saharan Africa. In 1997, the average life expectancy in the region was 49 years as compared in 63 in South Asia and 70 in East Asia, Latin America, and the Caribbean. In the same year, infant mortality rate per 1,000 live births was 91 in the region as compared to 77 in South Asia, 37 in East Asia, and 32 in Latin America and the Caribbean.[92]

The steady economic decline of sub-Saharan Africa would suggest the need for some serious economic and political strategies for the region. However, World Bank authorities persist in applying an educational formula of human capital that was developed for Western industrialized countries. It is important to note that educational planning based on human capital ideas developed after the industrialization of the West. It is not clear what would have happened in Western countries if 19th-century educational leaders had actually attempted to organize schools to meet the labor needs of developing industrialism. Given the inadequate ability to actually predict how industrialism would develop and the type of society that might result, 19th-century educational planners using human capital ideas might have actually slowed industrial development.

Neglecting the lack of historical proof that human capital planning actually works, World Bank experts declared, "Development strategies designed to reduce poverty must thus be grounded in sound economic policy and centered on human capital development programs .... Longer-term economic performance will depend on improvements in human capital and the associated ability to use modern technology."[93]

Another assumption is that a knowledge economy is essential to solving the issue of poverty in sub-Saharan Africa. One wonders if World Bank experts question their own world view that leads to the conclusion that "the most important determinant of the pace of Africa's development may be its ability to create, acquire, absorb, and communicate knowledge."[94] Also, Western faith in science as the key to economic progress is projected onto the region. As a solution to economic problems, World Bank leaders declared that to "take advantage of the new knowledge economy, Africa needs well-trained scientific, technological, and processing personnel–including some with sophisticated research skills–who can participate in advances in key fields (physics, materials science, computer science, technology, engineering)."[95]

World Bank leaders persist in applying the Western models of science, industrialism, and human capital to sub-Saharan Africa despite the actual inability of governments in this region to sustain Western forms of schooling. As the World Bank report indicates, "Between 1985 and 1995 regional spending per student on primary education fell by 6 percent. In stark contrast to this decrease, primary education spending increased approximately threefold in every other developing region over the same period."[96] In addition, there was an equal decline in spending for secondary and postsecondary education.

Two major reasons for regional economic decline are war and diseases such as HIV/AIDS. The end of colonialism left many unstable nation-states. The organization of these nation-states had forced an artificial unity on previously disparate tribal structures and kingdoms. According to the World Bank, "In 1996 alone a third of African countries experienced armed conflicts. One African in five lives in a country severely disrupted by war."[97] The World Bank's educational response is to "support conflict resolution and instill civic values and principles of democracy, tolerance, and cooperation."[98] Bank officials do not suggest that the political structures of the postcolonial period might be inappropriate for the region.

Regional diseases, such as river blindness, sleeping sickness, and malaria, seriously hinder economic development. The region accounted for 70% of all new HIV infections and 80% of all AIDS-related deaths in 1998. Besides the actual costs of treatment and prevention, many infected people in the 20 to 30 age group are removed from the productive workforce, further reducing the ability of governments to spend more on education.

In the case of diseases, education and science are obvious answers. However, the actual conditions of development contribute to unhealthy environmental conditions. Urban slums lacking basic sanitary conditions are created with rural migration and the breakdown of village and family life. In the West, similar unhealthful urban conditions were created in the 19th century as workers moved from farms to industrial centers. Nineteenth- century London and New York were noted for their unsanitary tenement areas.

In summary, political and social conditions in sub-Saharan Africa do not seem ideal for the application of Western models of the nation-state, industrialism, and education. In fact, there is no proof that World Bank plans will actually improve conditions. There is a need for new concepts of economic, political, and educational organizations that take into account African cultural and political traditions, and the aftermath of a brutal period of colonialism. I discuss other possibilities in later chapters on the possible worldwide role of indigenous forms of education in the postcolonial period. Obviously, sub-Saharan African tribes and kingdoms will never be able to return to precolonial times. However, like former colonialists, World Bank leaders seem hopelessly trapped by their own fixed beliefs on how society should be organized.

THE WORLD BANK IN LATIN AMERICA
AND THE CARIBBEAN: THREE STARTLING FACTS

There are three startling facts about the World Bank's educational strategy for Latin America and the Caribbean. First is the attempted global homogenization of economies and political systems into free-trade markets and representative governments. The same educational, economic, and political vision is applied to Latin America and the Caribbean that is applied to Africa and the rest of the world. If World Bank development plans are successful, the whole world would be organized into similar societies.

The second startling fact is the unwillingness of World Bank officials to consider the maintenance of indigenous cultures. For these officials, indigenous cultural practices are to be utilized solely for the purpose of achieving the Bank's objectives. It is surprising that World Bank planners neglect the interests of indigenous peoples who—from Aztecs and Mayans of Mexico and Central America to Amazonian, Columbian, and Bolivian tribes and the Incas of South America—are struggling for autonomy and protection of their languages and cultures. Tribal organization and cultural traditions might offer important alternatives to the free market and representative government, and to the urban slum life created in the process of modernization.

World Bank planners approach indigenous cultures as something to be utilized in the development process rather than as alternatives to the mass consumer cultures. For utilitarian purposes, World Bank authorities created an "Indigenous Knowledge Program" for the purpose of "mainstreaming indigenous/traditional knowledge into the activities of development partners and to optimize the benefits of development assistance, especially to the poor."[99] I don't want to be overly critical of the use of indigenous knowledge because it does represent an important advance over previous activities by the World Bank. For instance, the World Bank is supporting efforts in Malawi to develop indigenous crops for food emergencies. In northern Uganda, local elders are being utilized to prevent and manage conflict. In Burundi, indigenous knowledge is being used in the fight against HIV/AIDS.[100]

The utilitarian approach of the World Bank to indigenous knowledge is most evident in their educational examples. Indigenous methods are treated as bridges to Western-type schooling and modernization. For instance, one example provided by Bank officials involves three men who were educated in traditional Islamic schools in Ghana, Burkina Faso, and Guinea. "In all three cases," the report states, "adults schooled in Koranic instruction have assumed key accounting functions in local businesses and community enterprises."[101] In another example, 200 traditional leaders in Niger were brought together to discuss the survival and protection of women. The traditional leaders agreed to develop strategies to persuade communities to send girls to school.[102] Based on the methods of storytelling used by Maasai elders, it is proposed to use these "traditional methods of conveying information ... in awareness campaigns or in the participatory preparation of projects."[103]

In these examples, there is no suggestion that traditional governing structures utilizing elders might be a positive alternative to representative government or that traditional storytelling might be a reasonable alternative to human capital education. Even traditional Koranic schools are highlighted because graduates can get jobs in modern businesses and not because of the religious values that are learned. This utilitarian approach reinforces the single-minded World Bank vision of a global society organized around a mass consumer market.

The third startling fact is that students in a Communist country, Cuba, score higher on international tests used by the World Bank than students in all other Latin American and Caribbean countries. Cuba has a centrally planned economy and educational system. These test results would seem to contradict World Bank planners' claims that educational improvement requires free markets and the privatization of the educational systems. The World Bank's strategy document *Educational Change in Latin America and the Caribbean* (Fig. 3.9, Third Grade Language Achievement Scores from UNESCO) shows Cuban student scores ranging from 300 to about 400 while all other countries range from a low of about 190 to a high of about 300.[104] The World Bank document does not comment on this Cuban achievement. UNESCO test scores for fourth-grade reading and math provided by the Inter-American Development Bank show Cuban students scoring at 103 in reading and 104 in math while students in other Latin American and Caribbean countries range from a low in reading of 68 in the Dominican Republic to a high of 83 in Brazil and a low in math of 67 in Venezuela to a high of 79 in Argentina and Brazil.[105]

Shouldn't World Bank educational strategists be considering the Cuban educational model if they want successful schools? Consider comparative scores on the Third International Math and Science Survey (TIMSS) for 1997 and 1999. The World Bank strategy document for Latin America and the Caribbean reports scores for selected countries but does not include the results for Cuba or offer any comparisons with the United States.[106] On the other hand, the Inter-American Development Bank offers the following commentary on the TIMSS results:

> On this basis [in reference to test scores], Latin American countries would be likely to score similar to or lower than Chile and Colombia on the international tests, equivalent to at least a half deviation below the United States, which itself generally scores a half to a full standard deviation below countries such as Japan and Singapore. *The only Latin American country which would score at a level similar to that of the United States would be Cuba* [emphasis added].[107]

Cuban students' achievement scores on international tests are similar to those of students in the United States and higher than those of all other Latin American and Caribbean countries! Why? The Inter-American Development Bank report suggests, "Cuba's success has been attributed to the high quality of its teachers (who are paid relatively well in comparison with other professions), rigorous teacher evaluation, universal pre-schooling, adequate and equitable school inputs, and strong community involvement."[108] Reporting for *Education Week* on the success of Cuban schools, Robert C. Johnson suggested that one possible cause is the lack of economic inequality. Describing the arguments of Martin Carnoy, a Stanford University professor who studies Latin American educational systems, Johnson wrote, "The lack of extreme poverty in Cuba compared with elsewhere in Latin America, he [Carnoy] says, means fewer distractions in the classroom related to hunger, health, and students who work."[109]

What I call startling facts underscores the single-minded vision of World Bank authorities. There seems to be no place in their reasoning for the possibility that a Communist country with government-provided schools could actually maintain a superior educational system. Also, there is no place in their global vision for indigenous forms of education or social organization. And, as I discuss in the next section, World Bank authorities seem unwilling to recognize that free markets combined with schooling might contribute to growing economic inequalities.

LATIN AMERICA AND THE CARIBBEAN: SCHOOLING AND ECONOMIC INEQUALITY

The World Bank's educational strategy report for Latin America and the Caribbean identifies income inequality as one of the most pressing economic problems in the region. According to their figures, the region "continues to be one of the least egalitarian regions of the world."[110] The income gap between the rich and poor is increasing. A difficult thing for the World Bank to explain is why the region is becoming less equalitarian as free markets are expanded. Do free markets increase the income gap between the rich and the poor? In the United States, a similar phenomenon has taken place in recent years with the decline of the welfare state. According to U.S. census figures, income differences between the rich and poor in the United States have steadily increased since the 1980s.[111]

Of course, World Bank experts attribute the growing income gap to educational attainment and not the workings of the free market. Staff writers of the World Bank's regional strategy report concluded, "There is growing evidence that in Argentina, Chile, and Mexico, which have liberalized trade regimes in recent years, *wage disparities have increased, presumably because of growing gaps in skill* [emphasis added]."[112] Presumably, overcoming the gaps in skill by expanding educational opportunities will reduce income inequalities.

World Bank staffers admit that it might be illogical to equate increased educational opportunities with reducing income inequalities. They refer to the "paradox that education is a powerful means for reducing poverty and inequality, but at the same time it can lead to exclusion and marginalization."[113] In fact, the experience in the United States over the last 20 years does not prove any necessary relationship between expanded educational opportunities and reduction of income inequalities.[114]

There is an assumption that raising a person's educational level will allow him or her to get a higher paying job. There are a number of possible fallacies in this reasoning. First, the higher paying job must exist. Second, if the supply of educated workers for a job increases, then, as a result of competition for the job, wages might fall. And third, unless everyone attains the same educational level, such as a nation's doctors, then educational attainment might simply be equated with social class. The poor could be high school graduates and the rich college graduates. In other words, not only is there no proof that expanded educational opportunities reduce income inequalities, but there is also no logical reason why they should. Consequently, the World Bank regional strategy document's statement that "education reduces inequality and poverty by enhancing the skills and productivity of the whole population by equipping them with the skills they need to adapt in volatile economic times,"[115] is an unproven assumption and not a fact.

Also, to overcome poverty and inequality, the strategy document proposes concentrating on nutrition, health, and early childhood education. There is little doubt that nutrition and health are important. However, early childhood education raises the issue of protection of indigenous cultures. Is the purpose of early childhood education to change the culture of tribal children so that they will more easily fit into Western-style schools?

For instance, the World Bank report, *Peruvian Education at a Crossroads: Challenges and Opportunities for the 21st Century*, early childhood education is highlighted as a means of preparing indigenous children for school and overcoming significant differences in school completion rates and learning outcomes between the rich and the poor, between rural and urban areas, and between indigenous and nonindigenous populations.[116] Peru is a multilingual country with Incan and Amazonian tribes. Out of a population of 24 million, 8 million are indigenous peoples with 4 million speaking Quechua.[117] Among Incas, according to the report, "about 63 percent of Quechua speaking children are over-aged. For children who work in the countryside, 68 percent are over-aged, and the dropout rate among them is as high as 55 percent."[118] The report proposes the use of bilingual and multicultural methods for educating indigenous children. It recognizes the problems in educating indigenous children but warns, "Given that Peru has many indigenous groups who speak different languages, and that indigenous communities in the Amazon regions are small and dispersed, such intervention is predictably expensive. Nonetheless, given the cost of marginalizing indigenous people, the benefit of poverty alleviation and social cohesion is high."[119]

Although recognizing that Peru's indigenous peoples are marginalized in the modern mass consumer society, the report does not suggest protecting their cultural traditions as an alternative to modernization. Instead, the strategy suggested is changing traditional family childrearing practices. Bilingual and multicultural education are to be used as utilitarian methods for socializing indigenous peoples for a mass consumer society. Regarding indigneous peoples, the report suggests "besides the interventions through textbook provision and teacher training, educating parents about good child-rearing practices and the positive effects on achievement of school attendance."[120] This type of intervention recalls the worst 19th-century practices of the U.S. government toward indigenous peoples when attempts were made to change childrearing practices and destroy Native American culture.[121] Again, referring to indigenous children, the report continues to emphasize using schools as a means of cultural change: "The policy of universalizing early childhood education to enhance students' school readiness might help reduce late entry and repetition and reduce the between-student differences."[122] The goal of changing indigenous cultures is underscored by the Peruvian Ministry of Education. The Ministry, which is in charge of early childhood education, defines its mission as "developing the character of the individual, improving the quality of life, and facilitating social development in Peru through promotion of culture, science and technology, physical education, and pursuit of excellence."[123] There is no suggestion that education will promote indigenous cultures for the purpose of maintaining their social, political, and economic structures.

These educational activities are being pursued despite the Peruvian government's commitment to protecting indigenous cultural rights. The strategy document for Peru's Rural Education and Teacher Development

Project admits that "Peru's Political Constitution mentions that all individuals have the right to preserve their ethnic and cultural identity; that the Peruvian state recognizes and protects ethnic and cultural plurality in the nation; that bilingual and inter-cultural education must be fostered, recognizing each area's characteristics while preserving the various cultural and language manifestations."[124] However, in the actual plan for rural education, preserving language and cultural identities is placed in the framework of integration into the nation's life and learning Spanish.

> The new Primary Education Regulations create[s] the ways to provide Andean and Amazonian communities with inter-cultural bilingual education schools, with education provided in the indigenous mother tongue and Spanish progressively taught as a second language, thus helping to build among the students a stronger language and cultural identity in the framework of the nation's life.[125]

However, fitting indigenous people's cultural identity into the "nation's life" means adapting cultural traditions to economic development plans. In fact, the very act of sending indigenous children to Western-style schools could be considered a violation of cultural integrity. Ensuring the continued existence of indigenous cultures might require allowing traditional forms of education to be promoted and continued without outside interference.

There is little proof that attempts to restructure indigenous cultures will remove them from the margins of a mass consumer society. After more than a century of educational efforts, many Native Americans in the United States still remain in tribal communities with high rates of poverty and alcoholism. And, it is not clear that all indigenous groups in Latin America want to embrace a mass consumer society. Trapped by their single-minded vision of the future, World Bank officials are planning cultural changes that will force indigenous peoples to compete in a free-market system designed for modern consumerism.

LATIN AMERICA AND THE CARIBBEAN: COLONIALISM AND THE NEOLIBERAL STATE

Unlike their position toward Africa, World Bank educational experts do consider the effects of colonialism on Latin American countries. The Bank's strategy report recognizes that after the defeat of European colonialism in the 19th century, educational systems were used for nation-building. According to this argument, nation-building required the centralization of government control and financing. Now, the World Bank envisions these former centralized, welfare governments as joining the global march to a neoliberal state with reduced public services. Regarding Latin America, the report states,

The decline of the welfare state across the world is affecting all of the countries in the region. What has been called the "reinvention of the state" is based on several different goals: increasing the efficiency of public finances and the essential services provided by the government, limiting the involvement of governments to those activities that cannot be effectively performed by the private sector, making service providers more responsive to their clients, and promoting equity and the participation of stakeholders in all aspects of the management of social services.[126]

Again, applying the same global vision to Latin America and the Caribbean that it is using in Africa, the Bank calls for more community involvement and privatization of schools. While governments in this region are still charged with promoting "basic education for all, it is no longer solely responsible for actually providing education itself."[127] This approach is exemplified by World Bank loans to the Dominican Republic to support early childhood education as part of a poverty reduction program. In keeping with the Bank's vision of the neoliberal state, one goal is to "enhance private sector participation" in the provision of early childhood education.[128] Consequently, "loan money is spent to carry out 200 initiatives involving … public-private collaboration for early childhood services."[129]

Consequently, World Bank loans appear as self-fulling prophecies. While World Bank leaders imagine a global trend toward the neoliberal state, they are in fact causing this to happen by demanding that their loans be used to encourage private educational ventures. Consequently, education loans serve the dual purpose of preparing populations for globalized markets and promoting the Bank's attempt to undermine the welfare state.

THE WORLD BANK: EAST ASIA AND THE PACIFIC

World Bank educational loans for East Asia and the Pacific repeat the ideological stance behind the Bank's work in Africa and Latin America. The loans are to both former colonies and uncolonized societies, such as China. In 1998, Indonesia, a former Dutch colony, received 37% of the Bank's total regional educational loans followed by China, Korea (former Japanese colony), Thailand, the Philippines (former Spanish and U.S. colony), Malaysia (former British colony), and Vietnam (former French colony).[130] Regional loans support projects ranging from early childhood to university education. And, similar to those in Africa and Latin America, they support a vision of a globe linked by free trade with neoliberal governments and mass consumer societies. Under colonial rulers, many of these countries already experienced Western-style education. World Bank loans continue support for these colonial models.

For instance, World Bank authorities use the language of human capital to describe the economic downturn of the early 21st century. The World Bank reports,

Indonesia's economic crisis is expected to hurt the poor as a result of reduced incomes, increasing prices, higher unemployment, and underemployment. The poor's ability to invest in human capital, and hence their potential future income earning capacity, will be impaired as parents face higher prices of schooling and lower incomes to pay for schooling.[131]

Again using the language of human capital, the World Bank responds to Asian financial problems in this way: "In order not to jeopardize its long-term investment in human capital, the Government of Indonesia is already taking steps to counter the effects of the crisis."[132] One important measure is a stay-in-school campaign providing scholarships for poor children.

In the Philippines, the primary concern is with rural education. In Manila almost 100% of children graduate from primary school, whereas in rural areas less than 30% of students finish. School organization, as a result of U.S. colonization, follows Western patterns. From the viewpoint of World Bank authorities, "The Philippines failed to capture the benefits of education—productivity growth, poverty reduction, and social development. Slow-growth and import-substitution policies failed to generate jobs, and 4 million Filipinos went abroad. The new emphasis on export-led growth, however, has increased the demand for skilled labor, and exposed the deteriorating quality of education."[133] As in other countries, the World Bank holds out the hope that education will eliminate poverty and prepare the population in skills needed for the global economy.

ONLINE LEARNING AND THE AFRICAN VIRTUAL UNIVERSITY

The Internet is a powerful force in disseminating the World Bank's vision of a world organized around free markets and neoliberal governments. The Banks most important online learning project is The African Virtual University. This World Bank-supported virtual university was started in 1997 as a pilot project in six English speaking African countries–Kenya, Uganda, Tanzania, Ethiopia, Zimbabwe, and Ghana. Eventually, The African Virtual University extended its work into French-speaking African countries.[134]

The globalizing effect of The African Virtual University is its ability to reach across the borders of nation-states and create regional learning projects, and its use of online learning packages from around the world. During its early development, according to World Bank officials, "a number of course providers were identified from all over the world and courses were broadcast live from the United States, Canada, and Europe to students in the partner institutions, who could participate in a live virtual discussion *across Africa and beyond* [emphasis added]."[135]

The use of packaged online instruction from around the world highlights the potential of the World Wide Web to create global uniformity of knowledge and learning. The World Bank contracted with 30 non-African universities to supply online courses. Reflecting the continued domination of former colonial powers over the intellectual life of Africa, the Bank reports, "Leading universities in the North, academics and professionals with highly specialized skills who could understand Africa's needs and build tailor-made courses to meet these, were enlisted to develop the courses."[136] In fact, the major changes in these online courses developed by non-African academics was the introduction of African examples. Or, in the words of Bank officials, "Knowledge has to be conceptualized in order to add value to a different setting."[137] In a startling example of the World Bank's support of the continued domination of Western intellectuals, the Bank's report on The African Virtual University states, "For instance, a course in advanced economics in the US may have *the same theoretical content* as one being taught in South Africa, but *the case studies* used to test the theories *may vary* [emphasis added]."[138]

Besides helping to globalize knowledge, The African Virtual University is focused on preparing students for the global economy. Current courses include business communication, web design, computer repair, starting and planning your business, information technology, remedial science and math, and economic, business, and investigative journalism.[139] Of course, the World Bank has encountered problems in providing the infrastructure to support the work of the virtual school. However, World Bank officials see the future in positive terms and believe that this style of virtual university will spread around the world. According to Bank officials, the virtual university is playing a key role in developing African nations for participation in the global economy: "AVU [The African Virtual University] training courses are helping shape tomorrow's business managers, women entrepreneurs, scientists and other professionals who will make effective use of the knowledge economy, to stimulate growth and development in Africa."[140]

CONCLUSION: THE WORLD BANK: EXTENDING THE REACH OF COLONIALISM

Most of the World Bank's educational loans go to countries that emerged from colonialism in the 19th and 20th centuries. Through their loans, the World Bank continues to reinforce Western educational structures and methods that had been imposed on regions by colonial powers. In this context, the World Bank contributes to globalization of educational practices initiated by Western colonialism. Similar to most former colonial powers, the World Bank attempts to adapt and change indigenous educational practices to support the economic requirements of a globalized society.

World Bank officials have adopted a single vision for the best form of government and economy for the entire world. In actualizing this vision through development loans and its use of information technology, the World Bank is contributing to the uniformity of global society. Within the Bank's vision, neoliberal governments rely on privatization and the free market for the provision of educational services. This represents a significant shift from the control exerted by the traditional nation-state over public schools. In neoliberal states, governments reduce their provision of public services and focus their concerns on regulation of private markets in areas ranging from health care to schooling.

The World Bank's ideological purposes are important because the World Bank is the largest external financer of education in the world. Its actions are undermining the power of the traditional nation-state and are contributing to a uniform global consumer society. Highlighting the Bank's attempts to shift the provision of schooling from the nation-state to free market regulated by a neoliberal state is its project called "EdInvest" which is billed as "Facilitating Investment in the Global Education Market."[141] In promoting private investment and control of schools, EdInvest's March, 2003 claims, "Education companies, especially those in higher education, are performing well as evidenced by their strong performance in the equity markets."[142] And, in keeping with the World Bank's use of human capital theory, EdInvest suggests that people are willing to pay for schooling because of the promise of higher incomes: "Private (i.e., to the individual) rates of return to schooling are a useful indicator of the productivity of schooling .... In the United States, another year of schooling generates about a 10 percent annual return, while in the Philippines it is 12.6 percent and 12.0 percent in Chile."[143]

A possible outcome of World Bank efforts to support privatized schooling might be the growth of global learning corporations that sell educational products. This economic model would integrate education into a consumer market where advertising claims would be used to sell educational services. Such an outcome would certainly ensure global uniformity in learning as education products are marketed under brand names similar to those of Coca-Cola, Nike, and Honda. The role of the nation-state in education would disappear as control shifted to privatized multinational corporations.

Globalizing Morality:
Human Rights Education

"Ultimately I do not think that a 'true' human rights culture will exist until every citizen on the planet has an 'allegiance to humanity' ... rather than to their nation-states," argued Joseph Wronka in a 15-nation 2003 Internet Listserv debate on human rights education and culture.[1] Human rights organizations comprise the largest group of NGOs in the global civil society.[2] Along with the United Nations, these NGOs are actively promoting human rights education. The rapid growth of human rights NGOs and human rights education is, in part, a result of the rapid flow of information over the Internet.

I begin this chapter by considering the general ideology of human rights education. It should be noted that there is a distinction between human rights education and education as a human right. Education as a human right is provided for in Article 26 of the Universal Declaration of Human Rights. The Article proclaims the principle that all children have a right to an education. I have explored the issue of education as a human right in two other books.[3]

Human rights education is concerned with the transmission of knowledge about human rights doctrines and the development of attitudes that will protect, enforce, and expand rights doctrines. The audience for human rights education is global. Rights educators are interested in creating a global culture of human rights. Within this particular concept of a global culture, human rights doctrines establish standards for human conduct.

This global framework for human rights education is presented in the 1996 Report of the United Nations High Commissioner for Human Rights. This report contains policies for implementation of the Plan of Action for the United Nations Decade for Human Rights Education. The High Commissioner's report defines human rights education "as the training, dissemination and information efforts aimed at the building of a *universal culture of human rights* [emphasis added]."[4] The building of this global human rights culture is to be achieved

> through the imparting of knowledge and skills and the molding of attitudes and directed to: (a) The strengthening of respect for human rights and fundamental freedoms; (b) The full development of the human personality and the sense of its dignity; (c) The promotion of understanding, tolerance, gender equality and friendship among all nations, indigenous peoples and racial, national, ethnic, religious and linguistic groups; (d) The enabling of all persons to participate effectively in a free society; (e) The furtherance of the activities of the United Nations for the maintenance of peace.[5]

HUMAN RIGHTS EDUCATORS AS A GLOBAL TEACHING FORCE

Human rights educators are the new global missionaries spreading the ethical and attitudinal standards for the conduct of human life. With the goal of creating a global culture, human rights teachers play an activist role in promoting human rights. Many are trained as teachers in universities and NGOs around the world. They are linked through the World Wide Web by the Listserv operated by Human Rights Education Associates (HREA), which defines itself as "an international non-governmental organization that supports human rights learning; the training of activists and professionals; the development of educational materials and programming; and community-building through on-line technologies."[6]

Training for human rights educators consists of instructional methodologies and knowledge about the content and issues related to international human rights agreements. One of these teacher-training NGOS, the Canadian Human Rights Foundation, offers the following chart to distinguish a human rights educator from an activist. This chart is part of a training exercise that requires the participants to "Complete the chart below. Describe the main goal, responsibilities, skills, knowledge and personal characteristics desirable for each role." It is important to note that this chart represents an instructional methodology based on the idea that human rights teachers should participate in the creation of knowledge.

Throughout this chapter I discuss instructional methods used by human rights and peace educators. As noted in the previously presented chart, the primary distinction between a human rights teacher and an activist is knowledge of instructional skills. They both have the same goal of promoting social change but using differing methods. The human rights educator is interested in teaching people how to be human rights activists. In some ways, human

Our Roles as Human Rights Educators and Activists		
	Human Rights Activist	*Human Rights Educator/ Trainer*
Goal	To promote social change through taking action	To promote social change through education
Responsibilities	To ensure defense of human rights To monitor human rights violations ...	To promote human rights through education To develop educational programs and materials and deliver training ...
Knowledge and Skills	Knowledge of international HR instruments Understanding political situation Knowledge in specialized areas, e.g., forensics Negotiation skills Conflict resolution skills ...	Knowledge of human rights theory Knowledge of educational theory and techniques Interpersonal skills Facilitation skills Instructional design skills ...
Personal Characteristics	Single-minded in the pursuit of their goals ...	Open to various perspectives ...

Source: Canadian Human Rights Foundation, *Module: Building a Global Culture of Human Rights* (Montreal: Canadian Human Rights Foundation, 2002), p. 25.

rights educators might have a broader vision of their responsibilities than an activist. Human rights teachers are marching to the drum beat of a historical mission to create a global culture of human rights. In this context, they are the missionaries of a new gospel to regulate human behavior.

A GLOBAL CULTURE OF HUMAN RIGHTS

There are two approaches to creating a global culture of human rights. One envisions a uniform global culture that protects human rights. The other sees human rights doctrines embedded into local cultures. Education is by its very nature involved in either the maintenance of culture or cultural change when culture is defined as shared customs, attitudes, institutions, and intellectual traditions. Human rights educators want to teach a global set of customs, values, and attitudes that will ensure the spread and maintenance of rights doctrines. In addition, they want their teachings to effect the actions of institutions, including governments, and to change intellectual traditons in many societies.

What is unique about a human rights culture is that it is "not geographically located" and it is "not created by a shared language."[7] Human rights culture is a declared culture. As Olive Moore of Youth for Human Rights, Ireland, insightfully stated, "Human rights only exist because they are talked about, it remains a declared culture and therefore it carries a heavier burden of representation."[8] From the standpoint of human rights educators, their teachings are creating a culture of human rights rather than maintaining some previous cultures.

As a declared culture without a geographical location or growing out of a shared language, human rights embraces all other cultures. Some argue that human rights culture assumes a guardianship role over other cultures. From this perspective, if cultural traditions violate human rights, then that culture should be changed to conform to the superior culture of human rights. For instance, Maria Teresa Gutierrez of Argentina is disturbed by the cultural relativism implied in the idea of "live and let live." Referring to the degrading treatment of women by some cultures, Gutierrez worried, "I think it will be an interesting issue to think how long we respect other cultures if we see that some human rights aren't being respected there. We live and let others live?"[9]

Therefore, human rights educators are endeavoring to create a particular type of global culture, which, as I explain later, is in conflict with the World Bank's vision of a world dominated by free markets and neoliberal governments. The question of what is a global human rights culture was debated in the previously mentioned 15-nation 2003 Internet Listserv discussion. The fact that this debate took place on the Internet highlights the important role of the Internet in linking NGO members and spreading human rights ideas.

The global debate on human rights culture focuses on educating individual consciousness, interpretative frameworks, and emotions to motivate people to resist human rights abuses and not just the transmission of knowledge about international rights agreements. From the perspective of the debaters, a global human rights culture will be composed of people whose education prepares them to actively work to ensure the protection of the human rights of all people. This approach requires educators to develop in students a conscious awareness of human rights protections and abuses, and a desire to defend the human rights of others. Greta Nemiroof of the Sisterhood is Global Institute contended, "A culture of human rights means that we see the world through the lens of human rights and that our agency is focused on both acting and desisting, in small as in big acts, in a respect for human rights that becomes automatic."[10]

Sometimes in the debate a global human rights culture is portrayed as a sharing of a consciousness or awareness of human rights issues. This includes a sharing of an interpretative lens for viewing human activities. In this context, consciousness or awareness of human rights requires all people thinking actively about rights issues. A shared interpretative lens requires all people to make sense of human events using a common set of human rights values. In other words, people are to think about how their own behavior and the behavior of others might or might not violate human rights. Instruction alerts students to abuse and protection of human rights. Also, it prepares them to interpret their own actions according to whether or not they support or violate human rights. Donna Habsha of the University of Windsor (Canada) stated it this way, "a 'culture of human rights' seeks to cultivate a high level of consciousness and compassion for the inalienable rights of all beings. Such a growing consciousness within communities around the world will form a universal lens through which we are able to inform our legal, political and moral decisions."[11]

Another version of a global human rights culture was based on the concept of self-ownership. Bernie Weintraub of the organization Facing History and Ourselves argued for a belief in the value of self-ownership as the shared value of a global culture. Weintraub argued, "A culture of human rights is one in which people are not thought of as belonging to anyone, or any entity, other than themselves. This is usually taken to apply to family structures: women are not their husbands' property, children are not their parents' property."[12] Weintraub made a clear distinction between human rights culture and cultures defined by the boundaries of a nation-state. In this regard, a human rights culture undermines the concept of national cultures. Weintraub stated, "I mean also that people in such a culture [human rights] aren't seen as belonging to the state either, or to the ideology to which the state adheres, or even dedicates itself ...."[13]

A shared global value of self-ownership means that people cannot be used without their consent to serve the ends of others or the nation-state. Weintraub referred to this as the "means/ends" issue. In other words, the nation-state should not be allowed to force people to join a military engagement when the goal is to expand the power of the rulers of the nation-state. People could volunteer to work for others or the nation-state, but they could not be forced to work for them. Weintraub contended, "In a culture of human rights no one should be used as a means to someone else's, or to the state's ends, without their voluntary consent .... The line between the legitimate interests of the state, or even of society as a whole, would have to be drawn very, very cautiously in a culture of human rights."[14]

Another foundation for a global culture is a shared belief that human rights embraces welfare issues. Welfare issues include the right to shelter, nutrition, medical care, and employment at a living wage. If people share this belief in welfare rights, then people's interpretative lenses would be calibrated to include an evaluation of the welfare of others. This would mean seeing the world through a framework that asks whether or not all people have adequate shelter, nutrition, medical care, and employment. Shulamith Koenig of the Peoples Movement for Human Rights Education urged, "Let us not forget the Roosevelt definition 'freedom from fear and freedom from want' .... So, a human rights culture is where we are free from fear and want."[15] Reflecting a concern about the acute shortage of water in India, Anna Pinto of the Center for Organization, Research and Education, New Delhi, included protection from corporate exploitation in the idea of welfare rights. As examples, she gave the marketing of Coca-Cola and the building of water-consuming golf courses. From her perspective, human rights education should include a critical awareness of how corporate actions might interfere with the welfare needs of humanity.[16]

Educating for a human rights' consciousness, an interpretive human rights lens, an acceptance of the idea of self-ownership, and protection of human welfare requires a global sharing of similar behaviors and ideas. Mike Pates of the American Bar Association places this notion of shared values in a legal framework. He defines human rights as "a dynamic body of law." Therefore, he argued, "A 'culture of human rights' constitutes the set of shared attitudes, values, goals, and practices characterizing a collective recognition of, and adherence to, these laws."[17]

A GLOBAL HUMAN RIGHTS CULTURE AND CULTURAL DIVERSITY

Promoting educational programs designed to create shared global values and beliefs raises issues of cultural imperialism and relativism. One issue is whether or not the Universal Declaration of Human Rights reflects universal values. The ongoing debate over this issue has not provided any satisfactory answers.[18] Consequently, human rights teachers present the question of universality as a topic to be debated. This is exemplified in the Canadian Human Rights Foundation module for preparing teachers, titled *Module: Building a Global Culture of Human Rights*. The second unit of the module utilizes a "fishbowl" method for debating the universality of the values contained in the Universal Declaration of Human Rights. The fishbowl method divides the class of future human rights teachers into two groups with one group adopting the position that the Declaration "should not be considered a universal declaration" and the other group arguing that it "should be considered a universal declaration."[19] Each group is given time to organize their arguments. Some suggestions are made in the unit. For instance, those taking the "not universal" position are asked to consider arguments that not all nations have adopted the Declaration and that the meaning of rights is relative to a particular culture. Those taking the "should be considered" position are to consider that 250 delegates from 56 countries have accredited the Declaration and that a detailed questionnaire sent to leading politicians and scholars found a general agreement about basic rights. Using the "fishbowl," the debate is started with five or six members of one group sitting in the middle of the class discussing their position while the rest of the class sits on the outside listening. After 10 minutes, the positions are reversed with five or six members of the opposing group taking seats in the middle. After 15-minute intervals, positions are again reversed with each group responding to the other.[20]

This teaching module does not resolve the question of universality of human rights values. What it does do is help teachers understand the arguments on both sides of the issue. This prepares teachers to discuss this issue with their students. However, teachers are to remain dedicated to the proposition that they should create a global culture of human rights.

It remains an open question whether or not creating a global culture of human rights is a form of cultural imperialism. Cristina Sganga of Amnesty International–Netherlands and a board member of the Human Rights Education Associates rejects the idea that a human rights culture is singular and uniform. She advocates embedding human rights doctrines into local cultures. Rather than being superior to other cultures, human rights doctrines unify all cultures by giving them a common set of values. Local customs are protected as long as they do not violate human rights. "Always respecting those customs, which do not violate human rights," she argued in reference to infusing human rights into local cultures, "preserving them or letting them change as time and life change ideas, experiences and customs. And transform or eliminating those [customs] which are violatory according to those standards that the international community agrees ... [provides] a common denominator which unites us all in dignity, [while] maintaining our diversity."[21]

There is a consensus among human rights educators that the implementation of human rights doctrines and human rights education will change local cultures. However, human rights culture is not considered a substitute for local cultures. It is a cultural corrective that eliminates customs, behaviors, and values in local cultures that violate human rights. Of course, no matter how you describe it, this is a form of cultural imperialism. It is similar to the World Bank's attempt to reshape the values of local cultures to fit its image of globalization. While lip service might be given to protecting indigenous cultures, the infusion of human rights values will result in cultural change.

Human rights educators admit that they are trying to strike a balance between respecting local cultures and establishing a uniform global rights culture. Vibeke Eikass of Amnesty International–Norway endorses a statement made by Ed O'Brien of Street Law, Inc.

> A culture of human rights may sound to some people as if there is a movement to substitute a culture of human rights for their cultures. However, isn't what we want to achieve through human rights education: cultures which support human rights, include human rights principles as part of their core values, recognize and incorporate human rights into their laws, customs, traditions etc., value knowledge and respect for human rights, and recognize the need for human rights education?[22]

An approach to this issue that attempts to avoid the charge of cultural imperialism is to claim that an evolutionary process can embed human rights in local cultures. Rather than forcing human rights doctrines on societies, the persuasive power of educators is regarded as a means for gradual cultural change. From this framework, it is claimed, the work of human rights educators is not imperialistic but is part of the evolution of global societies. However, what is the difference between the work of human rights educators and the preaching of religious missionaries?

Another way of avoiding the charge of cultural imperialism is to assert that human rights educators are not claiming that one culture is superior to another but that human rights are superior to some values in local cultures. Within this conceptual framework, a human rights culture assumes a guardianship over other cultures. Olive Moore of Youth for Human Rights contended, "A human rights culture is not a pinnacle in a hierarchy of cultures, but rather a culture which is situated on [a] higher level englobing [sic] local cultures. The fact that a human rights culture asserts itself through englobement [sic] does not necessitate or facilitate a claim of superiority."[23]

While these educators do not see a human rights culture as taking over all aspects of local culture, there is a belief in the necessity of globalizing human rights culture. From this perspective, human rights educators are creating a global culture that will permeate all other cultures. Gauri Bhopatkar of the Center for Empowerment, Pune, India, considers his work as contributing to the building of a global human rights culture. In fact, Bhopatkar argues that creating a global human rights culture should be the central goal of educators. "I feel such a culture may evolve automatically once we ensure to create a respect for human rights as values for the existence of human beings and not attach any legal or jurisprudential dictums to it. But, as the international human rights discourse is not void of politics, those involved in human rights education need to work hard towards this goal."[24]

TEACHING ABOUT CULTURAL DIFFERENCES

However, the difficulty of infusing human rights into local cultures is illustrated by another teacher training module distributed by the Canadian Human Rights Foundation. Called *Seeking Common Ground*, the instructional module forces human rights instructors to confront their own cultural assumptions and deal with the problem of cultural uniformity versus diversity. A goal is to identify diversity of cultural values and then find common ground for working for human rights. In essence, the module assumes the protection of personal values that are not in conflict with the values of a global human rights culture. The module's introduction claims, "Only by acknowledging our differences can we find common ground on which to work together for human rights. And only when we perceive human dignity as the foundation of all human rights can we fully understand their universality and interdependence."[25]

The module's first unit confronts human rights instructors with their own personal values regarding cultural unity and diversity. Participants are asked to create a "Personal Web of Connections" which is composed of a series of circles connected by lines to a circle containing the name of the participant. In the web's circles, teachers write personal identifiers, such as religion, ethnicity, workplace, social status, friendship, belief/ideology, political affiliation, hobbies, community service, family role, sexual orientation, and state of health. After completing the personal webs, participants form groups of four. Each group member presents his or her web and addresses questions designed to elicit cultural values and conflicts, and cause discussion. Many of the questions deal with discrimination and marginalization because of membership in a certain group (circle). Some provocative and powerful questions are "Can you think of factors within yourself or your society that might lead you to discriminate against others? To what extent are these factors within your control? To what extent are they embedded in society?"[26]

Following the self-revelation of personal values to the small group, the class meets as a whole to create a web based on personal webs for the purpose of discussing cultural unity and differences. A discussion is generated about the possibility of cultural unity around human rights doctrines. For instance, two questions asked the class are "What would be the advantages or disadvantages to this course if almost everyone belonged to the same categories [circles]? If most categories [circles] contained only one or two names?"[27] These questions directly confront the class with the issue of the desirability of global cultural uniformity. Questions are also designed to highlight problems occurring because of cultural diversity, such as "Can anyone cite examples from personal experience where a failure to recognize differences has prevented well-intentioned people from working together?"[28]

Clearly, in the module's first unit, future human rights teachers are confronted with the idea that it would be easier to work with groups that share their own cultural values. However, the reality is cultural diversity. How do you teach human rights in the context of cultural diversity? The teaching module's second unit alerts teachers to this problem with "The Fatal River Story." The goal is "to clarify values and help participants focus on the bases, perhaps unconscious, of their moral judgements. It helps to throw into relief the contrasts in individual value systems and raises issues of whether concepts such as justice, honesty, power, or honor have different meanings when applied to men or women."[29]

The unit confronts human rights teachers with the question, "Can human rights be truly universal when such differing values exist?" as presented in a morally complex case study, "The Fatal River Story." The story involves an engaged couple, deeply in love, who live on opposite sides of a river. One night the woman, Leit, receives a message that her fiancé, Han, is ill and might die. A storm destroys the one bridge across the river. Leit's only hope is to ask the owner of a power boat, Roni, to take her across the river. He agrees on the condition that she goes to bed with him. She consents and, after sleeping with him, Roni takes her across the river. Her fiancé eventually gets well and she confesses to her deal with Roni. Enraged, Han casts her aside and declares that he will never marry her. Leit's brother and male cousins are angered by Han's actions and beat him severely. After hearing about the beating, Leit laughs.[30]

After reading the story, teachers write a personal assessment of who they think are the most honorable and least honorable, and the most powerful and least powerful, characters in the story. Teachers then work with another teacher to fill in a worksheet containing questions designed to highlight differences in values, such as "Do you and your partner agree on the most honorable character? Do you and your partner agree on the most powerful character?" The two teachers are asked for reasons for their agreements or disagreements. Teachers are then placed in groups of four to fill in a group copy of the worksheet.

The goal of the Fatal River unit is to raise the issue of whether or not human rights can be universal when there might exist major differences in personal values as might result from differing interpretations of the story. No answers to this issue are provided in the instructional module. However, the assumption is that the problem is resolvable and that human rights can be adjusted to complex clashes in cultural values. The burden for this resolution is on the shoulders of the human rights teachers who must understand their own personal values, recognize value conflicts, and work to resolve them within the framework of human rights doctrines.

In summary, human rights educators consider themselves as doing more than simply providing information about human rights documents and laws. Their agenda includes creating a global consciousness about human rights that extends to the interpretation of human experience through a human rights' lens. Students are to be taught to automatically evaluate the actions of governments, civil institutions, business activities, and individual actions according to human rights standards. This consciousness includes a sense of self-ownership where individuals protect themselves and others from being forced to serve the ends of governments, civil institutions, and corporations.

In essence, human rights educators are creating global ethical or moral standards. A human rights culture is based on these global ethical standards determined by internationally agreed-on human rights doctrines. These ethical standards are to regulate human behavior. Consequently, when human rights educators declare that they are not intent on replacing local cultures with a global human rights culture, what they mean is that their primary concern is affecting local ethical standards, institutions, and government actions that violate human rights principles. These ethical standards of conduct or morality are to permeate all cultures while cultural diversity is maintained.

Similar to the World Bank officials, human rights educators use the language of cultural diversity while acting in ways that will fundamentally change local cultures. World Bank officials claim they want to support diversity while introducing significant changes in traditional family structures through the education of women and by championing Western concepts of urbanization and industrialization. Within the World Bank framework, local cultures are commodities to be sold to tourists. Human rights doctrines, through their support of women's and children's rights, welfare rights, and other political and social rights, will significantly change local cultures. Human rights educators are contributing to a uniform world culture.

HUMAN RIGHTS AS THE MORALITY
OF A GLOBAL CIVIL SOCIETY

Human rights educators are creating a global ethical system. As I discuss later, there is an inherent conflict between the global values propagated by the World Bank and those embodied in the efforts of human rights instructors. Human rights educators are not unique in their desire to create a self-regulating civil society through education. This has been a traditional goal of Western forms of public schools since the 19th century. Public schools try to generate self-regulating societies through moral and civic instruction.

The best historical example is the American educator Horace Mann. He provides an historical backdrop for understanding the implications of the work of human rights educators. Mann is often identified as the key ideologist in organizing the U.S. public school system. In laying out the framework for U.S. public schools in his reports as Secretary of Massachusetts' State Board of Education in the 1830s and 1840s, Horace Mann, similar to human rights educators, questioned the ability of the nation-state to create a just society. According to Mann, a just society depends on personal values and actions rather than laws decreed by the nation-state. Mann expressed this distrust of the actions of the nation-state in his 1848 Annual Report: "With the existence of private relations between men, came fraud; and with the existence of public relations between nations, came aggression, war, and slavery ... and for every new law there may be a new transgression."[31]

Mann believed that moral education in public schools would create a civil society that would correct the evils of the nation-state and the ineffectiveness of the legal system to bring justice to humanity. Mann envisioned the schoolmaster as the new guide to social justice. By implanting morality in each child, the public school could create a self-regulative civil society. With a dramatic style not often found in government reports, Mann declared education as the remedy for the defects of the nation-state:

> But to all doubters, disbelievers, or despairers, in human progress, it may still be said, there is one experiment which has never been tried. It is an experiment which, even before its inception, offers the highest authority for its ultimate success. Its formula is intelligible to all; and it is as legible as though written in starry letters on an azure sky. It is expressed in these few and simple words:—'Train up a child in the way he should go, and when he is old he will not depart from it.' This declaration is positive .... In all the attempts to reform mankind which have hitherto been made, whether by changing the frame of government, by aggravating or softening the severity of the penal code, or by substituting a government-created, for a God-created religion;—in all these attempts, the infantile and youthful mind, its amenability to influences, and the enduring self-operating character of the influences it receives, have been almost wholly unrecognized.[32]

An important difference between Mann and human rights educators is that Mann proposed teaching a morality that is a product of a historical culture in contrast to the declared culture of human rights. Mann believed that schools, without advocating the views of a particular Christian religious domination, should imbue in all students the basic ethical principles of Christianity. Similar to human rights educators, Mann believed this could be accomplished without undermining the diversity existing between Christian religious groups. In teaching human rights doctrines, educators also hope to promote a self-regulating civil society without undermining cultural diversity. As a declared culture, educators feel that the ethics of human rights can apply to all of humanity.

Issues surrounding the role of a human rights morality in forming a global civil society are highlighted in a Canadian Human Rights Foundation instructional module for teachers called *The Global Human Rights Context*. The objectives of this training module are to introduce human rights teachers to the "impact of globalization on human rights" and "issues related to global governance and their impact on civil society."[33] In this instructional module, globalization is presented as a complex phenomenon with both positive and negative effects. In the module's first unit, small groups of teachers are asked to read newspaper headlines with short quotes from the article. Examples of the headlines are "Amazon Tribe Sues for Survival," "Languages Are in Danger of Extinction," "Information Technology in the 21st Century," "Police Say Toronto a World Hub for Child Porn," and "New Front in Aids War."[34] They are then asked to compose lists of what they feel are the positive and negative influences of globalization and present them to the entire class.

The questions recommended for the class discussion illustrate how human rights educators accept the inevitable creation of a globalized society and how they want to ensure that globalization creates a civil society that protects human rights. The two recommended questions are "In what ways can globalization create opportunities to better promote and protect human rights? In what ways do certain dimensions of globalization threaten or pose a danger to human rights?"[35]

The second and third activities require human rights teachers to examine the impact of globalization on different world regions. In the second activity, teachers listen to a special resource person explain the impact on Pakistan of international financial institutions, international power politics, political/religious extremism, and the work of NGOs. This presentation serves as a model for the third activity, which divides the class into groups representing different world regions. Each group is asked to read an article titled "Globalization and Its Impact on the Full Enjoyment of Human Rights." The groups are then asked to consider, based on the article, the impact of globalization on human rights in the region they represent. The central question is "How would you try, in this context, to promote respect for human rights in your community and region?"[36]

As illustrated in these training modules, human rights educators believe their role is to regulate the effects of globalization. In Unit 2 of the module, they are trained to effect specific organizations by creating a "Spheres of Influence" diagram. Reflecting the almost Machiavellian approach of the lesson, the human rights teachers are told, "An understanding of power relations and structures at all levels of society (i.e., international, national and local) is an essential tool for the protection of human rights and social change. The aim of this activity is to identify the key actors and their influence on the globalization process in our societies."[37] The class is asked to consider how they might influence groups in the globalization process. These groups include

> Globalized Economic Institutions
> World Bank
> International Monetary Fund
> Regional Development Banks
> Multilateral Trade Institutions (such as the World Trade Organization)
> Transnational Corporations
> National Government
> Ministry of International Trade
> Ministry of Education
> Ministry of Finance
> Intergovernmental Institutions
> United Nations
> Association of South East Asian Nations (ASEAN)
> Council of Europe
> Global Communications Industry
> Internet
> CNN
> Civil Society
> NGOs
> Individuals[38]

The necessity for human rights educators to understand power relations is central to this lesson. After completing the "Spheres of Influence" web, the class is given a statement designed to provoke discussion about the role of human rights educators in influencing power relations in a global society. The statement is an excerpt from the International Consultation on the Pedagogical Foundations of Human Rights Education declaration "Towards a Pedagogy of Human Rights Education." It begins, "Human rights education should be approached in a fashion that includes the analysis, understanding and reading of power relations and social forces so as to enable a struggle to change those power relations that impede the full realization of human rights."[39]

Influencing the power relations in the globalization process becomes another method for making human rights doctrines the regulating ethics of a global society. Therefore, similar to some 19th-century advocates of public schooling, human rights educators recommend an enforcement of global ethics through power politics that will result in a just global society. By fostering a consciousness and a desire to actively protect human rights, educators hope to create a civil society that will curb the unjust actions of governments, corporations, and other institutions and people. This ethical system will supposedly create a common bond among the world's people in the process of creating a global culture.

HUMAN RIGHTS EDUCATION AND THE NATION-STATE

As I discussed in the previous chapter, NGOs are playing a major role in shaping the future global civil society. As part of their efforts, they are trying infuse human rights education into the public schools of nation-states. This is an important educational effort of Amnesty International, which was the first major international human rights NGO, founded in 1960. Government repressions in Greece, Chile, Uruguay, Uganda, and Argentina in the 1970s contributed to the rapid growth of Amnesty International from an organization of 3,000 to 50,000 members. Between 1983 and 1993, the total number of human rights NGOs doubled to reach 168.[40]

In recent years, Amnesty International has supported human rights education programs in countries of the former Soviet Union, South America, Southeast Asia, the Middle East, and Africa. Some national school systems are directly affected by these efforts. In Albania, human rights education is now replacing courses in Marxism–Leninism. In the Philippines, human rights education in public schools is mandated by the Constitution. Amnesty International–Philippines is part of an effort to build awareness of human rights efforts. In Guyana, Amnesty International is targeting a human rights training program for every teacher in the country.[41]

In some countries, such as the United States, human rights education is not mandated by the federal government, nor by most state governments. It is seldom found in official public school curricula. Consequently, there is an indirect approach to introducing these topics in public schools. One method is to try and influence future teachers who might surreptitiously introduce human rights education in their classrooms and other public forums. For instance, Amnesty International's teacher training book for U.S. colleges, *Human Rights Here & Now: Celebrating the Universal Declaration of Human Rights*, suggests work in a wide variety of settings including classrooms: "No matter what the setting—whether a classroom, a senior citizens' center, or a religious organization—common principles inform the methods used to teach human rights."[42]

The writers of the volume are aware of the political problems in introducing human rights education in U. S. public schools. After all, the United States never ratified the Universal Declaration of Human Rights. And, as Fateh Assam, Program Officer for Human Rights at the Ford Foundation in Egypt, observed, there is a problem "building a notion of economic justice in the United Sates, in other words, building a culture of economic rights in a society that values individual freedoms so highly as to accept the concept of exploitation of labor. This is a mammoth project."[43]

Given the potential controversy facing teachers who try to introduce human rights into U.S. public schools, the Human Rights Educators' Network and Amnesty International–USA provide a disingenuous answer to the question, "Isn't human rights education too political for schools?"[44] Their answer distinguishes between political skills and political ideology. They describe human rights education as teaching a set of political skills and disavow any attempt to impart a political ideology. They propose telling future teachers,

> Knowing about human rights makes people better able to participate in the social and political life of their communities. However, it is important to distinguish between political and analytical skills and party politics and political ideology. Educators have a great responsibility not to become propagandists or to push students towards a specific political position or party. Human rights education must be exploratory, open-ended, and problem solving. It should also call on the learner to identify and strive to eliminate injustice.[45]

However, human rights is an ideology or set of ideas about the organization of society. Human rights educators insist that they are attempting to create a global human rights culture. This sought-after culture is based on a human rights ideas. Human rights is a political ideology.

Despite the attempt to hide the political nature of the human rights agenda, the actual content of the teacher training conveys a strong ideological message. An important feature of this training is the linking of human rights concepts to developmental stages of children's growth. This allows public school teachers to make judgments about the appropriateness of human rights topics for particular school grades. For instance, for early childhood, which includes preschool and lower primary grades, it is recommended that human rights education begin with teaching respect for self, parents, teachers, and others. For this age group, the key learning concept is responsibility to the community; in group, students practice self-expression and listening to others. Age-appropriate lessons on racism, sexism, unfairness, and hurting people are introduced. For upper primary, ages 8 to 11, the emphasis is on teaching social responsibility and distinguishing wants from needs. The concept of needs, as opposed to wants, is then related to human rights. Concepts related to individual and group rights, freedom, equality, justice, and rule by law are introduced. Students learn to value diversity and to distinguish fact from opinion. Also, they perform school and community service. In lower secondary, ages 12 to 14, students are taught about the content of human rights documents. They learn about international law, world peace, world developmental and economic issues, and legal and moral rights. They are taught how to understand another person's point of view, to do research on human rights issues, and to practice sharing information about community activities. And in the final years of high school, students integrate human rights into their personal awareness and behaviors by participating in civic organizations and learning the power of civil disobedience.

Armed with this developmental and conceptual framework, teachers leave the course ready to integrate human rights education into their public school teaching. Future teachers learn to conduct lessons that emphasize human rights as a positive value system; promote debate over human rights issues; discuss human rights in relationship to cultural diversity; and link human rights to global concerns. And, of course, future teachers are urged to educate students to become human rights activists. The textbook stresses, "Include an ACTION DIMENSION that provides participants with opportunities to act on their beliefs and understanding. These actions should address problems both at home and elsewhere in the world."[46]

Political activism is stressed in human rights curricula for U. S. public schools. A good example is the college textbook, *Educating for Human Dignity: Learning About rights and Responsibilities*.[47] Written by Betty Reardon, a well-known leader in U.S. human rights and peace education, the book provides instructional guidelines and models of lessons on human rights that can be used in classes ranging from kindergarten to the 12th grade. An example of activist education is a 12th-grade lesson titled, "Moral Development–From Awareness to Commitment, the Making of Human Rights Heroes."[48]

Accompanying the lesson is a guide to "Phases in the Development of Moral Inclusion." These phases of "moral inclusion" move from "Spectator" to "Solidarity/Victim/Martyr." The guide emphasizes creating a global moral community: "The universal recognition of the full range of human rights for all peoples of the world depends in large part on widening our moral community and extending its boundaries to include all human beings."[49] Supposedly, members of a global human rights community would actively intervene, even to the extent of martyrdom, to protect universal human rights. "Moral inclusion" is defined as "a capacity that can be developed through both experiential and academic learning."[50] According to Reardon, proper instruction could change the mere spectator into a martyr. In her steps of moral inclusion, the first three stages involve progressively greater involvement in human rights issues from "Spectator," "Observer," to "Witness." At the next stage, "Advocate," moral concerns about human rights cause them "to join advocacy groups, write letters to the editor, speak to schools, church groups, etc. Such people *advocate* the cause of the victims." "Advocate" is followed by "Activist" when people are "moved to the acceptance of personal responsibility and risk [in defending human rights]."[51] Activists assume personal responsibility to try and stop human rights violations. At the final "Solidarity/Victim/Martyr," the person begins to take on personal risk in defending human rights. This stage highlights the attempt to surreptitiously train students to become active human rights defenders in U.S. schools. Reardon provides the following description of the "Solidarity/Victim/Martyr" stage of moral inclusion:

> Activism is most often pursued within one's own group or country, but some activists actually join in *solidarity* with the struggle and suffering of victims to work for human rights as a member of the victimized group. Such an activist risks being victimized herself even to the point of losing her life and thus becoming a *martyr* in the struggle for human rights. Do you know of such martyrs who are now considered heroes of human rights?[52]

In the actual lesson, students view films depicting responses to human rights violations. They are then given the guidelines on phases of moral inclusion. Students are asked "to write a reflective essay on the significance of individual learning and personal development to the process of moral inclusion and the growth of the human rights movement."[53] Then they are asked to compose a list of outstanding people who defended human rights. This is a method for achieving the goal expressed in the lesson's title of "Moral Development ... Making Human Rights Heroes."[54]

So despite claims of not teaching a political ideology, Human Rights Educators' Network, Amnesty International–USA and other U.S. human rights leaders are offering material that teachers can use to promote an activist human rights culture. Included in the compendium of recommended lessons by Amnesty International for teachers to use in classrooms is a section devoted to training student advocates. Under the subtitle "Students as Advocates for Human Rights," teachers are told that after pupils start seeking information about events they are witnessing, "they are moving from being spectators to being active observers ... [then] they are moved to action."[55] In the process, teachers offer "Ten Tips for Taking Action" ranging from choosing a problem to carrying out a solution and, lastly, "10. Don't give up. Problem solving means eliminating all the things that don't work until you find something that does. Don't pay attention to people who try to tell you that the problem can't be solved. Keep on keeping on!"[56] Following the 10 tips are lessons, "Stories of Students Who Took Action," "Getting to Know the Activists Among Us," "Strategizing for Action," "The Power of the Pen: Writing Letters for Human Rights," and "The Power of Petition."[57] As the titles of these lessons indicate, human rights education for U.S. public school teachers is highly political even to the point of preparing students to carry out an ideological program in support of human rights doctrines.

Unlike in the United States where in most cases teachers must hide the political nature of their instruction, in the Philippines, the Filipino Constitution mandates human rights education. The hope is that human rights education will strengthen the nation-state by reducing police and military violence against the population, and create a public that will not tolerate dictatorial governments. Also, the Philippines is an important example of the influence of human rights doctrines as an international code of ethics on the actions of nation-states. In 1986, after the overthrow of dictator Ferdinand Marcos, the government issued Executive Order No. 27, "Education to Maximize Respect for Human Rights," ordering the Ministry of Education "to include the study and understanding of human rights in the curricula of all levels of education and training in all schools."[58] In particular, human rights education was targeted at the police and military personnel who had helped maintain the brutal Marcos regime. The year before the ratification of the Constitution, the government issued the memorandum, "Education of Arresting and Investigating Personnel on Human Rights," which called for "a continuing education and training program on human rights for existing military, police and other arresting and investigating personnel, especially those in charge of detention and convicted prisoners."[59]

In 1987, the new Filipino Constitution was ratified with Article 3 detailing a bill of rights that includes all the civil and political rights provided for in the Universal Declaration of Human Rights. Section 17 of Article 13 created an independent Commission on Human Rights that, among a list of duties, would "establish a continuing program of research, education, and information to enhance respect of the primacy of human rights."[60]

Symbolizing the attempt to use human rights to maintain the nation-state, the Filipino Constitution merges human rights and nationalist education. The Constitution's Article 14 prescribes a curriculum that blends the national heroes and citizenship training methods of nationalist education with the teaching of human rights. Section 3 of Article 14 orders,

> All education shall … inculcate patriotism and nationalism, foster love of humanity, respect for human rights, appreciation of the role of national heroes in the historical development of the country, teach the rights and duties of citizenship, strengthen ethical and spiritual values, develop moral character and personal discipline, encourage critical and creative thinking, broaden scientific and technical knowledge, and promote vocational efficiency.[61]

Human rights education for the police and military is a product of this constitutional mandate. The curriculum stresses learning about human rights to guide future behavior in contrast to training human rights activists. The hope is that police and military actions will be self-regulated by internalized human rights principles. The "Human Rights Education Curriculum for Police/Military" contends, "Human rights education is a process of imparting both values and knowledge. It involves the awakening of conscious commitment to the values embodied in the International Bill of Human rights–an understanding of value conflicts and how they can most equitably be resolved."[62]

The global influence of the Universal Declaration of Human Rights and its potential effect on nation-states in creating rules of conduct is exemplified by the Filipino police and military curriculum. The curriculum is based on the "principles which underlie the Charter of the United Nations, the Universal Declaration of Human Rights, the International Covenants on Human Rights, and other international human rights instruments."[63] In other words, the globalizing effect of human rights documents and education directly affect the training of police and soldiers of a nation-state. In this manner, these international ethical guidelines become directly embedded in the actions of a government.

In most circumstances, nation-states are not interested in training employees who actively work to change the fundamental structure of society to meet human rights standards. Most likely, government workers will be trained to not violate human rights. This is a passive approach to human rights education. Government workers are to act according to the ethical standards of human rights. Action on the part of government workers is limited to advocacy and regulation of behavior. For instance, the objective of the curriculum's first unit is a commitment "to promote or uphold human rights." The first unit is devoted to forming values, such as "Values of Self," "Values of Fellowmen," "Values of Community," and "Values of Country."[64] The second unit involves "Theory Formation" in which participants receive instruction in human rights law. Specific parts of this unit are planned for the police and military. The first seven parts of the second unit focus on knowledge about human rights standards. The eighth unit involves military training in "Your Rights and the Rights of Others in Times of Armed Conflict," which includes topics on "Fundamental Rights and Liberties in Times of Armed Conflict," International Humanitarian Law Principles Proper to the Rules of War," and "International Law and the Armed Forces of the Philippines: Existing Rules and Procedures."[65] Police training topics include "Standard Minimum Rules for the Treatment of Prisoners," "Conventions Against Torture and Other Cruel, Inhuman or Degrading Treatment or Punishment," and "The Rights of Offenders."[66]

Introducing human rights education in Filipino schools is much harder than training for the police and military. In his study of human rights education in the Philippines, Richard Pierre found that the resistance of the educational bureaucracy makes it difficult to introduce human rights curriculum into schools. The problem is the lack of human rights questions on the test used for certifying teachers. Pierre argued that the exam determines the content of instruction in teacher training courses. Without human rights questions on the exam, there is no incentive for professors to include human rights education in their courses. Consequently, Filipino teachers are not prepared to teach about human rights in the schools.

In summary, the United States and the Philippines provide contrasting examples of the effect of human rights education on the nation-state. In the United States, some teachers clandestinely introduce human rights education into classrooms. The nation-state's politicians and public school establishment remain resistant to human rights instruction. In part, this could be a result of the threat of international human rights to sovereignty of the nation-state. In contrast, the principle ethics of international human rights doctrines are included in the present Filipino Constitution as a means of strengthening the nation-state by protecting it against the charges of corruption and brutality leveled against the police and army of the previous government. Consequently, the emphasis is on human rights education for the police and military in order to ensure popular acceptance of the new government. However, as in the United States, human rights education in the Philippines remains neglected in the public schools. Does this mean that human rights education in public school systems is a threat to the sovereignty of the nation-state?

THE UNITED NATIONS CYBERSCHOOLBUS

The 1945 founding of the United Nations and the issuance of the 1948 Declaration of Human Rights set the stage for an international movement for human rights education and the creation of global ethical principles.[67] The United Nations is central to the efforts of human rights educators. To understand the organization's approach, I focus on the recent use of the Internet by the United Nations to provide a global curriculum for human rights education. Cyberschoolbus, as it is called, can be found at the U.N. Web site http://www.cyberschoolbus.un.org. The site can be accessed in English, French, Chinese, Arabic, and Russian. Besides human rights, the cyber schoolbus offers curricula on peace, poverty, cities of the world, health, and the environment. The human rights curriculum includes resources, such as a simplified version for school children of the Universal Declaration of Human Rights and the Declaration of the Rights of the Child, linkages to other human rights Web sites, a bibliography, a human rights fact sheet, a human rights vocabulary list, and letter-writing tips for advocating human rights.

The letter-writing tips demonstrate the activist aspects of human rights education. The goal is to prepare future citizens to interpret events through a human rights lens and to actively protect human rights. This goal is most evident in the educational game "Pook in the World." The game is designed for students 6 years and up. Similar to American comic book characters Superman and Batman, "Pook wants to be a superhero …. Help Pook and her animal friends save the world … at least a little bit."[68] The game is designed to capture the imagination of students so that they can envision themselves struggling to save humanity.

There is a radical element to the game. Pook starts out by asking others how she can save the world. Businesspeople, teachers, judges, and politicians attempt to discourage her. The only encouraging person is a shabbily dressed junk man who pushes a shopping cart filled with empty bottles. Symbolically, the game contrasts the attitude of a member of the underclass with the political and economic establishment. The mayor is presented as a member of an entrenched administration when he exclaims, "Pook, as long as I am mayor, there is nothing wrong with the world." The judge expresses self-importance with, "Pook, leave that sort of thing up to me." And the teacher is the ultimate pedant: "Pook, you've got to stop dreaming and get serious." The businessperson, as represented by the baker, grocer, and butcher, express, respectively, the uncaring views: "Pook, I've got my own problems, I can't worry about the world." "Pook, forget about it, the world will never change." " Pook, the world's full of problems, no one can save it."

Discouraged by the phalanx of officials and businesspeople, Pook falls on the sidewalk near the Junk Man while hurrying home in a mood of discouragement. When the Junk Man expresses concern Pook sobs, "I was on my way to become a superhero and save the world." The Junk Man, representing the underclass, is the first to offer encouragement and add realism to Pook's quest. He advises, "Maybe you can't save the whole world but you can help a little." "How?" Pook asks. "Well, for example," he replies, "I collect bottles and cans and recycle them. That helps a little."

Combining a lesson in environmentalism with one on social activism, the Junk Man tells Pook that superheroes are for comic books and gives her a stamp book filled with a U.N. list of endangered species, including a Secretary Bird, Orang-Utan, Hyacinth Macaw, Chinchilla, and Pelican. These endangered animals become Pook's friends, and when the game player clicks on the computer screen image of the animal, there appears a description and a given name.

Playing the role of the activist teacher, the Junk collector explains to Pook that she must now go on a mission to gain an understanding of the world. Three rolled pieces of paper appear on the screen representing three different missions. The first mission requires protecting Hereandnow from an epidemic. To begin the mission, various choices are displayed ranging from playing in the river to going to a health clinic located 20 miles from Hereandnow. The selection of wrong choices sends Pook home to go to bed. The correct choice sends Pook to the health clinic where she meets Dr. Doomuch. After Pook announces that she wants to stop the epidemic, Dr. Doomuch replies that Pook must find out the nature of the disease and possible vaccines. The viewer is then asked to select from the various stamps an endangered species that might help Pook get to Hereandnow. The correct answer is the Pelican who flies Pook to the village where she finds out the problem is measles. After the Pelican flies Pook back to the clinic, another problem is discovered. The solar power unit on the cooler for the transporting of vaccines and medicines is only working at 50% efficiency. Pook remembers a school experiment using a magnifying glass to concentrate the sun's rays. Using the lens from the Secretary Bird's glasses to intensify the sun's rays onto the solar panel, a flock of Pelicans return the medical cooler, Pook, and Dr. Doomuch to Hereandnow. The inevitable happens when Pook, with a little help from her friends, saves the village from the epidemic.

Pook is the most sophisticated of the available games on the cyberschoolbus Web site. The others, such as The Professor's Postcards, Water Quiz, Flag Tag, Urban Fact Game, and Health Game, are simple geography and fact games. These other games do contribute to an increased consciousness of the world's geography, cultures, and problems. However, they do not, as compared to Pook, attempt to mold a social activist.

Project is a Cyberschoolbus instructional unit designed to promote activism to protect human rights. "The project," the Cyberschoolbus Web site states, "hopes to demonstrate that young people around the world are active in and concerned about their world ... and that young students can, indeed, make a difference."[69] The *Project* utilizes rather traditional methodologies associated with the project method. These involve cooperative student activity requiring the acquisition of knowledge and the application of the knowledge to real social problems. Information technology is used to expand the work of a single cooperative group to that of other global participants. It is a means of globalizing knowledge, cooperative activities, and social action. Around the globe, students are encouraged to actively engage in the protection of human rights.

A spin-off of the *Project* is a global atlas of student actions to protect human rights. The Cyberschoolbus Web site is designed to collect stories of "classes or schools defending and promoting human rights in their neighborhoods and cities."[70] By broadcasting and exchanging these stories by e-mail and the World Wide Web, the project is training students to use the Internet to promote activism and share information in the same manner as members of other human rights organizations.

The *Project*'s classroom guide, which I want to remind the reader is available in multiple languages, begins with an explanation of the project's methodology to teachers. Teachers are told to begin with the concept of rights embodied in the Universal Declaration of Human Rights and then expand the rights notion to other international agreements. Then they are told to help students apply the notion of rights to issues in their own communities and to analyze through discussion what they are doing to protect human rights. Teachers encourage students to submit reports for the global atlas of student actions. In keeping with the activist tone of the project, teachers tell students to "get active to increase respect for human rights ... [and] plan an action in their own communities and then carry it out." Teachers are cautioned to select "appropriate" projects.[71]

As part of the knowledge-building aspects of the project method, student participants must gather and understand information about human rights. It is recommended that teachers use a plain language version of the Universal Declaration of Human Rights. This version simplifies the wording of articles of the Declaration to make the document accessible to young students. This is problematic because rewording the Declaration might result in giving particular interpretations to the meaning of each article. In some cases, simplification doesn't seem warranted. For instance, Article 3 of the 1948 Declaration declares, "Everyone has the right to life, liberty and security of person."[72] The plain language version is "You have the right to live, and to live in freedom and safety."[73] In addition, an interactive version of the Declaration is available where each article is introduced with an explanation of key issues, suggested activities, and discussion questions. There is also an indexed guide to specific issues such as children's rights, the rights of organized labor, and women's rights.[74] The availability of the "The Interactive Declaration" on the Internet in multiple languages is a power tool for globalizing human rights concepts. Students with access to the internet can easily familiarize themselves with a broad range of human rights concepts. This is a major contribution to creating a uniform global morality based on human rights.

Based on what they have learned about human rights, students involved in the *Project* are asked to apply a human rights lens to interpreting activities in their communities. The suggested "Hints" for initiating community rights projects underline the development of consciousness that interprets local and global events from a human rights perspective. The "Hints" require students to actively think and apply human rights doctrines. Initiating student involvement is prompted by classroom discussions of historical situations involving rights issues, analyzing media for human rights stories, and relating these discussions to appropriate articles in the Declaration, and relating human rights to classroom and school situations.

The participation of students in creating a global atlas requires thinking about human rights and active involvement in protecting rights. In the first part, students examine their communities for examples of how human rights are protected. The second part requires student activism to protect rights. The Cyberschoolbus provides online submission forms for both types of projects.

The global submission forms contain a pedagogical method that combines an analysis of the social construction of knowledge with the importance of struggling for human rights. Students learn that historical documents do not magically appear but are the result of human action or, in other words, they are socially constructed. For instance, after asking about school and class, the first submission form asks students to fill in a blank section following the statement, "In our community, one of the well-respected rights is the right to."[75] Then the form requires filling in a blank that relates this right to an article in the Universal Declaration of Human Rights. Then, to help students think about the historical struggles and social construction that helped establish this particular right, students are asked to fill in a blank giving the date when "there was a movement/struggle to promote this right."[76] Finally, students are asked to write "70 words or less about the movement, its key figures and the main issues."[77]

Instructional methods are also embedded in the second submission form, which is devoted to student activities to protect human rights. After filling in blanks identifying the school, class, and project, students are asked to fill in a blank next to the statement, "Describe how the human right was not being fully respected [in the student's community]."[78] As in the first form, students are asked to identify the appropriate article in the Declaration related to this right. Finally, students must "summarize the action [to protect this right] taken by students (max. 150 words)."[79]

The Pook game and the *Project* are the most interesting and activist aspects of the instructional material that can be found on the Cyberschoolbus Web site. Most of the other material is primarily informational. Briefing papers for students are offered ranging in topics from biodiversity to globalization. Descriptions are given of the plight of the world's children, emphasizing violations of the rights of the child.

The Cyberschoolbus's global influence in forming an international human rights ethic is exemplified in the section on Human Rights Questions and Answers. Questions are sent from students around the world and they are answered by Philip Alston, Chairman of the U.N. Committee on Economic, Social and Cultural Rights; Elsa Stamatopoulou, Acting Director of the Office of the High Commissioner for Human Rights; and Cynthia Brown, Program Director for Human Rights Watch. A question from Surbhi Army Public School (India) is, "Regarding Article 5 on punishment and torture: Is it not necessary to control evil and hooliganism by giving punishment accordingly?"[80] Cynthia Brown provides a lengthy answer dealing with humane and inhumane methods of social control that can be used by governments. Manuela Perez of the Colegio Internacional SEK wonders, "Do countries take children's rights seriously?"[81] Philip Alston replies with a lengthy explanation of the problems faced in gaining recognition and enforcement of the 1989 Convention on the Rights of the Child. From the Hondsrug College (Netherlands) is the question, "Regarding Article 16 of the Universal Declaration, what is marriageable age? And does this vary by race, nationality or religion?"[82] Elsa Stamatopoulou explains why, on the basis on human rights documents, the United Nations recommends that governments establish 18 years as the age of marriage.

In summary, the Cyberschoolbus exemplifies the role of the Internet in building a global ethical culture. Instructional methods foster a consciousness of human rights, teach students to interpret the world through the lens of human rights doctrines, and attempt to motivate students to become human rights activists.

PEACE EDUCATION AS GLOBAL MANNERS

Peace education strives to limit violence by creating global rules for interpersonal and governmental relations. The peace education movement has ties to U.N. activities and to NGOs. For instance, leading American peace educator Betty Reardon gave up her position as a high school social studies teacher in 1963 to head the secondary education program of the Institute for World Order, an NGO devoted to peace research and education.[83] In the 1960s, leaders of the Institute for World Order made a distinction between their concerns and those influencing the international and global education movements of the 1960s. While international and global education movements claimed to be value-free, the World Order approach emphasized the necessity of changing value systems to promote peace. They also distinguished their organization from others regarding violence. According to Betty Reardon, international and global education worked from the premise "Large-scale violence [is] considered an acceptable means to implement policy goals." In contrast, the Institute for World Order and, consequently peace educators, declared, "Large-scale violence [is] ordinarily considered unacceptable."[84] The work of the Institute for World Order, and that of Betty Reardon, linked peace education to issues of values and social justice. The social justice embraced aspects of human rights doctrines. Writing in the 1973 yearbook of the Association for Supervision and Curriculum Development, Reardon described the general approach of the Institute for World Order,

> World order seeks not only nonviolent solutions to conflicts but, even more important, *just* solutions to conflicts. It is a normative, value-centered discipline which aspires to more than the elimination of war, aiming also at relieving human suffering resulting from the drastically disparate distribution of the world's wealth ... and from the wanton exploitation of the earth's resources by that powerful minority which controls and uses them without regard to the interests of people of this and succeeding generations.[85]

In 1971, the Peace Education Commission was formed by the International Peace Research Association (IPRA). IPRA was organized in 1963 at a conference called by the Quaker International Conferences and Seminars in Clarens, Switzerland. The stated purpose of IPRA is

> to advance interdisciplinary research into the conditions of peace and the causes of war and other forms of violence. To this end, IPRA shall encourage worldwide cooperation designed to assist the advancement of peace research and, in particular: to promote national and international studies and teaching related to the pursuit of world peace; to facilitate contacts and cooperation between scholars and educators throughout the world; and to encourage worldwide dissemination of results of peace research.[86]

The Peace Education Commission expanded their endeavors to include human rights education and development education. Development education dealt directly with problems of world poverty and economic exploitation. In the early 1970s, the Peace Education Network (PEN) was formed to work with U.S. primary and secondary school educators.[87] By the 1980s, peace education had expanded to include environmentalism and multiculturalism. In 1986, the Juniata report (named after the meeting place at Juniata College in Huntingdon, Pennsylvania) was adopted by peace educators which included in its objectives "the five 'world order values': peace, social justice, economic equity, ecological balance, and political participation."[88]

Further expanding the peace education effort was a 1979 resolution of the General Assembly of the United Nations to establish a University of Peace. With land donated by the Costa Rican government, the University of Peace was founded in 1980 with the Secretary-General of the United Nations as its honorary president. The University of Peace was given the mission of providing "humanity with an international institution of higher education for peace and with the aim of promoting among all human beings the spirit of understanding, tolerance and peaceful coexistence, to stimulate cooperation among peoples and to help lessen obstacles and threats to world peace and progress, in keeping with the noble aspirations proclaimed in the Charter of the United Nations." The University's charter declares that peace requires the "most effective resource that man possesses: education." Furthermore, in language similar to that of American education leader Horace Mann who felt public schools were the undiscovered solution for crime, the charter states, "Peace is the primary and irrevocable obligation of a nation and the fundamental objective of the United Nations; it is the reason for its existence. However, the best tool for achieving this supreme good for humankind, namely education, has not been used."[89] The University of Peace is only part of the United Nation's involvement in peace education. The United Nations Decade for Human Rights Education includes in the building of global human rights culture, as stated previously, "(e) The furtherance of the activities of the United Nations for the maintenance of peace."[90]

How is peace education different from human rights education? Peace education encompasses human rights education but places an emphasis on conflict resolution. Betty Reardon, a leader in the field of peace education, stated, "The conceptual core of peace education is violence, its control, reduction, and elimination."[91] She described its evolution from a study of how to eliminate the causes of war to how to create conditions of peace. In the context of promoting conditions of peace, there is concern about the conditions leading to war but also conditions that cause other forms of violence, such as poverty, unequal political and economic structures, racism, sexism, ethnocentrism, and other forms of cultural violence. Within the framework of peace education, protection of human rights creates the conditions that makes peace possible.

Included under the banner of peace education are human rights and environmental education, conflict resolution, and multicultural, development, and world order studies. All of these studies contribute to conditions needed for peace. In conflict resolution, peace educators study and teach methods for avoiding and settling struggles between people and institutions. Environmental education is considered necessary for protecting the human species, which, of course, is the central purpose of human rights doctrines. Betty Reardon argued that environmental education "brings an ecological or living systems perspective to the study of global problems .... It provides a way of considering the possibility that the human species as a unit has rights, a possibility implied in the designation of some human rights abuses as 'crimes against humanity'."[92] In addition, multicultural education promotes peace by reducing conflict between cultural groups and by promoting cultural harmony within the framework of human rights. Peace educators argue that development plans and discussions of the world order should be analyzed according to their effect on the conditions of global peace.

Peace educators focus on teaching global rules of conduct, or in other words good manners, that will promote social harmony and reduce conflict. I do not intend to demean or understate the goals of peace education by using the phrase "good manners." In the case of peace education, good manners extend beyond the realm of interpersonal relations to relationships between governments, social groups, institutions, and the environment. Hitting someone is an act of interpersonal violence, war is an act of governmental violence, and pollution is environmental violence. In this sense, good manners, or rules for social conduct, prohibit actions that lead to personal, institutional, governmental, and environmental violence just as bad manners might be throwing trash on the ground, emptying oil cans in a river, or governments initiating acts of war.

These good global rules of conduct are inscribed in a peace culture. Similar to human rights educators, peace educators desire the creation of a "global culture of peace."[93] As stated in a Cyberschoolbus lesson plan, "A culture of peace will be achieved when citizens of the world understand global problems, have the skills to resolve conflicts and struggle for justice non-violently, live by international standards of human rights and equity, appreciate cultural diversity, and respect the Earth and each other."[94]

In educating the world in manners that promote peace, the primary instructional concern is building good human relations among learners so that after leaving the classroom they will live in peace with others. Again, it needs to be emphasized that this means peace between humans along with peace between humans and the environment. The classroom becomes a minisociety for conflict resolution and the practice of peace. British peace educator Patrick Whitaker described the practice of classroom peace as a necessary part of learning how to create a peaceful world. "If peace is both the destination and the journey then what we teach and how we teach it must not be separated in our preparations for working with students."[95]

Peace educators want to understand violence and transform it into peacefulness. Peace educators divide violence into personal and institutional. Personal violence includes "assault, rape, brutality, terrorism, murder and ethnic cleansing."[96] Institutional violence involves "war, state-sponsored terror, industrial destruction of plant and animal life."[97] This broad definition encompasses environmentalism along with human rights concerns. Peace is defined as the "absence of personal and institutional violence" and the "presence of well being, social justice, gender equity, and human rights."[98]

As part of a global morality, peace educators define proper modes of human relationships. These social conduct skills or manners include "active listening and reflection, cooperation, empathy and compassion ... patience and self-control ... tolerance, [and] gender sensitivity"[99] These are modes of conduct which, in some cultures, might separate "well-mannered" people from the boorish. The assumption is that the value of being well-mannered is peaceful relationships and world peace.

Classroom instruction is an opportunity to teach standards for global manners that will contribute to a culture of peace. "In the classroom," the Cyberschoolbus site on peace education states, "peace education aims to develop skills, attitudes, and knowledge with co-operative and participatory learning methods and an environment of tolerance, care, and respect."[100] Besides teaching active listening and reflection skills, peace education includes the imparting of knowledge about things ranging from nuclear weapons and international law to AIDS and the drug trade. In the classroom, teachers are to develop attitudes regarding self-respect, ecological awareness, tolerance, cultural differences, caring, social responsibility, and world-mindness.

For instance, in a peace education lesson on "Ecological Thinking and Respect for Life," students learn to "demonstrate a co-operative approach to learning, practice active listening, develop an ability to participate and express their opinions, [and] display care for others and the planet."[101] These human relations skills are attained by working cooperatively in small groups to complete an assignment. The process of "Checking In" develops skills in listening to others and expressing opinions. The "Checking In" part of the lesson can be contrasted to a family meal where relatives all talk at the same time, do not hear what others say, and, consequently, do not actually respond to the opinions expressed by other family members. The breakdown in communication can result in misunderstandings that could result in family conflict. In the "Ecological Thinking and Respect for Life," "Checking In" takes place at the end of the exercise with the question, "What did we learn?" The teacher is instructed to "sit in a circle and ask students to share one or two things they learned in this activity. The teacher should also share something she or he learned in the activity .... The teacher's openness will hopefully encourage students to trust and share in the learning environment."[102]

Often peace education lessons appeal directly to the emotions. Affective education is absent from most, if not all, educational strategies of World Bank officials and human rights educators. Obviously, moods and feelings are directly related to acts of violence and, consequently, to creating peaceful relations. The World Bank's neglect of affective education might be considered strange when they are educating people for the instability and insecurity of free markets. And, of course, thoughtfulness and action regarding human rights embodies many levels of emotions particularly compassion.

Therefore, peace education realistically addresses the education of the emotions. Accompanying a lesson called "Tolerance and Respect for Dignity and Identity" is a Cyberschoolbus peace poem submitted by a middle school in Zagreb, Croatia: "Wherever I go, peace is with me, because without peace there is no me."[103] The lesson incorporates articles from the Convention on the Rights of the Child dealing with the protection of a child's national and family identity. Included in the skills to be learned is practicing "empathy and compassionate treatment of others" and demonstrating attitudes of "self-respect" and "tolerance for differences."[104] Students are asked to keep a reflective journal about their personal responses to the reading of *The Diary of Anne Frank*. For students, the book can be an emotional experience if they are able to place themselves in her situation. The lesson focuses on her efforts to maintain her self-identity and self-respect. To help students gain empathy for Anne Frank, they are asked to construct individual identity cards with symbols and logos of self-representation and to write a story dealing with an event of emotional impact to themselves or someone close to them. Students then share their cards and stories with the rest of the class. Interacting with the class about their identity and a personal emotional episode exposes students' emotions. The goals of this emotional training are revealed in the responses students are asked to provide to a series of assessment questions, such as "Have your feelings about others in the class changed at all? If so, in what way? Have your perceptions of others in the class changed? If so, in what way?"[105] Their own sense of self-worth is tied to their display of personal identities before the class.

Emotions are linked to imagination. There are many uses for imagination. Nationalistic education uses imagination to train people to think of their country as the best. Education promoted by the World Bank relies on imagination for the making, selling, and consuming of products. In the Pook game, children dream of being superheroes who save the world from injustice. Peace educators want students "to enhance [their] abilities in imagining alternatives to violence."[106] In all these situations, imagination becomes an instrument for achieving a specific social objective. These examples demonstrate how much personal imagination has become public property. It is played to by media, arts, and advertising. It is used in the quest for national glory, corporate profit, and a humane and peaceful world. The conquest of personal imagination is important in all commercial and social enterprises.

For instance, peace educator Betty Reardon provides a second-grade lesson where imagination is used in "Wishing a World Fit for Children—Understanding Human Needs."[107] Reardon instructs the teacher, "Tell the children that when we make wishes we use our imaginations. When we imagine good things and a better world, we actually begin to make the world better."[108] In the lesson, children are to make gifts for a newborn baby and give it to a model baby wrapped in a wish. The gifts represent things the baby will actually need, such as a bed, clothes, and food. The wishes are for something that will make the child's life more secure and happy. A class discussion of wishes and needs yields two lists, "Needs of a Child" and "Wishes for a Better World." The lesson concludes with teachers asking the second graders, "Look at the list of wishes for a better world and think about what we need to learn to make a better world."[109]

Another example of the use of imagination for ending violence can be found in the Cyberschoolbus peace education lesson, "Critical Thinking and Active Non-Violence." This lesson is accompanied by a section of the Preamble of the Constitution of the United Nations, Educational, Scientific and Cultural Organization: "Since wars began in the minds of men, it is in the minds of men [and women] that the defenses of peace must be constructed."[110] It is assumed that the elimination of violence will require people to find creative alternatives. Classroom instruction should prepare people to use their imaginations in creating new scenarios for peaceful resolution of conflicts.

In the lesson, critical thinking is linked to the use of imagination through the medium of student "Detectives." A student is designate as Storyteller to relate a personal incident or one they have knowledge about that involves conflict. Student Detectives listen, trying to identify any assumptions underlying the story. In this exercise in critical thinking, the Detectives are asked to consider, "Does the Storyteller have any biases related to the story? What do they appear to be? What assumptions or conclusions has she/he drawn about what took place? What is stated as an assumption and what seems to be implied or unstated? What are some alternative interpretations that could be given based on the same facts and circumstances?"[111] After the Storyteller is done, the Detectives offer alternative interpretations of the story. This is followed by a discussion analyzing all aspects of the story and interpretations.

The stage is set for unleashing the imagination after critical thinking has been used to analyze the story. The consideration of assumptions, bias, and alternative interpretations leads logically to imagining other endings to the story and other ways of handling the conflict represented in the story. Students are asked to imagine how they might deal with similar conflicts in the future.

In summary, peace education develops a complex set of skills to guide personal conduct so that social harmony is enhanced and violence is reduced. In peace education, students learn the moral standards embodied in human rights doctrines. They learn how to apply this morality to their own actions. Students learn to think of violence as something that is not only committed by individuals but also by governments, corporations, and other institutions. They learn to consider environmental destruction as a form of violence. They learn to use emotions that promote peace, such as compassion, and to restrain emotions that contribute to conflict, such as anger. They learn to listen and reflect on the opinions of others. Also, they learn to think critically about their own biases and assumptions about others, and the assumptions and biases of others. Finally, they learn to imagine how to resolve conflicts and create a peaceful world. All of these lessons compose rules of conduct or good manners that will help to end global violence.

CONCLUSION: HUMAN RIGHTS NGOS
AND CREATING THE RULES OF CONDUCT
FOR A CIVIL SOCIETY

The major human rights NGOs are contributing to the educational work of building a morality and rules of conduct for a global civil society. They actively distribute educational material. In addition, they work for the implementation of Article 26, the educational rights provision of the Universal Declaration of Human Rights, and the Rights of Children. In this regard, human rights NGOs are helping to spin a web of morality around the actions of nation-states and the global civil society.

There is a connection between the enforcement of educational rights, as given in Article 26, and human rights education. As I have suggested in other works, the right to an education includes an education in human rights.[112] The linkage is similar to the plans of the World Bank, where its support of schooling is designed to educate students who will support the activities of free markets and neoliberal governments. In this case, support of the right to an education makes possible the educating of people about human rights and preparing them for active protection of the human rights of others.

There are potential clashes between the global educational ideologies of nation-states (e.g., Singapore), the World Bank, and human rights groups. As a strong nation-state, Singapore, similar to the United States, resists interference in its internal affairs. However, Singapore, along with other nation-states, must worry about global condemnation if human rights groups complain about their actions. A major clash with human rights groups is over the issue of the death penalty. An example is a notice of condemnation posted on the Amnesty International Web site: "SINGAPORE: Norishyam Mohamed Ali and Shaiful Edham Adam (EX 77/99 issued June 29, 1999). Norishyam Mohamed Ali and Shaiful Edham Adam were hanged at dawn on 2 July 1999."[113]

Claims rights to adequate nutrition, shelter, health care, and employment are a major area of conflict. These rights are considered necessary to the welfare of all human beings. They are a claim right against all of society, particularly when that society is represented by a government. From a human rights perspective, people should actively work to ensure that all people have adequate nutrition, shelter, health care, and employment. This thinking is completely contrary to ideology supporting free markets and neoliberal governments. Within this framework, societies and government are not obligated to provide these services or ensure these social and economic conditions. Whereas neoliberal governments might not provide these services and conditions, NGOs are free to act.

Cultural diversity issues present the greatest difficulty for human rights and peace educators. Both groups are trying to create global standards of conduct that would change or eliminate many practices of local cultures and of nation-states. A universal culture of human rights and peace will be used to judge all cultural practices and the actions of nation-states. It will be the global standard for judging human actions. For better or worse, human rights and peace educators are missionaries proclaiming the best social order for all.

Love the Biosphere:
Environmental Ideologies
Shaping Global Society

I am convinced, along with many others, that environmental education is the most radical pedagogy shaping global society.[1] Also, because of its broad definition of environment, environmental education encompasses human and peace education, and concerns about economic justice. Similar to human rights and peace educators, environmental educators often find themselves in disagreement with neoliberal education policies of organizations such as the World Bank and educational policies tied to support of the nation-state. Environmental education may provide the central core of a global ethic and civil society.

By *radical*, I mean that environmental education attempts to fundamentally change concepts of the good society that are based on industrial expansion and consumerism. First, it replaces the human-centric focus of most educational theories with a broader focus that is centered within the biosphere. In other words, the survival of all species of animals and plants is considered of equal value to the survival of humans. Second, educational goals articulated during the industrial development of the 19th and 20th centuries, such as training workers and consumers, and aiding economic growth, are replaced in environmental education by goals of reducing consumption and waste, achieving sustainable development, and improving the environment. Third, environmental educationists believe the nation-state often interferes with efforts to protect the biosphere and, consequently, support global organizations. The nation-state is a political form that allows for willful exploitation and destruction of the environment. Fourth, many environmental educators reject the proposition of past radical educational theories that the goal of schooling should be increased economic equality. In reality, economic equality means equality of consumption, which might be an impossible goal because of earth's

100

limited resources. Also, the pursuit of equality of consumption could literally destroy the planet.

Contemporary environmentalists reject the prevailing linear paradigm that frames most economic debates. Since the 19th century, arguments about industrial organization have been trapped between the two extremes of capitalism and communism. As a result, most proposed solutions to problems arising from industrialism involve some combination or variation of these two extremes. Advocates of either extreme promise that their economic plans will provide the most efficient means to produce consumer products and achieve equality of consumption. In this paradigm, progress is measured by the amount and equality of consumption. Environmentalists argue that this concept of progress and the economic systems of capitalism and communism, along with their many variations, are self-destructive because they result in the depletion of the planet's resources and the destruction of the biosphere by the waste products of consumerism.

In general, environmental education is also radical in form. It rejects the idea that schooling involves the study of separate disciplines. It calls for an interdisciplinary and wholistic approach to learning in which a broad concept of environmentalism is woven through all areas of study. In most discussions, environmental education includes issues of human rights, social and economic justice, peace, protection of living species and cultures, and peace studies. This broad definition of environmentalism is used to frame the curriculum, methods of instruction, and goals of learning.

Environmental education promotes the growth of an activist global civil society that is influencing the actions of nation-states, intergovernmental organizations, and corporations. Similar to other educational ideologies shaping global society, the ideology of environmental education supports global changes in human attitudes and behaviors. Reflecting the activist element in environmental education, the North American Association for Environmental Education declares, "A knowledgeable, skilled, and active citizenry is a key to resolving the environmental issues that promise to become increasingly important into the next century."[2]

The environmental imperative is a driving force in global unity. Inevitably, after humans connected across oceans and populations grew, the environment became a common global concern. Today, the second largest international group of NGOs, after human rights organizations, are environmental organizations. Between 1953 and 1993, the number of international environmental groups leaped from 2 to 90, making them the fast growing sector of the global civil society.[3] Environmental education is shaping global attitudes and knowledge about human interaction with the planet, including relationship between humans, and between humans and other species. Environmental education is the most all encompassing educational ideology shaping global society.

THE BIOSPHERE: FORMULATING THE NEW PARADIGM

The "biosphere" is the conceptual paradigm underlying most current environmental thought. The term *biosphere* was first coined in 1875 by Austrian geologist Edward Suess. However, it was Russian scientist Vladimir Vernadsky's 1926 book *The Biosphere* that created a framework for integrating all life with an environmental system.[4] University of Geneva's Jacques Grinevald, a historian of science, considered Vernadsky a "cosmic prophet of globalization."[5] Grinevald claimed that Vernadsky's *The Biosphere* is of the same importance in changing human views of life and the planet as Charles Darwin's *Origins of Species*.[6] Vernadsky developed a wholistic and globalizing paradigm that makes it impossible to separate life from its surrounding environment. Acceptance of Vernadsky's paradigm results in seeing the protection of the total environment of the planet as necessary for the sustaining human life. In Vernadsky's words,

> In most of their works studying living organisms, the biologists disregard the indissoluble connection between the surrounding milieu and the living organism. In studying the organism as something quite distinct from the environment, the cosmic milieu ... they study not a natural body but a pure product of their thinking.[7]

While Western scientists were trying to understand life by reducing it to its smallest parts, such as the genome, Russian scientists were trying to understand life as part of an integrated whole, such as how forests exist and sustain life. Physics Professor Freeman Dyson described these differences: "Russian biologists aimed to understand life by integrating it into ecological communities and planetary processes. Meanwhile, in the West, biology developed in a strongly reductionist direction, the aim being to understand life by reducing it to genes and molecules."[8]

In Vernadsky's concept of the biosphere, the conditions necessary for sustaining life include the interrelationships between solar radiation, the atmosphere, oceans, and the earth's surface. Important to his formulation of the biosphere is the effect of life on geology as part of the biosphere's interdependence. In the foreword to the Russian edition of his book, he wrote, "Let us consider all empirical facts from the point of view of a [w]*holistic mechanism* that combines all parts of the planet in an indivisible whole. Only then will we be able to perceive the perfect correspondence between this idea and the geological effects of life .... Included in the [wholistic] mechanism is the biosphere, the domain of manifestation of life."[9]

From this perspective, the human species is not free but is part of a larger collective. Vernadsky stated, "Basically man cannot be separated from it [biosphere]; it is only now that this indissolubility begins to appear clearly and in precise terms before us .... Actually no living organism exists on earth in a state of freedom."[10] Emphasizing the interdependence of life and natural conditions, Vernadsky argued, "All organisms are connected indissolubly and uninterruptedly, first of all through nutrition and respiration, with the circumambient material and energetic medium."[11]

Setting the stage for the leap in environmental activism after World War II, Vernadsky recognized that humans above all other species had the greatest impact on the biosphere. In words that would be echoed in different forms and for differing reasons across the spectrum of environmental educational ideologies in the 20th and in the 21st centuries, Vernadsky wrote, "Chemically, the face of our planet, the biosphere is being sharply changed by man, consciously and even more so, unconsciously. The aerial envelope of the land as well as all its natural waters are changed both physically and chemically by man .... Man now must take more and more measures to preserve for future generations the wealth of the seas which so far have belonged to nobody."[12]

In the 1960s, the concept of the biosphere became part of environmental education. In 1965, the International Union for the Conservation of Nature and Natural Resources (IUCN), also known as the World Conservation Union, called for "environmental education in schools, in higher education, and in training for the land-linked professions."[13] Historically, the IUCN represents a major step in the development of a global civil society. It was organized in 1949 as a union of government organizations and NGOs interested in environmental problems. In 1968, the IUCN played a major role in the Biosphere Conference held in Paris with support from the United Nations Educational, Scientific and Cultural Organization (UNESCO). At the conference, curriculum materials were developed for schools to create global awareness of environmental problems.

What is called the "greatest landmark in the history of attempting to define the term 'environmental education'" occurred in 1970 at a joint meeting of IUCN/UNESCO on the Environmental Education in the School Curriculum held in Carson City, Nevada.[14] The meeting issued what is now called the "classic" definition of environmental education. The definition reflects the integrating influence of the biosphere paradigm.

> Environmental education is the process of recognizing values and clarifying concepts in order to develop skills and attitudes necessary to understand and appreciate the inter-relatedness among man, his culture and his biophysical surroundings. Environmental education also entails practice in decision-making and self-formulation of behavior about issues concerning environmental quality.[15]

The 1972 U.N. Conference on the Human Environment in Stockholm, Sweden, highlighted global acceptance of the biosphere concept. Preceding the Stockholm meeting, international treaties and government initiatives had dealt with protection of migratory birds, some forms of wildlife, forests, and mineral deposits. The Stockholm meeting made environmental protection a major global concern and directed attention to the concept of the biosphere. According to environmental historian Lynton Caldwell, "The change marked by Stockholm is from the view of an earth unlimited in abundance and created for man's exclusive use to a concept of the earth as a domain of life or biosphere for which mankind is a temporary resident custodian."[16]

Humans are dependent for their very lives on the biosphere and, consequently, environmental worries propel the human species into an all-encompassing global awareness. From ocean floors to the ozone layer, humans need to maintain supportive living conditions. While human rights education attempts to regulate behavior between people, environmental education hopes to define behaviors between species and the globe. As I discussed in chapter 3, peace education embraces environmental education as protection against violence to the earth. A twist on this perspective is to subsume peace education, and for that matter human rights education, under environmentalism. A healthy planet might require peace and well-regulated human behaviors.

ENVIRONMENTAL EDUCATION
AND A GLOBAL CIVIL SOCIETY

Framed by the biosphere paradigm, environmental education requires active citizenship in a global civil society. Calling for a global alliance, the 1991 Second World Conservation Report, *Caring for the Earth* declared, "We must act globally .... The environment links all nations."[17] There was a demand for global civil action at both of the two major world environmental summits in 1992 and 2002. In 1992, the Rio Earth Summit issued a declaration defining the basic elements of civic action from local to national levels. Meeting in Rio de Janeiro, the summit attracted representatives from 172 governments, including 108 heads of state, along with 2,400 representatives from NGOs. "Environmental issues," stated the *Rio Declaration on Environment and Development* or as it has been called *Agenda 21*, "are best handled with the participation of all concerned citizens, at the relevant level. At the national level each individual shall have appropriate access to information concerning the environment that is held by public authorities, including information on hazardous materials and activities in their communities, and the opportunity to participate in decision-making processes."[18] This was a call for direct participation and action by citizens as opposed to a reliance on elected representatives. The

Rio Declaration called on governments to ensure that the public is given information about environmental issues. "States shall facilitate and encourage public awareness," the Declaration demands, "by making information widely available."[19]

Ten years later, another earth summit was held in Johannesburg with the same global participation. Meeting at the Johannesburg summit, the Global People's Forum issued a Civil Society Declaration. This declaration claims that the Global People's Forum represents those oppressed social groups named in *Agenda 21* of the Rio summit, including "women, youth, labour, indigenous peoples, farmers, NGOs, and others including disabled people, the elderly, faith-based organizations, peoples of African descent, social movements, people under foreign occupation and other under-represented groups,"[20] in other words, the dispossessed and disadvantaged who feel their interests are not represented by nation-states. The declaration asserts, "As the key agents of social change and sustainable development, we are determined to take leadership for our future with utmost seriousness."[21]

Important for environmental education, the Johannesburg declaration took a wholistic approach to environmental issues. Among educators, *wholistic* has two important meanings. The first meaning reflects the biosphere paradigm in which all human social issues and environmental conditions are seen as interrelated. The second considers all arenas of human knowledge as a whole rather than separated in specific disciplines such as history, economics, physics, and biology. The Johannesburg declaration emphasized the wholistic nature of human and environmental issues in its description of a global civil society and its role in environmental protection.

> The definition of civil society includes the major groups defined in Agenda 21, formal and informal community-based organizations, NGOs that work with and represent peoples who are victims of racism. Organizations of civil society have a central role to play in the translation of the Rio Principles and Agenda 21 into concrete programs, projects and implementation strategies for sustainable development .... We affirm that solidarity and partnerships for sustainable development are those entered into on the basis of clearly defined human needs and related goals, objectives and actions for the elimination of poverty and the enhancement and restoration of the physical, social, and universal spiritual environment.[22]

As a result of this wholistic approach, the Civil Society Declaration provides a list of Core Issues similar to those that fall under the umbrella of peace education as described in chapter 3. These wholistic Core Issues are equality, human rights, economic justice, redistribution of natural resources and wealth, corporate accountability, debt eradication, antiprivatization, political transparency, right to self-determination, militarism, environmental sustainability, genetic engineering, marine and coastal resources, and renewable energy. As evidenced by the list of issues, the Declaration opposes most of the neoliberal economics of organizations such as the World Bank. Specifically, the declaration rejects free-trade doctrines for "fair-trade" doctrines which it contends "reinforces and supports the right of developing countries to protect their own industries and natural resources against outside externalities including currency fluctuations and such as imposed by the WTO [World Trade Organization] and other global organizations." The declaration also rejects the neoliberal call for privatization of government services.

Environmental education is an important part of the "Programme of Action" accompanying the Civil Society Declaration. The educational proposals are in the context of a global civil society and contain some elements in other global educational proposals, such as lifelong learning and human rights education. Those proposals specifically related to environmental education deal with sustainable development, the preservation of indigenous environmental knowledge, and the development of technical and research expertise. Specifically, the action program asserts:

> Governments and civil society should:
> a. Implement educational methods enhancing ethos and methods of sustainable development, including the mainstreaming of indigenous knowledge systems.
> b. Ensure that financial and technical support is provided for the development of dynamic national systems of innovation in developing countries, with technology policies geared towards poverty reduction and environmentally sustainable development, integrated with poverty reduction strategies.
> c. Provide support for technological R&D relevant to the poor, focused upon creating R&D capacity in developing countries, and support for investment in R&D and innovation by low-income producers themselves to develop their own technologies that are most suitable to local needs.
> d. Ensure international and national regulatory frameworks that support the development of technological capabilities in developing countries, including the regulation of trade and investment by national governments, and intellectual property rights regimes that enable access to new and existing technology knowledge.[23]

There are a number of items mentioned in the Global People's Forum that are discussed in greater detail later in this chapter, particularly education for sustainable development, the role of indigenous peoples' knowledge, and the education of environmental experts. But before turning to these aspects of environmental education, I want to discuss the argument for a global environmental ethic, and the internal differences in the environmental education movement with respect to opposition to speciesism, naturalism, humanism, and sustainability. These differences in approaches to environmental issues are reflected in differing forms of educational programs.

A GLOBAL ENVIRONMENTAL ETHIC

Philosopher Peter Singer argues for a global environmental ethic and for recognition that animals have rights. In *One World: The Ethics of Globalization*, Singer analyzes the concept of the nation-state and he concludes that people have an ethical responsibility to a world community.[24] Part of his argument is based on a consideration of human rights and the global economy. Regarding the environment, Singer illustrates his case for a global ethic by analyzing the effect of pollution on atmospheric warming and the shrinking of the ozone layer.

Singer asks whether or not nation-states such as Singapore and the United States, which have the world's highest average carbon emissions in relationship to gross national product, have a primary ethical responsibility to protect the economic interests of their citizens or do they have an ethical responsibility to the global community? The key question is national interests. As Singer points out, President George W. Bush rejected the Kyoto Treaty designed to reduce world pollution because it threatened the economic interests of U.S. citizens. Bush asserted, "We will not do anything that harms our economy, because first things first are the people who live in America."[25]

Is there an ethical responsibility to protect the interests of the citizens of one's nation-state in opposition to the interests of the global community? Singer's answer is an emphatic no! First he argues that the nation-state is a historical construct dating from 17th-century Europe. It is an imagined community created by patriotic schooling and media. Citizenship is granted arbitrarily depending on immigration laws. Often citizens share more interests with people of other nation-states than with some citizens living in their own nation. Loyalty to the nation-state is a false ethical responsibility. Singer likens loyalty to fellow citizens to racism. He argues, "If we reject the idea that we should give preference to members of one's own race, or those 'of our blood', it is difficult to defend the intuition that we should favor our fellow citizens, in the sense in which citizenship is seen as a kind of extended kinship."[26] He further illustrates the issue by considering the difference between rescuing a child drowning within 10 yards of oneself and helping people dying of starvation in India at a distance of 10,000 miles. Of course, he argues, a person has an ethical responsibility to try and save the child. But what about those in India? Singer asserts, "It makes no moral difference whether the person I help is a neighbor's child ten yards from me or a Bengali whose name I shall never know, ten thousand miles away … no one has disputed this claim in respect of distance per se—that is the difference between ten yards and ten thousand miles."[27]

Regarding the necessity of a global ethic and the environment, Singer asks the reader to imagine a village where everyone puts their wastes down a common sink. Initially, there are no problems with this method because the environment can absorb the wastes. Consequently, there are no issues raised regarding the inequitable disposal of waste. Some people consume more than others and therefore dump more waste down the sink. This, of course, is similar to the problem of air pollution. Highly industrialized countries dump more pollutants into the atmosphere than nonindustrialized countries. What happens when disposal through the village sink increases to the point where it begins to pollute the village's water supply and to create unhealthy environmental conditions? Should those villagers who consume the most, and consequently have the most waste, be asked to reduce their consumption level? Should all villagers reduce their consumption by equal amounts which then allows some villagers to continue to consume more than other villagers? Is there an ethical justification for rich nations to continue destroying a resource, namely the atmosphere, needed by all the world's peoples?

First, Singer considers these ethical questions from the standpoint of arguments provided by John Locke and Adam Smith regarding private property. Does the right to private property allow owners to use their property to destroy the environmental resources of others? Singer concludes, "Neither Locke nor Smith provides any justification for the rich having more than their fair share of the finite capacity of the global atmospheric sink. In fact, just the contrary is true. Their arguments imply that this appropriation of a resource once common to all humankind is not justifiable."

Do leaders of a nation-state have the right to dump inordinate amounts of waste into the atmosphere in order to protect the economic interests of the their fellow citizens? Singer answers, "There is no *ethical* basis for the present distribution of the atmosphere's capacity to absorb greenhouse gases .... If industrialized countries choose to retain this distribution ... they are standing simply on their presumed rights as sovereign nations. That claim, and the raw military power these nations yield, makes it impossible for any one else to impose a more ethically defensible solution on them."[28]

What is needed to protect the environment for all the world's peoples, according to Singer, is a global ethic that overrides the particular interests of nation-states. As I illustrate throughout this chapter, this global environmental ethic is being articulated by a variety of international organizations. One aspect of Singer's argument that is particularly important is his consideration of humans as a species rather than as nationalities or races. Considering humans as a single species allows for the consideration of environmental conditions that are in the interests of the entire species.

And, as I illustrate in the next section, consideration of humans as a single species among other species provides a justification for animal rights.

DIFFERING APPROACHES
TO AN ENVIRONMENTAL ETHIC

Like any intellectual movement, the environmental movement has differing schools of thought about the content of a global environmental ethic. For the purpose of discussion, I am dividing these differing schools of thought into opponents of speciesism, naturalism, humanism, and sustainability. These are not mutually exclusive sets of ideas. There is an overlapping of concepts. However, they all provide a basis for developing a global environmental ethic. Also, they share a concern about indigenous cultures and their storehouses of traditional knowledge about the biosphere. Most environmental programs recognize the importance of traditional knowledge. There are several ways of thinking about humans and the environment.

Speciesism

Opposition to speciesism is influencing the development of a world environmental ethic. Speciesism is manifested as human discrimination against other animals. The struggle against speciesism, or a human-centered view of nature, fosters an environmental education based on animal rights and protection of all species. Peter Singer uses "speciesism" to characterize ideas and behaviors that ensure the triumph of humans over other animals. Speciesism is a form of discrimination, comparable to racial and gender discrimination among humans, in which humans, in order to maximize their survival and power, discriminate against other species. In the preface to the 1975 edition of *Animal Liberation*, Singer wrote,

> This book is about the tyranny of human over nonhuman animals. This tyranny has caused and today is still causing an amount of pain and suffering that can only be compared with that which resulted from the centuries of tyranny by white humans over black humans. The struggle against this tyranny is a struggle as important as any of the moral and social issues that have been fought over in recent years.[29]

Singer argues that humans share important characteristics with other animals such as suffering and self-interest. Also, if intelligence is used to distinguish species, then it should be recognized that members of some species are more intelligent than some humans. Language, according to Singer, embeds this discrimination in the human mind. In English, the word *animal* is used to distinguish humans from other nonhuman animals. Singer wrote, "This usage sets humans apart from other animals, implying that we are not ourselves animals—an implication that everyone who has had elementary lessons in biology knows to be false."[30] Therefore, according to Singer, humans cannot justify discrimination against other animals by claims of superiority.[31]

Equality among animals, as Singer defines it, does not mean equality of physical characteristics but equality in ability to experience suffering. In his words, "The principle of the equality of human beings is not a description of an alleged actual equality among humans: it is a prescription of how we should treat human beings."[32] In other words, equality among animals should involve equality of treatment.

As a result of speciesism, humans willfully make other animals suffer on farms and in cages, experiments in laboratories, and other forms of torturous situations. However, animals do kill each other for food and in the process cause suffering. Singer's response is that this does not justify humans killing and torturing other animals because "while humans can live without killing [by being vegetarians], other animals have no choice but to kill if they are to survive."[33] Therefore, animal rights activists and other environmentalists, similar to Hindus, are often vegetarians. Singer claims that there is no evidence that plants experience suffering. What about conflict between humans and other animals over food sources such as rabbits eating farm crops? In these situations, Singer argues, "The problem is how to defend our own essential food supplies while respecting the interests of these animals to the greatest extent possible."[34]

People for the Ethical Protection of Animals (PETA) is an example of an animal rights organization attacking speciesism and promoting a nonhuman-centric view of nature. The organization is engaged in a massive educational campaign to protect animal rights. PETA crusaders criticize humans for using other animals as sources of food and clothing, and campaigns against the use of animals in research. This means, of course, that animal rights advocates promote a vegetarian diet. PETA makes a distinction between animal rights and animal welfare. According to PETA, animal rights means "recognizing that animals are not ours to use—for food, clothing, entertainment, or experimentation."[35] In contrast, PETA considers the animal welfare position a form of speciesism, "Animal welfare theories accept that animals have interests but allow these interests to be traded away as long as there are some human benefits that are thought to justify that sacrifice."[36]

Naturalism and Deep Ecology

Naturalists object to animal rights advocates limiting their concerns to animals rather than being concerned about all species, including plant species, and the condition of the land, air, and water. The term that characterizes naturalists is *Deep Ecology*. One aspect of Deep Ecology is humans' relationship to all of nature. Humans respond to all aspects of nature, such as birdsongs, mountains, waves, clouds, sunsets, flowers, animals, and waterfalls. Humans have always gained a great deal of happiness, inspiration, and fulfillment through contact with their environment. Destruction of that environment reduces the quality of human life that is a result of contact with nature. From this standpoint, humans should protest not only cruelty toward animals but also actions that reduce human pleasure and personal development through the destruction of, for example, mountains, forests, planet species, coral, air, and oceans.[37]

Another aspect of Deep Ecology is that it identifies anthropocentrism as the cause of the current environmental crisis. *Anthropocentrism* is a broader term than speciesism. Anthropocentrism assumes that the biosphere exists to serve humans. It assumes that humans are at the top of the chain of being and are more developed than all other life forms. Whereas speciesism refers to discrimination by humans against other animals, anthropocentrism refers to the assumption that the earth, air, and water, and all living species exist for the benefit of humans. Anthropocentrism is a central assumption of most economic theories, including capitalism and communism, and most religions. From the perspective of anthropocentrism, humans have the right to destroy mountains and forests, change the direction of rivers, pollute oceans, and exploit and destroy animal and plant species.

Naturalists want nature to evolve with a minimum of human interference. Dave Foreman, one of the founders of Earth First!, explains this attitude and the difference between Deep Ecology and animal rights: "Deep Ecology is naturalistic, believing that nature knows best, going beyond good and evil to simply *letting being be*; Animal Rights in its more extreme forms is anti-nature ... to even claiming that nature is not perfect, that windstorms, forest fires, and predation are bad because they cause suffering. For instance, a primary concern of naturalists is the effect on nature of the burning of fossil fuels."[38] In *Green Rage: Radical Environmentalism and the Unmaking of Civilization*, a book that Earth First!'s Dave Foreman calls a "manifesto for the radical environmental movement," Christopher Manes provides a summary of naturalist ideas and themes that includes "the persuasion that humankind is not the center of value on this planet, the conviction that the other species on Earth have just as much right to exist as humans do, the belief that wilderness and not civilization is the real world."[39]

An example of the naturalist position is action-oriented Earth First! Founded in 1979, the organization rejects the modernization trends resulting from industrialization. The doctrines espoused by Earth First! include opposition to speciesism. "While many environmental groups are members of the American political establishment and essentially adopt the anthropo-centric (human-centered) world view of industrial civilization," the Earth First! organization proclaims, in differentiating itself from other environmental NGOs, "we say the ideas and manifestations of industrial civilization are anti-Earth, anti-woman, and anti-liberty. We are developing a new biocentric paradigm based on the intrinsic values of all natural things. Earth First! believes in wilderness for its own sake."[40] Adopting a nonhuman-centric interpretative framework, Earth First! defines the problem as human interference with the "continuous flow of evolution." Deforestation, desertification, the poisoning of the earth's water and air, and a human war on large animals, Earth First! claims, is resulting in a loss of almost one third of all species. Rejecting a humanist or human-centric approach to environmental issues, Earth First! demands complete protection of all existing wilderness and species.

Humanism and Sustainability

In contrast to animal rights and naturalist activists, humanists believe environmental conditions should maximize the growth and health of the human species. The humanist or human-centered perspective is quite different from that of the animal rights and naturalist activists. Singer would call the humanist position a form of speciesism, whereas naturalists would accuse it of anthropocentrism. The humanist perspective interprets changes in the global environment according to its effect on humans. The humanist approach to environmental education stresses clean water and air, and conservation of nature in order to provide a healthy environment for the human species. This form of environmentalism uses an interpretative perspective that evaluates conditions according to their human benefits.

An example of a humanist NGO is the Earth Day Network. Launched on April 22, 1970 by U.S. Senator Gaylord Nelson, Earth Day activists focus on industrial pollution, global warming, and destruction of water and air quality. According to the Earth Day Network, "Earth Day 1970 achieved a rare political alignment, enlisting support from Republicans and Democrats, rich and poor …. The first Earth Day led to the creation of the United States Environmental Protection Agency and the passage of the Clean Air, Clean Water, and Endangered Species acts."[41] The Earth Day Network involves a major educational effort to influence school curricula. Earth Day activists do not advocate animal rights or criticize speciesism. Protection of the environment is proclaimed necessary for the protection of human life or, in the words of the Earth Day Network, for "the common good."[42] The annual celebration of Earth Day every April 22 is a "collective expression of public will to create a sustainable society. Linking citizen activists, Earth Day educates and mobilizes people worldwide for environmental protection."[43]

An important part of the humanist perspective is the concept of "sustainable development." Supporters of sustainable development label naturalist organizations such as Earth First! and PETA as extremists. Referring to these naturalist groups as "ecological fundamentalists who will accept no compromise," a report of the 1997 UNESCO conference on sustainable development in Thessaloniki, Greece, expressed concern that the extreme methods used by these groups hurts the effort of advocates of sustainable development. The report contended in reference to the action of naturalist groups, "More moderate and reasoned voices often go unheard in the din. Extreme positions, while they may be useful in catching the public's attention and alerting it to pending dangers, make it difficult to move from declarations and debate to action."[44]

The idea of sustainable development was presented in the 1980 *World Conservation Strategy* report and became a central theme of the World Commission on Environment and Development. The *World Conservation Strategy* was prepared by the IUCN, the World Wildlife Federation (WWF), and the United Nations Environment Program. It contains a clear statement of the role of environmental education in creating a global ethic supporting sustainable development. The report states,

> Ultimately, the behavior of entire societies towards the biosphere must be transformed if the achievement of conservation objectives is to be assured ... the long term task of environmental education [is] *to foster or reinforce attitudes and behavior, compatible with a new ethic* [emphasis added].[45]

In 1992, sustainable development became the integrating theme for the United Nations Conference on Environment and Development.[46] The objective of sustainable development is to meet human needs without jeopardizing the environment. The 1992 United Nations Conference defined sustainable development as "development that meets the needs of the present without compromising the ability of future generations to meet their own needs."[47]

The idea of meeting human needs broadens the concept of sustainable development from just protection of environment to securing human rights and overcoming poor economic conditions. This means that environmental education for sustainable development will encompass these topics. The 1997 UNESCO conference in Thessaloniki, Greece included improving the quality of life for all, particularly the poor, as part of the idea of sustainable development: "Perhaps the most widely used definitions [of sustainable development] focus on the relationship between social development and economic opportunity, on the one hand, and the requirements of the environment of the other ... on improving the quality of life for all, especially of the poor and deprived, within the carrying capacity of supporting ecosystems."[48]

Sustainable development is important in plans such as those of the World Bank for modernizing societies. In fact, the World Bank is funding the Economics of Industrial Pollution Control Research Project. Through its program "New Ideas in Pollution Regulation," the World Bank offers information on the environmental effects of its developmental programs including interactive "maps that illustrate new international estimates of pollution damage, natural resource degradation, genuine savings, pressure on water resources, threats to biodiversity, and World Bank project responses."[49]

Global ethics for supporting sustainable development were promulgated in the Earth Charter issued on June 29, 2000 at the Peace Palace in The Hague. The drafting of the Earth Charter was initiated at a 1987 meeting of the United Nations World Commission on Environment and Development. Work was done on the Charter at the 1992 Rio Earth Summit and continued under the leadership of Maurice Strong, the Secretary-General of the Earth Summit and Mikhail Gorbachev, former leader of the Soviet Union and President of the Green Cross International.

The official Web site for the Earth Charter asserts that it is playing an important role in forming a global civil society. It claims the participation of a large number of international representatives. The Web site states,

> The drafting of the Earth Charter has involved the most open and participatory consultation process ever conducted in connection with an international document. Thousands of individuals and hundreds of organizations from all regions of the world, different cultures, and diverse sectors of society have participated. The Charter has been shaped by both experts and representatives of grassroots communities. It is a people's treaty that sets forth an important expression of the hopes and aspirations of the emerging *global civil society* [emphasis added].[50]

The officially stated mission of the Earth Charter "is to establish a sound ethical foundation for the emerging global society and to help build a sustainable world based on respect for nature, universal human rights, economic justice, and a culture of peace."[51]

Moacir Gadotti, the Director of Brazil's Paulo Freire Institute, advocates planetary citizenship with the Earth Charter serving as an ethical guide. He asserts, "The Earth Charter … [provides] a universal code of ethics and it should lend an important contribution, not only by its proclamation through Member states, but especially through the impact that its principles may have on the daily life of a planetary citizen."[52]

The Earth Charter's ethical imperative is set forth in its Preamble: "We must join together to bring forth a sustainable global society founded on respect for nature, universal human rights, economic justice, and a culture of peace. Towards this end, it is imperative that we, the peoples of Earth, declare our responsibility to one another, to the greater community of life, and to future generations."[53] The Charter asserts the necessity of global unity through "a sense of universal responsibility, identifying ourselves with the whole Earth community as well as our local communities."[54] The sweeping approach of the environmental movement is exemplified by the four categories of ethical principles. The first is the "Respect and Care for the Community of Life," with ethical standards ranging from respect for the diversity of the Earth to transmitting to future generations traditions that support ecological communities. The second set of principles covers "Ecological Integrity," which includes a commitment to restore Earth's ecological systems, prevent harm to the biosphere, support sustainable development and consumption, and promote knowledge about ecological sustainability. The third set of principles deals with "Social and Economic Justice" and requires people to work for the eradication of poverty, the initiation of economic activity that supports sustainable human development, the assurance of gender equality, and the abolition of discrimination. The final set of principles covers "Democracy, Nonviolence, and Peace." This section of the Earth Charter includes the ethical values advocated by human rights and peace educators.

Sustainability and the Earth Charter are major elements in the development of a global ethic centered on concerns about the biosphere. However, it would be wrong to discount the importance of animal rights and naturalist activists in the evolution of a global ethic. Their contributions are not only in their assaults on speciesism and anthropocentrism, but also in their very public forms of education.

Indigenous Cultures

Most environmental perspectives and education programs recognize the importance of indigenous peoples' cultures and traditional knowledge about the biosphere. Indigenous cultures contain storehouses of knowledge about the interrelationships between plants and animals supporting the biosphere. For instance, indigenous understanding might be the key to preservation of rain forests. Also, from a commercial perspective, indigenous knowledge of the medicinal properties of plants is valuable to pharmaceutical companies. All of these concerns were expressed in the "Indigenous Peoples' Caucus Statement at the World Summit on Sustainable Development" issued at the 2002 Johannesburg World Summit. The statement was supported by 300 representatives of indigenous peoples from 52 countries.

> Our key message in all these events is to ask the world to recognize Indigenous Peoples' Rights to self-determination and our rights to our territories, our cul-

tures and our traditional knowledge. A major step in the achievement of sustainable development is the recognition of our rights.[55]

The importance of maintaining and passing on to future generations the environmental knowledge of indigenous peoples was recognized in the Report of the Commission on Intellectual Property Rights, an international commission appointed by the British Government. A concern of the Commission was ensuring the protection of the commercial value of indigenous knowledge, particularly regarding biodiversity, agricultural practices, and the medicinal uses of plants. The Report states that "the custodians of traditional knowledge should receive fair compensation if the traditional knowledge leads to commercial gain."[56] Also, the Report gives the reasons for protecting indigenous knowledge as:

- conservation concerns—the protection of traditional knowledge contributes to the wider objective of conserving the environment, bio-diversity and sustainable agricultural practices
- preservation of traditional practices and culture—protection of traditional knowledge would be used to raise the profile of the knowledge and the people entrusted with it both within and outside communities
- prevention of appropriation by unauthorized parties or avoiding "biopiracy"
- promotion of its use and its importance to development.[57]

Traditional indigenous knowledge also provides a deep understanding of natural phenomenon, such as forests, as integrated systems. This was recognized in "Principle 22" of the Declaration of the 1992 Rio Earth Summit which states, "Indigenous people and their communities and other local communities have a vital role in environmental management and development because of their knowledge and traditional practices."[58] This idea was reiterated in the Political Declaration of the 2002 United Nations' World Summit on Sustainable Development (WSSD) in Johannesburg, South Africa in Johannesburg, South Africa, which declares, "We reaffirm that indigenous people and local communities are important for the sustenance of biological diversity and the preservation of indigenous knowledge systems, and must participate in and benefit from the implementation of the Johannesburg Commitment."[59] This affirmation reflects two important aspects of indigenous peoples regarding the environment.

The Johannesburg declaration integrates the idea of cultural diversity, which in this case means protection of indigenous cultures, as an important part of sustainable development. The Declaration states, "We respect cultural diversity and different value systems, as well as the promotion of the interests of indigenous peoples."[60] Tom Goldtooth, Dakota/Diné of North America and a member of the Indigenous Environmental Network, used the following words to describe the relationship between indigenous rights and environmental protection, "The battle we face everyday is the protection of our environment, way of life, spirituality, self-determination and the recognition as peoples. The WSSD has an obligation to respect Indigenous Peoples and our place in the world. Indigenous Peoples are the most affected by uncontrolled development and are at the mercy of governments and multinational corporations. We need respect, protection and a say in development that affects our lives."[61]

Indigenous groups at the Johannesburg meeting gave a spiritual meaning to their environmental concerns. The link between nature and some spiritual world is an important aspect of environmentalism. These beliefs are not confined to indigenous peoples. They provide another set of reasons for protecting the biosphere other than simply maintaining human life and sustainable industrial development.

Spiritualism

The spiritual aspects of indigenous peoples' concerns are clearly expressed in the "Kimberley Declaration" issued by the Indigenous Peoples' Summit at the 2002 Johannesburg World Summit. The Declaration contains the following statement of the spiritual importance of nature, which resonates with the ideas of Deep Ecology: "Our lands and territories are at the core of our existence—we are the land and the land is us; we have a distinct spiritual and material relationship with our lands .... We are the original peoples tied to the land by our umbilical cords and the dust of our ancestors. Our places are sacred and demand the highest respect."[62]

Education in traditional spiritual knowledge and cultural values is explicitly recognized in the "Indigenous Peoples' Plan of Implementation on Sustainable Development" issued at the Johannesburg Summit. The plan's first section after the introduction is titled "Cosmovision and Spirituality" and recognizes the importance of traditional indigenous education as the method for retaining spiritual and environmental knowledge. The plan states, "We will direct our energies ... to consolidate our collective values and principles which spring from the interrelation of the different forms of life in Nature."[63] In this context, tribal elders become the keepers and teachers of traditional knowledge which is presented as an alternative to the environmentally destructive forces of industrialization. "We will strengthen the role of our elders and wise traditional authorities as the keepers of our traditional wisdom," the plan maintains, "which embodies our spirituality and cosmovision as an alternative to the existing unsustainable cultural models."[64]

Spiritualism is also identified in the plan's section on the intellectual property rights of indigenous peoples. In the plan's discussion of "biopiracy activities" and attempts to steal indigenous knowledge by profit-making corporations through patents, copyrights, and trademarks, it is asserted, "We commit ourselves to safeguard, protect and reaffirm the use of indigenous knowledge and practices, respecting the spiritual values and dimensions of such knowledge."[65]

There are other groups who also link spirituality with protection of the biosphere and turn environmentalism into a religious quest. Again, this spirituality can be considered another aspect of Deep Ecology. Examples can be found in the Spring 2003 issue of the *Nature Conservancy*, the official publication of the international NGO of the same name. The Nature Conservancy donates money to buy and protect lands throughout the world. The organization embraces sustainability. The organization's president Steven McCormick asserts, within the biosphere paradigm, "It is a concept [sustainability] that The Nature Conservancy is increasingly committed to exploring, for our mission preserving Earth's biological diversity will succeed only if we can maintain the full benefits of that diversity for the well-being of humankind."[66]

Connecting spirituality to sustainability, the same Spring 2003 issue containing McCormick's statement is devoted to the spiritual aspects of nature with an essay by Paul Gorman, who is described as a noted religious and environmental activist, and interviews with Nature Conservancy members representing a variety of religious faiths. Gorman's essay opens with questions suggesting a strong link between environmental causes and religion: "How does faith foster a conservation ethic? In what ways does nature inspire one's beliefs?"[67] Gorman begins answering these questions by pointing out that, "In the fall of 1986, at the direction of the World Wildlife Fund president Prince Philip, the organization convened its 25th anniversary in Assisi to affirm what Prince Philip called the 'spiritual and religious dimensions of conservation'."[68]

The 12 interviews following Gorman's article stress the idea of nature and earth embodying a god or spirit. Sudaryanto, a Muslim and the Nature Conservancy's Mariculture Broodstock and Grow-out Coordinator at the Komodo Field Office in Indonesia, said, "I was taught how people should behave in the eyes of God and about the connection between people and nature .... I studied biology at university and developed a strong awareness of the power of God through His creation."[69] Sam Gon III, Haipul Hawai'i practitioner, Roman Catholic, and Director of Science of the Nature Conservancy Hawai'i, said, "I have been studying chants and dance with Kumu John Keolmaka'āinana Lake, a master of Hawaiian religion .... [It] helps you connect with the land in a very intimate way, as the ancient natives did.

The winds, the trees, everything becomes living, personified."[70] At the Nature Conservancy in Indonesia, Marcy Summers, Senior Conservation Planner and Quaker, asserted, "For me, faith and spirituality are not just what you believe, but what you live .... I really value that the Conservancy's mission is based on the assumption that all species are valued."[71]

There is a "New Age" quality to these testimonials linking environmental activism to religious faith. The New Age movement is composed of people who combine varieties of spiritual practices, such as practices from indigenous peoples' religions, astrology, witchcraft, and crystal healing, with formal religions. New Agers tend to believe that God is an attainable state of higher consciousness which allows for the fulfillment of human potential.[72] Identifying herself as New Age, Rosita Scarborough-Owusu, Grants Specialist at the Nature Conservancy Mid-Atlantic Region, United States, explained, "I'm from Nairobi, Kenya. My mother and aunt helped start a grass-roots environmental organization called the Green Belt Movement .... In my culture there is a lot of folklore about humans interacting with wildlife .... We [at her grandmother's place in Kenya] sat in the dark on her homestead, very rural, with the insects chirping and smelling the breeze, and I felt this must be what God is all about. It was so peaceful, so beautiful, so perfect."[73]

A feeling of global unity can occur among those who relate their religious beliefs to environmental causes. Environmental concerns can create a sense of global spiritual unity. Certainly, Vernadsky's biosphere paradigm lends itself to a religious interpretation that integrates gods and spirits into the natural world. Another dimension to this global spirituality might be a world ethic that dictates human action in the biosphere, for those who combine spirituality with a world environmental ethic are united in a worship of the biosphere. And, of course, spirituality can be considered another aspect of Deep Ecology.

World Ethic for Sustainable Future

Whereas Peter Singer provided a philosophical justification for a global environmental ethic that overrides the interests of nation-states, advocates of sustainable development have specified the rules of conduct that will comprise this ethic. One set of ethical standards can be found in the 1991 Second World Conservation Report, *Caring for the Earth: A Strategy for Sustainable Living*. Participating in the writing of this world ethic were 11 international environmental groups working in collaboration with 14 intergovernmental organizations including UNESCO, the World Bank, the Asian Development Bank, the World Health Organization, and the Organization of American States.[74] The report's "Elements of a World Ethic for

Living Sustainably" called for protection for all species and animal rights. However, unlike organizations such as PETA, it did not advocate vegetarianism and the end to killing animals for food for humans.

"Elements of a World Ethic for Living Sustainably" established global rules for human interaction with the biosphere. Similar to teaching rules of conduct through human rights and peace education, the proposed "World Ethic" could serve as a homogenizing force in bringing together global cultures. The opening statement of the proposed World Ethic reflects the wholistic ideas of Vernadsky's biosphere: "Every human being is a part of the community of life, made up of all living creatures. This community links all human societies, present and future generations, and humanity and the rest of nature. It embraces both cultural and natural diversity."[75]

The equating of "cultural and natural diversity" overlooks the fact that a world ethic on sustainability will contribute to cultural uniformity in the same manner as the neoliberal policies of the World Bank, and human rights and peace education. A similar equation between natural diversity and linguistic diversity was made by Tove Skutnabb-Kangas in her monumental work, *Linguistic Genocide in Education or Worldwide Diversity and Human Rights.*[76] She argued that human languages are disappearing as rapidly as many species of life. Ironically, all these educational endeavors preach cultural diversity while advocating some form of global standards for human conduct.

Despite the contradiction between advocating cultural diversity and a world ethic, it is important to note the inclusion of cultural diversity as part of the wholistic approach of the "World Ethic." Human rights doctrines were also included:

> Every human being has the same fundamental and equal rights, including: the right to life, liberty and security of person; to the freedoms of thought conscience, and religion; to enquiry and expression; to peaceful assembly and association; to participation in government; to education; and, *within the limits of the Earth, to the resources needed for a decent standard of living. No individual, community or nation has the right to deprive another of its means of subsistence* [emphasis added].[77]

The ethic stressed human rights activism: "Each person and each society is entitled to respect of these rights; and is responsible for the protection of these rights for all others."[78]

After establishing the rules of conduct between humans, the proposed world ethic for sustainability called for protection of all species. The proposal parallels some of the propositions of animal rights advocates but still places emphasis on "human development."

> Every life form warrants respect independently of its worth to people. Human development should not threaten the integrity of nature or the survival of other species. People should not threaten the integrity of nature or the sur-

vival of other species. People should treat all creatures decently, and protect them from cruelty, avoidable suffering, and unnecessary killing.[79]

The protection of other species is followed by the rules of sustainability which emphasize protection of resources used by humans and their equal distribution.

> Everyone should take responsibility for his or her impacts on nature ... ensuring that their uses of renewable resources are sustainable.
> Everyone should aim to share fairly the benefits and costs of resource use ....
> Each generation should leave to the future a world that is at least as diverse and productive as the one it inherited. Development of one society or generation should not limit the opportunities of other societies or generations.[80]

The concluding statement of the proposed world ethic highlights the wholistic and globalizing aspects of this approach to sustainable development. It places an emphasis on the collective nature of the human community and interdependence of that human community with the rest of nature. Human actions within this concept of the biosphere are to be governed by human rights and environmental concerns: "The protection of human rights and those of the rest of nature is a worldwide responsibility that transcends all cultural, ideological and geographical boundaries. The responsibility is both individual and collective."[81]

The proposal for a world ethic for sustainability recognizes the problem raised by animal rights experts and naturalists on the equality of species. The report states, "The obligation to respect every species independently of its worth to people may conflict with human interests, if a species endangers human health or survival."[82] For instance, should humans eradicate viruses and animals that carry pathogens harmful to human life? What about campaigns such as those against fur trade that undermine the livelihoods of indigenous peoples?

The report recognizes that these ethical dilemmas represent a fundamental split in environmentalist ranks. "Perhaps there is no other issue," the report states, "over which human rights and animal rights have collided with such emotional force. Such conflicts reveal radically different cultural interpretations of the ethic for living sustainably."[83] The only suggestion made to remedy this split is the development of new ethical principles that would resolve these dilemmas.

A world environmental ethic for instruction in schools was formulated at the 1997 UNESCO conference in Thessaloniki, Greece. The conference specifically called for the changing of behaviors and lifestyles. The Declaration of Thessaloniki states, "In order to achieve sustainability, an enormous co-ordination and integration of efforts is required in a number of crucial sectors and *rapid and radical change of behaviors and lifestyles, including chang-*

ing consumption and production patterns [emphasis added]."[84] The globalizing effect of environmentalism was recognized in the Conference's general statement about education: "Education is an indispensable means ... to learn throughout life *without frontiers, be they geographical, political, cultural, religious linguistic or gender* [emphasis added]."[85]

Teaching global ethical standards of conduct as part of environmental education was called for in the Thessaloniki Conference's report, *Educating for a Sustainable Future: A Transdisciplinary Vision for Concerted Action* in sections titled "Ethics, Culture and Equity: Sustainability as a Moral Imperative" and "Towards a Common Ethic."[86] The report specifically sees the development of a common global ethic based on the biosphere paradigm. "Perhaps," the report states, "we are beginning to move towards a new global ethic which transcends all other systems of allegiance and belief, which is rooted in a consciousness of the interrelatedness and sanctity of life."[87]

The global ethical standards that are to serve as the basis for environmental education include the original "Elements of a World Ethic for Living Sustainably." In addition, the Thessaloniki Conference's report emphasizes the importance of teaching the "ethic of time." The ethic of time refers to stopping the irreversible damage that is being done to the environment. "The notion of the 'ethic of time'," the report states, "is the moral imperative to take action before reaching the point of no return."[88] The moral imperative is that people be taught to anticipate irreversible ecological damage and to take action. Similar to educators who want people to act according to the moral imperative to take action to stop violations of human rights, the "ethic of time" is a moral imperative to do something *now* to save the biosphere.

A New Consumerism?

Concerns about consumerism are an important part of the development of environmental education and a global ethic. As I discuss in a recent book, consumerism is a dominant global ideology with advertising-driven media convincing shoppers to seek personal satisfaction in the purchase of a constant stream of newly manufactured products.[89] There is global recognition of brand icons such as those representing Coca-Cola, Nike, and McDonald's. Articulated in early 20th-century United States, consumerist economics assumes the desirability of continuous industrial growth. Continuous industrial growth requires creating an insatiable need in shoppers for more and more manufactured goods and processed foods. Consumerism is considered an important alternative to the possibility that advanced industrialism would mean more leisure time for workers. Advertising, changing fashions, and planned obsolescence are to motivate people to work harder for the purchase of an endless stream of goods. Rather than personal contentment, consumerism is driven by a feeling of dissatisfaction, caused in part by advertising, that can only be gratified through shopping. Consumerism evolved into what is known as the throw-away and polluting culture in which the consumerist lifestyle are a key element in the destruction of the biosphere. Neoliberalism's stress on free markets is one aspect of consumerism. Supporters of free markets argue that it is the best means for ensuring the production, distribution, and access to consumer items.

In opposition to consumerism, the 1991 Second World Conservation Strategy report, *Caring for the Earth*, warns that, "with a few notable exceptions, the most powerful influences on popular attitudes in upper-income countries—advertising and entertainment–promote over-consumption and waste."[90] This report proposes that environmental education should attempt to counter the consumer lifestyle promoted by media and advertising. It contends that, "Not enough people in high-income countries adopt a driving style that conserves energy, recycle their garbage, or place 'environmental friendliness' above 'convenience' when shopping."[91] Two approaches are suggested to change lifestyles associated with wasteful consumption. One is formal education to teach people to value environmental friendliness over wasteful consumption in the purchase of products. The other is influencing media and advertising so that they are guided by an ethic that promotes consumption that is not environmentally destructive and that instills values of conservation and environmental awareness in the general population.

Educating a "caretaker consumer" using the principle of "eco-efficiency," "sustainable consumption" and "sustainable lifestyles" are called for in the 1997 Thessaloniki Conference's report on *Educating for a Sustainable Future*.[92] These concepts are developed under a section titled, "Shifting To Sustainable Lifestyles: Changing Consumption and Production Patterns." In this section, the report emphatically states its intention to change global behaviors.

> The effectiveness of awareness raising and education for sustainable development must ultimately be measured by the degree to which they change the attitudes and behaviors of people, both in their individual roles, including those of producers and consumers, and in carrying out their collective responsibilities and duties as citizens.[93]

However, this proposed education does not reject the idea of consumerism. It proposes transforming consumerism into "sustainable consumption." In fact, working harder to buy more remains the economic principle of sustainable consumerism. In the report, "a high quality life" is equated with consumerism. The report assures the future consumer, "Sustainable consumption does not necessarily mean consuming less. It means changing unsustainable patterns of consumption by *allowing consumers to enjoy a high quality of life by consuming differently* [my emphasis]."[94]

Educating the "caretaker consumer" requires making the purchaser think about the environmental effects of products. "The caretaking consumer," the report states, "insists upon purchasing products that are kind to the environment."[95] According to the report, consumption should be guided by the principle of eco-efficiency. The consumer is to be taught to evaluate purchases according to their eco-efficiency. "Eco-efficiency," the report contends, "calls for better management of existing processes or products to reduce waste, use less energy and facilitate reuse and recycling."[96] The consumer should be taught to ask: Does the manufacturing process for a product reflect a concern about reducing the use of resources? Can the product be recycled?

The reports, and apparently most arguments for sustainable development, assume that consumerism is the key to a "high quality life." In this context, environmental education is simply to train an environmentally responsible consumer rather than preaching against consumerist ideology. This issue is important to consider with regard to indigenous cultures and Deep Ecology. Deep Ecology considers humans' relationship with nature as being more important than consumerism. Some indigenous groups are concerned about their spiritual relationship with nature rather than seeking satisfaction in the accumulation of manufactured goods. Indigenous cultures may provide ways of thinking about human happiness that are independent of consumerism. They could be an inspirational source for finding ways of escaping the environmentally destructive effects of consumerism rather than trying to modify consumer behavior.

Ecotourism

Tourism is the neocolonial aspect of Michael Hardt and Antonio Negri's famous statement quoted in the preface, "*A specter haunts the world and it is the specter of migration*."[97] While workers from poor countries migrate in search of work to rich countries, tourists from rich countries descend on the poor. Tourism is the largest global employer according to Martha Honey, Executive Director of The International Ecotourism Society and Center for Ecotourism and Sustainable Development (a joint project of the Institute for Policy Studies and Stanford University). "International tourism to the third world," Honey wrote, "is increasing 6 percent annually, compared with only 3.5 percent to developed countries. About 80 percent of these foreign travelers come from just twenty developed countries, with destinations in Asia, Africa, and the Americas growing at the expense of those in Europe."[98] Published in 1999, Honey's study did not anticipate the uncertain effects on travel caused by what I call the "war on tourism" initiated by the terrorist attacks on the United States in 2001. However, tourism will probably continue to be an important factor in globalization and environmentalism.

In European countries, the development of the tourist industry paralleled the expansion of empire and the rise of a strong middle class. Both Thomas Cook and American Express, the two oldest Western tourist companies, were formed in the 19th century. In the 20th century, vacation time became a regular part of company benefits with the belief that both blue and white collar workers needed revitalization through leisure activities. In fact, vacation time became an expected worker's 'right'. With the expansion of relatively inexpensive jet airline travel, more tourists could travel to foreign countries. In the 1970s, World Bank leaders decided that the funding of the tourist industry in nonindustrialized countries would contribute to their overall development through the foreign funds spent by vacationers. The Bank believed that it would be a method for redistributing wealth from richer to poorer nations. Neocolonialism could be a descriptor for the growth of tourist resorts utilizing local populations to serve the foreign traveler from wealthier nations.[99]

Ecotourism as a form of neocolonialism might have the positive effect of protecting the environment. This trend is noted in 2003 article in the widely distributed travel magazine *Condé Nast Traveler*. With the trendy title, "The New World's New Groove," the article opens, "Forget rough-around-the-edges eco-outposts, Central America's latest wave of nature lodges is all about creature comforts."[100] The author, Allison Humes, describes her visits to ecotourist facilities in Belize, Honduras, and Costa Rica that offer spa facilities, yoga classes, gourmet meals, and luxury accommodations. Humes identifies the source of this trend as the 2002 World Summit on Sustainable Development and the work of the Central American Bank for Economic Integration. As a result of their efforts, she states, "*sustainable development is the phrase du jour.*"[101] Also, national tourist boards have adopted the sustainable development approach with Honduras limiting tourist development in pristine areas to small and exclusive lodges. The Costa Rican government has created a scale for rating the environmental sensitivity of resort establishments. This provides an indirect pressure on resorts to become more environmentally friendly if they are to attract the ecotourist.

Ecotourism as a form of education emerged in the 1980s in Latin America and Africa and quickly spread around the globe in the wake of the environmental destruction being caused by tourism. Ecotourism turns environmental protection into a valued asset. Ecotourism is a form of sustainable development since the goal is to promote tourism while limiting its damage to the environment. Or, in the words of an ecotourism course description, "How do we ensure that natural attractions are not loved to death?"[102] In 1991, the International Ecotourism Society adopted the following definition: "Ecotourism is responsible travel to natural areas that conserves the environment and sustains the well-being of local people."[103] Ecotourism is now considered part of sustainable development where tourist industries are developed in conjunction with environmental and cultural preservation. In her article, Honey listed education as an important aspect of ecotourism because it *"builds environmental awareness*. Ecotourism means education, for tourists and residents of nearby communities. Well before departure, tour operators should supply travelers with reading material about the country, environment, and local people."[104] The International Ecotourism Society proclaims that an important part of ecotourism is "Educating the traveler on the importance of conservation."[105]

In 2002, the United Nations recognized ecotourism as part of sustainable development by declaring the U.N. International Year of Ecotourism and sponsoring the World Ecotourism Summit in Québec City, Canada. The 2002 Summit was co-sponsored by the United Nations Environment Program and the World Tourism Organization. Conference participants adopted the Québec Declaration on Ecotourism. Also, participants regarded their work as related to the 2002 World Summit on Sustainable Development in Johannesburg. An important part of the Québec Declaration is the role of ecotourism in protecting indigenous cultures. The Declaration contains the following requirements for ecotourist groups.

> Affirm that different forms of tourism, especially ecotourism, if managed in a sustainable manner can represent a valuable economic opportunity for local populations and their cultures and for the conservation and sustainable use of nature for future generations.
> Emphasize that at the same time, wherever and whenever tourism in natural and rural areas is not properly planned, developed and managed, it contributes to the deterioration of natural landscapes, threats to wildlife and biodiversity, poor water quality, poverty, displacement of indigenous and local communities, and the erosion of cultural traditions.
> Acknowledge that ecotourism must recognize and respect the land rights of indigenous and local communities, including their protected, sensitive and sacred sites.[106]

In 1991, the International Ecotourism Society began offering courses to participants from 30 countries whose occupations ranged from park rangers and landscape architects to tour operators and government planners. The integration of environmentalism and economics is typical of the education offered by the International Ecotourism Society. For instance, at the Québec Summit a course was offered in Spanish and English on "Conservation Planning for Ecotourism." The course description provides a good definition of ecotourism along with highlighting its economic dimensions.

> Ecotourism relies upon the protection of natural attractions for its survival, and indeed, natural attractions whether landscapes, wildlife, rain forests or

coral reefs, are increasingly to be found in protected areas .... This one day course is aimed at ecotourism planners, developers, operators and conservation managers. It will cover the ecotourism planning process and key ecotourism management strategies for ensuring the *sustainability of tourism* in protected areas [emphasis added]."[107]

Another course offered in English, Swahili, and Gujarati dealt with the economic fundamentals of sustainable tourism. Called "Ecolodge Design and Development," the course description refers to the expanding ecotourism industry.

As the ecotourism industry expands worldwide, well-planned, ecologically sensitive facilities are in high demand. This demand can be met by ecolodges. These are small-scale facilities that provide visitors with a window to the natural and cultural world of the region. This course offers an introduction to the design and development of a successful ecolodge.[108]

And nothing better expresses globalization, environmentalism, and travel as a consumer product than a course titled "Ecotourism Internet Marketing."[109]

As part of sustainable development, the ecotourist industry works with indigenous groups to maintain vacation spots. In this symbiotic relationship, indigenous groups are able to earn money while protecting important aspects of their cultures and environment. Unfortunately, this relationship can turn indigenous peoples into simple objects for viewing by tourists and, in turn, might be destructive of local cultures. For instance, protection of indigenous peoples and ecotourism are important elements in the creation of the Mamirauá Sustainable Development Reserve in the Brazilian Amazon. This is the largest protected flooded forest in the Amazon. It is considered the first sustainable development reserve in which local indigenous peoples actively participate in its management along with government and international NGOs, including the Department of International Development and the Wildlife Conservation Society. Ecotourism is an important part of the sustainable development plan at the Uakari Floating Lodge in the Mamirauá Reserve. The Institute of Sustainable Development Mamirauá provides the following statement on ecotourism:

Why does ecotourism exist in Mamirauá? The Mamirauá Institute has implemented a series of economic alternatives to the local population in order to dislocate the traditional pressures on the natural resources. Thus, ecotourism was designed to be a source of income to the local population living in this protected area. Besides, it is a source of income to the protection of the area, environmental education and local community projects.[110]

Despite the commercial aspects of ecotourism, the movement represents another form of environmental education that is contributing to global unity. Both tourists and members of the tourist industry are being taught to value the biosphere. Despite the ecotourism movement, there is still criticism of tourism as a form of neocolonialism and of tourist industries that only appear "green" while continuing to be environmentally damaging. Eco-environmental leader Martha Horney warns that many hotel chains are simply trying to appear concerned about the environment by asking lodgers to reuse their towels and to reduce the frequency of changing bed sheets. Some new resorts are claiming to be eco-friendly while building elaborate golf courses. And, of course, tourism continues to be primarily a one-way road between rich and poor countries.[111] In *Sex, Money, and Morality: Prostitution and Tourism in Southeast Asia*, Thanh-Dam Truong wrote, "The general trend in integration in international tourism is that firms from industrialized countries tend to dominate the market .... This entails a division of labor ... [in] which Third World countries ... merely provide the social infrastructure and facilities with little or no control over ... production and distribution of the tourist-related services at an international level."[112]

CONCLUSION: ENVIRONMENTAL EDUCATION AND A GLOBAL ETHIC

Environmental educators are attempting to form a global ethic to regulate human interaction within the biosphere. There are disagreements about the standards for human conduct that will form this global ethic. These differences, as I discuss in chapter 5, are reflected in differing approaches to environmental education.

The sharpest ethical differences are between those identified as naturalist and opponents of speciesism and anthropocentrism, and those associated with sustainable development. Naturalists decry the anthropocentric view of the biosphere and demand a combination of equal rights between species and an end to human interference in the "natural" evolution of the biosphere. Supporters of sustainable development share an anthropocentric perspective while wanting to stop the destruction of other species. The goal of proponents of sustainable development is to use the biosphere to enhance human life while reducing human destruction of the biosphere and other forms of life.

Environmental education is influenced by the critique of industrial progress and consumerism embedded in these differing ethical perspectives. These critiques give a strong radical direction to environmental education. Of course, there are differing solutions to the problems of industrial progress and consumerism. Some naturalists suggest abandonment of industrialism and consumerism for simpler forms of living. Some advocates of sustainable development want sustainable consumption. Whatever the solution, the critique of industrialism and consumerism is influencing the development of a global environmental ethic and education.

Finally, the biosphere paradigm has given added importance to the preservation of indigenous cultures and traditional knowledge. It has been mainly indigenous peoples who have retained an understanding of how the biosphere works as an interrelated system while Western science pursued an interest in particular parts of life and lost a sense of the workings of the whole. Consequently, indigenous cultures and traditional knowledge are important parts of environmental education.

Educating for a Global Environmental Ethic

Environmental education is wide ranging in its goals and methods. At one end of the spectrum is education for simple awareness of environmental problems while at the other end is preparation for direct action against environmentally destructive governments and corporations. Between these extremes, as I indicated in chapter 4, education for sustainable development and consumption tends to be the dominant educational ideology. Environmental education takes many forms including school curricula, public demonstrations, advertising, web instruction, toys, and ecotourism.

A WWF (formerly known as the World Wildlife Fund) publication differentiates between a narrow and broad focus in environmental education. Instruction that is narrowly focused pursues local environmental issues and has the goal of developing a "caring interest in the environment." Hopefully, a caring interest will result in support of legal and technical efforts to improve the environment. This type of education does not attempt to engage the student in direct civic action. Activities are usually limited to picking up trash or planting a tree. In contrast, a broad instructional focus examines the relationship between "human behavior and global eco-systems" and develops "concerned awareness and participatory skills [civic action]."[1] These skills prepare students to engage in a range of activities from simply writing letters to political leaders to the direct action methods of Earth First! Civic action education contributes to the evolution of a global civil society, particularly when it is directed at changing the behaviors of nation-states and multinational corporations. A 1969 definition of environmental education in the United States made by William Stapp of the University of Michigan stressed civic action. Stapp would later coauthor important texts on environmental education. His 1969 definition is, "Environmental education is aimed at producing a citizenry that is knowledgeable concerning the biophysical environment and its associated problems, aware of how to help solve these problems, and motivated to work toward their solution."[2]

In general, environmental education tends to be wholistic in approach. This is a logical outcome of the biosphere paradigm. Embedded in environmental education are concerns about human interaction within the species and human interaction with the biosphere. For instance, human wars are very destructive to the biosphere. Therefore, peace education is high on the agenda of environmental education. Human rights education is important because it empowers people to protect the biosphere. Concerns about economic inequality are important because rich nations tend to exploit and destroy the natural environments of poorer nations. Ending poverty is crucial because the poor tend to be the worst victims of environmental pollution and the most exposed to hazardous waste. Political and economic knowledge is essential because it provides the tools to protect the biosphere. And, of course, science and math provide an understanding of the importance and the methods for protecting the biosphere. Environmental educators also emphasize the worth of traditional knowledge particularly indigenous peoples' wholistic knowledge, of the biosphere.

Most environmental educators advocate some form of interdisciplinary study where issues of the biosphere are taught across the standard disciplines. In fact, if you approach knowledge from the perspective of the biosphere paradigm, then knowledge becomes an integrated system where all the parts support the whole. In other words, interdisciplinary means more than just adding a unit on environmental problems to a science, literature, or history curriculum. It means teaching these subjects from the perspective of their interrelationship to the entire biosphere.

THE RADICAL ASPECTS OF ENVIRONMENTAL EDUCATION

At the beginning of chapter 4, I suggested that environmental education might be the most radical educational ideology, in the sense of making fundamental changes in education and the future of human society shaping global society. Criticisms of speciesism and anthropocentrism undermine the conceptual paradigm that has led humans to believe that the good life could be reached by the exploitation of resources and the search for technological solutions to human problems. Deep Ecology's recognition of the intimate human relationship/response to all elements of the biosphere creates a resistance to destroying the Earth in the name of industrial development and scientific living. It also supports educational programs that shift the conceptual paradigm from one supporting industrialization and technology to one based on the interests of the entire biosphere.

One sign of the increasing radicalness of the environmental education movement is the work of Brazil's Instituto Paulo Freire. In the 20th century, Paulo Freire's *Pedagogy of the Oppressed* launched a global education movement centered around the raising of human consciousness through dialogical methods. The Freirean method and philosophy is based on a anthropocentric Marxist paradigm that assumes that humans are different from other species because of their ability to make choices. The goal of the dialogical method is to raise the consciousness of learners so that they can understand the forces shaping their thinking and actions and, consequently, become liberated to make choices that will free all humans from oppression. Central to the method is the naming of the world through learning to read.

Shortly before his death in 1996, Freire began working on a book on ecopedagogy. His followers, as represented by the work of Moacir Gadotti, pursued the ecopedagogy idea. Richard Kahn, Ecopedagogy Chair of the Paulo Freire Institute at the University of California at Los Angeles, sent me the following e-mail statement on July 29, 2003 regarding the development of ecopedagogy. Kahn wrote,

> There is the question regarding whether or not Freireans are moving in a more ecologically-focused direction. This I can assure you is definitely occurring and represents one of the more exciting developments in this particular tradition at the moment. Freire himself was at work on a book of Ecopedagogy when he died in 1996, and this work has been taken up by his colleague and friend, the noted Freirean Moacir Gadotti. Under Gadotti's direction, a number of Paulo Freire Institutes have been opened around the world—with our Institute at UCLA being founded last summer (for which we held the 3rd annual International Freire Forum, which brought noted scholars from around the globe) and another to open for business in Argentina soon. At the UCLA Forum, the issue of Ecopedagogy was voted by the members at the conference's end as the leading theme generated from the proceedings, and my own work both at and beyond the conference allowed me to be given the position of Ecopedagogy Chair of the UCLA Paulo Freire Institute. To this end, I was scheduled to open the Transformative Learning Center's (TLC) international conference on Global Citizenship with a discussion on the move towards Ecopedagogy, on a panel which included Gadotti and the TLC's director Ed O' Sullivan. This conference was delayed due to SARS, and will now occur in October, with another to follow devoted solely to the Ecopedagogy theme and a celebration of O'Sullivan's tenure. The TLC at OISE [Ontario Institute for Studies in Education] has recently put out two books on Transformative Learning that speak very well to the direction of Freirean critical pedagogy—the way in which it will bridge themes of social and eco-justice in new [w]holistic and critical approaches. So, there is no question that Freireans are seeking alliance to eco-justice and themes of sustainable practice, etc.[3]

Moacir Gadotti, the head of Instituto Paulo Freire, is advocating a pedagogy of the earth or ecopedagogy. As mentioned in chapter 4, Gadotti is a leading proponent of building a global ethic around the principles of the Earth Charter. Accepting the arguments of Deep Ecology, Gadotti recognizes the interrelationship of humans with the biosphere. Gadotti writes, "We don't learn to love Earth by reading books on this subject, nor books on integral ecology. Our own experience is what counts."[4] While Freire celebrated the liberation of consciousness, Gadotti rhapsodizes about human connections with the environment. "To plant and live through the growth of a tree or a plant," he states in reference to the importance of experience for learning, "walking the city streets, or venturing into a forest, feeling the birds' chirping on sunny mornings, or ... watching how the wind sways the plants, feeling the warm sands of our beaches gazing at the stars on a dark night ... pollution and environmental defacement ... should remind us that we are able to destroy this wonder, and also to create our ecological awareness and move us to take action."[5]

Breaking with the paradigm that guided his mentor's thinking, Gadotti calls for a new pedagogy based on a planetary consciousness. He argues, "Classical pedagogies were anthropocentric .... Let us broaden our outlook. From man to the planet, above genus, species and kingdoms. From an anthropocentric vision to a planetary consciousness, for the exercise of a planetary citizenship, and for a new ethical and social reference the planetary civilization."[6]

In 1999, the Paulo Freire Institute in conjunction with UNESCO, hosted the First International Symposium on the Earth Charter in the Perspective of Education and in the following year the First International Forum on Ecopedagogy. The result of these two meetings was the Ecopedagogy Charter which contains the biosphere paradigm and the principles of Deep Ecology. The Charter represents both a major change in the Freirean thinking and a radical approach to changing the industrial world.

Ecopedagogy Charter

1. The planet is a single community
2. Earth as the mother, a living organism in evolution
3. A new awareness that knows what is sustainable, appropriate, or makes sense for our existence
4. Out tenderness towards this home. Our address is the Earth
5. A socio-cosmic justice: Earth is the great indigent, the greatest of all indigents
6. A biophile pedagogy (promoter of life): get involved, communicate, share relate, become motivated
7. A concept of knowledge that admits that it is only integral as long as it is shared

8. To walk with a meaning (daily living)
9. An intuitive and communicative rationality: emotional, not instrumental
10. New attitudes: reeducating the way we look at things, the heart
11. Culture gives sustainability: eco-formation. Broaden our outlook[7]

The Ecopedagogy Charter retains the concept of a biophilic personality but broadens its meaning from a desire to liberate all humans to loving the entire biosphere. The biosphere paradigm is contained in Principles 1, 2, 4, and 5 of the Charter while Deep Ecology is contained in Principles 7 through 10. The Charter reflects the radical trend in environmental education as represented in the United States by the writings of Chet Bowers and David Orr. Both Bowers' and Orr's arguments predate those of Gadotti and the Ecopedagogy Charter. Their writings provide an important background for understanding the direction of Freirean thought and the important and radical paradigm shift advocated by environmental educators.

THE RADICAL EDUCATIONAL PARADIGM SHIFT

Similar to Gadotti and the Principles of the Ecopedagogy Charter, Bowers and Orr criticize the neoliberal educational goals of economic growth. For Bowers, neoliberal goals are rooted in the Western idea of industrial progress where economic growth and technological development are considered the key to advancing the interest of the human species. Bowers and Orr agree that most current educational debates assume the same goals with the only differences being the best means of achieving them. In discussing these debates, Orr wrote that all sides "agree on the basic aims and purposes of education, which are to equip our nation with a 'world-class' labor force, first, to compete more favorably in the global economy, second, to provide everyone with the means for maximum upward mobility."[8] The industrial ideal, Orr argues, has turned all levels of schooling into knowledge factories and has corrupted universities through a "marriage between the academy and the worlds of power and commerce."[9] Bowers agrees with this assessment of current educational debates and argued that even so-called educational radicals share the same "cultural assumptions ... with the elites they criticize."[10]

What are these assumptions shared by most educators? They involve what I call the *industrial paradigm*, which includes consumerism and a faith in technology to provide humans with the good life. Chet Bowers identifies the assumptions of the industrial paradigm as "viewing change as progressive in nature, intelligence and creativity as attributes of the autonomous individual, science and technology as the source of empowerment, and the commodification of all areas as the highest expression of human development."[11]

Orr sees the industrial paradigm as part of the hidden curriculum of modern schooling. He argues, "We will have to challenge the hubris buried in the hidden curriculum that says that human domination of nature is good; that the growth of economy is natural; that all knowledge, regardless of its consequences, is equally valuable; and that material progress is our right."[12] He argues that inculcation of the industrial paradigm into students makes them unable to resist the "seductions of technology" and, I would add, the temptations of consumerism.

Another part of the hidden curriculum, according to Orr, teaches that technological development is a good thing and that it defines the meaning of progress. Orr states, "true believers [in technology] describe progress to mean not human, political, or cultural improvement but a mindless, uncontrollable technological juggernaut erasing ecologies and cultures as it moves through history."[13] The question that must be asked, he argues, is whether or not technology is improving the human well-being.

Both educators agree that the industrial paradigm causes social injustice rather than providing for a just social and economic system. Their arguments are based on both the internal problems within the industrial paradigm and the destructiveness of that paradigm to the biosphere. For instance, the industrial paradigm promises that schooling will provide an equal opportunity for all people to achieve wealth. Bowers asserts, "Educational institutions perpetuate the further creation of wealth at the top rather than nurturing at the grassroots level both material and social forms of wealth."[14] The primary result of the present paradigm governing educational discussions is to ensure that rich people within in nations get richer and that rich nations increase their total wealth in relation to poorer nations.

The industrial paradigm fosters social injustice by ignoring the limited availability of natural resources and the potential industrial destruction of the biosphere. These two factors guarantee that the distribution of consumer wealth will be limited in the biosphere. Wealth in the industrial paradigm is measured by the consumption of products. In claiming to provide equality of opportunity, schools are promising an equal opportunity to consume. Bowers notes that most often missing from lists "of educational goals are skills and knowledge needed for leading less commodified lives."[15] The result is a process of schooling that implants an acceptance of the industrial paradigm in each student and misguides them into thinking that everyone on the planet will eventually have an equal opportunity to consume.

Also, the waste products of consumerism have the most effect on low-income people. Upper-income groups can choose to live in minimally polluted areas, eat more expensive organic foods, and spend time as ecotourists. Of course, this does not mean that the rich can be completely insulated from the destruction of the biosphere. However, environmental destruction tends to reduce the standard of living for all people, particularly low-income groups. People's standards of living are not necessarily improving because they can purchase more goods. Air, water, and noise pollution, destruction of recreation areas, and environmental conditions that shorten life spans might actually be reducing living standards as consumption increases. Bower cites evidence of studies that show income and racial bias in the contact of humans with environmental hazards. Poor white and non-white populations are more likely to live near hazardous waste areas and to be exposed to hazardous materials at work.[16]

The industrial paradigm's assumption that economic growth is good supports the excesses of consumerist ideology. Most environmental educators reject consumerist ideology with its premise that the key to economic growth is increased consumption. Bowers asserts, "Unnecessary dependence on meeting needs through products and services that can be purchased has disruptive consequences that weaken the viability of the family, community, and environment."[17] Bowers argues that consumerist ideology results in lowering living standards. The more people become dependent on products, the more they have to work. The more they have to work, he claims, the less time they have for parenting and involvement in community projects.

The industrial paradigm creates a false sense of individualism which pervades neoliberal educational thought. In contrast, the biosphere paradigm embeds humans among other species living within the same environment. In reality, it is not possible to separate a person from his or her cultural background (unless he or she somehow managed to grow up alone), and it is not possible to live independently of other species of plants and animals and the Earth's atmosphere, water, and land (unless one is hurled into space and finds some other source of food, air, and water). The primary content, if not the entire content, of human consciousness is a product of interaction with other humans, other species, and with water, air, and land. This false sense of individualism pervades educational concepts of intelligence. Most people think of intelligence as rooted in the individual. An individual concept of intelligence makes it easy to judge one person as superior to another. Bowers claims, "The long-held myth that intelligence is an attribute of the individual (and now being argued as reflecting the genetic endowment of the individual) only makes sense when the encoding, storage, and reproduction characteristics of language are *entirely* ignored."[18] Bowers criticizes the industrial, and originally Western, idea of individualism in an article on creativity. As he points out, most current educational ideas about creativity assume the existence of an autonomous individual who can independently make great art. "The identification of creativity with the thoughts, imagination, and expression of the autonomous individual," he argues, "also sets the stage for transforming the traditional function of art in ways that made it receptive to the forces of commodification and nihilism ...."[19]

The neoliberal educational view of individualism is a form of speciesism. An assumption of neoliberalism and of the Western industrial tradition, according to Bowers, is that an autonomous individual, acting independently of social and cultural influences, can behave rationally and morally. This supposition allows humans to think of other humans as having differing worth, with some humans being smarter and more moral than other humans. This assumption also allows humans to claim superiority over other species. In Bowers' words, "The Western root metaphor of an anthropocentric universe represents humans in a one/many relationship with other forms of life—with humans placed at the top of a pyramid of unconnected life forms by virtue of their capacity for rational thought and moral judgment."[20]

Also, it is assumed within the industrial paradigm that the use of reason and science make some human cultures superior to others. This assumption denigrates the importance of societies organized around cultural traditions, particularly indigenous cultures. Those thinking and acting within the industrial paradigm have labeled indigenous societies as "primitive" and judged them as inferior to societies organized around the idea of progress through science and technology. It is now realized that many traditional cultures have retained principles of sustainable development. Bowers suggests one method for breaking the hold of the industrial paradigm is to study "what are now increasingly recognized as common characteristics of ecologically centered cultures that have developed profoundly different approaches to living within the limits of natural systems."[21] This approach does not mean abandoning scientific knowledge and methods. What Bowers and others propose is recognition of the value of traditional knowledge in helping people to live with each other and within the biosphere. Traditional knowledge is based on human experience and can provide an important means for understanding the workings of the biosphere, human interactions, and sustainable living.

Therefore, from the perspective of Bowers and Orr, a goal of environmental education is for students to interpret events through a biospheric paradigm; analyze the consequences of industrialism and consumerism; and consider the contributions of traditional knowledge. Supposedly a biospheric paradigm will result in students thinking about how their decisions and behavior are part of an interconnected web of life forms. Simply put, students must think about the consequences of knowledge and its effects on actions. Orr asserts, "we cannot say that we know something until we understand the effects of this knowledge on real people and their communities."[22] He uses the example of his own hometown near Youngstown, Ohio, which he claims was destroyed by corporate decisions to "disinvest" in the region. Orr argues that these decisions were made by graduates of business schools who were taught the importance of profit but were not taught to think about the consequences of their actions. As a result of their decisions, Orr claims, the Youngstown region experienced increased "unemployment, crime, higher divorce rates, child abuse, lost savings, and wrecked lives."[23] Orr asserts, "What was taught in the business schools and economics departments did not include the value of good communities or the human costs of a narrow destructive economic rationality that valued efficiency and economic abstractions above people and community."[24]

Similar to many participants in the global civil society, Bowers and Orr are critical of current democratic processes and concepts of citizenship. Orr criticizes American schools for overemphasizing "individualism and rights."[25] Of particular concern is the stress on patriotism to the nation-state. Orr argues that most uses of patriotism are devoid of ecological content. A new concept of citizenship and patriotism, he asserts, must include a responsibility to the entire biosphere. A good citizen, according to Orr, is one who actively works for the good of all humans and other species, and, consequently, feels a responsibility to ensure that the air, water, and land are not polluted and destroyed. A good citizen is not loyal to the nation-state but is loyal to the biosphere. Patriotism, within this meaning of loyalty, is an emotional attachment or love of the biosphere. The concept of patriotism matches the tenets of Deep Ecology.

Bowers questions the ability of democratic nation-states to deal with multinational corporations. He argues that "the ability of wealth to distort the democratic process in ways that favor the interests of the multinational corporations and other elite groups is too overwhelming for the educational process to have much influence."[26] Of course, Bowers accepts the idea that good citizenship involves working for the good of the entire biosphere. However, he believes the best approach is to educate for civic activism at the local level. He argues that "an eco-justice pedagogy should address the causes of poverty and wealth at the community level, which requires an understanding of how to regenerate the sense of local responsibility and mutual support that has been undermined by national and international market forces."[27]

These critiques of the industrial paradigm, economic inequalities, consumerism, and citizenship education result in specific proposals for the content of an environmental education. The following list of proposals combines the proposals of Orr and Bowers.

Proposed Content Areas for an Environmental
Education Curriculum

1. Methods of civic activism to protect all humans, other species, and
   the environment
2. The basic principles of ecology or, in other words, the biosphere
3. A study of the social, economic, and environmental impact and limits of industrialism and technology
4. History of science and its impact on humans and the biosphere
5. Sustainable consumption
6. Sustainable agriculture and forestry
7. Environmental ethics
8. The effect of poverty on the biosphere
9. Human rights as protection of the biosphere
10. Peace education as protection of the biosphere
11. The use of traditional knowledge for understanding relationships
    between humans and the interdependence within the biosphere

The preceding concerns are not, according to most environmental educators, to be taught as discrete units of knowledge. They are to be taught as
part of an interdisciplinary curriculum. Whereas the hidden curriculum of
contemporary schooling is teaching the value of the industrial paradigm,
the hidden curriculum of environmental education is teaching the worth of
the biosphere paradigm. By the very nature of a wholistic approach, the student is taught to think of the interconnections of the biosphere.

An example of an interdisciplinary approach is provided by Bowers in
his critique of standard teacher education programs. He complains that environmental education has become a separate discipline within colleges of
education and is too often associated with science education. The effect of
this separate categorization, he states, is that other branches of teacher education ignore environmental issues. Even more important is the effect of
categorization on reinforcing the industrial paradigm. Bowers wrote, "The
association of environmental education with the sciences helps to perpetuate the modern myth that science and technology provide the most effective
means of restoring the environment. This, in turn, makes it more difficult
to recognize the ways in which humans interact with the environment (including their ameliorative uses of science and technology) are influenced by
generally unconsciously held cultural assumptions."[28]

Environmental education should, according to Bowers, become a part of
all teacher education courses. Future teachers should be made aware of how
the industrial paradigm influences public school instruction and teaches
students to accept a world of consumerism. All teachers should be trained to

think within the biosphere paradigm. For instance, teachers of reading and literature should understand and teach that the meaning of the written word is dependent on a cultural context and that culture is product of human interaction, interaction with other species, and the environment. For instance, it is misleading to analyze literature outside of a cultural and historical process. To do this perpetuates the idea of the autonomous creator. Authors are members of the biosphere and their work should be analyzed in that context. Social studies teachers should be trained to understand the potential destructiveness of the industrial paradigm and learn to prepare their students for a form of citizenship and patriotism dedicated to the well-being of all species and the environment. The study of science should include an analysis of the impact of science on the biosphere. In other words, the biosphere paradigm and environmental issues are appropriate for all fields of study. What should hold the curriculum together in both teacher training institutions, and elementary and secondary schools, is instruction within the biosphere paradigm.

To illustrate the wholistic approach advocated by Bowers and Orr, I discuss the possibilities in teaching a secondary school unit centered on Henry David Thoreau's book *Walden Pond*. Any analysis of *Walden Pond* requires understanding Thoreau's relationship to other species and the surrounding conditions of the water, land, and air. In other words, it is a book about humans living within the biosphere. Thoreau's relationship to nature represents part of Deep Ecology. The book also exemplifies the myth of the autonomous individual. Even though Thoreau is isolating himself at Walden Pond, his ability to write about the experience is a result of his cultural experiences. Also, the book can be examined from the standpoint of environmental history, particularly the noise that intrudes in Thoreau's world at Walden Pond from the railroad being built in the distance. The discussion of the industrial noise invading Thoreau's attempt at solitude opens the door to a discussion of environmental change since the 19th century. Because of the book, Walden Pond is now a major tourist spot. Students can visit Walden Pond or read descriptions of its present-day condition with its parking lots, and water and air pollution. Science can be used in analyzing the current quality of water in the pond or some other body of water. There can be class discussions of changes in air quality. What did Thoreau smell at Walden Pond in the early 19th century as compared to visitors to the pond in the 21st century? Working within the biospheric paradigm, teachers can make any topic interdisciplinary.

The restructuring of school studies to reflect a biospheric paradigm is typically based on the ideas of sustainable development and the importance of utilizing traditional knowledge. In stating this, I do not wish to discount the importance of naturalist groups such as PETA and Earth First! The integration of sustainable development into environmental studies took place at a series of UNESCO-sponsored conferences. Important for environmental educators like Bowers and Orr, and for advocates of education for sustainable development, is the role of civic activism in a global society.

GLOBAL EDUCATION FOR SUSTAINABLE DEVELOPMENT AND CIVIC ACTION

Global planning and strategies for implementing the type of ideas articulated by Bowers and Orr have evolved from a series of international conferences beginning in the 1970s. These important educational plans support the idea of sustainable development or, as it is now called, sustainable education. This global planning includes the idea of shifting from an industrial paradigm to a biosphere paradigm. In David Orr's introduction to the authoritative book by Stephen Sterling, *Sustainable Education*, he stressed the importance of a paradigm change in education.[29] Orr wrote, "That paradigm [industrial] must be replaced by one that places us in the web of life as citizens of the biotic community. We must come to see ourselves as implicated in the world, not simply isolated, self-maximizing individuals."[30]

The global spread of sustainable education ideas can be traced to the 1975 Belgrade Charter, the 1977 Tbilisi Report, and the 1997 Thessaloniki Declaration. Beginning with the 1975 International Workshop on Environmental Education in Belgrade, sponsored by UNESCO and the newly founded United Nations Environment Program (UNEP), global educational plans moved quickly to the idea of organizing education around the idea of sustainable development. The 1975 meeting issued the Belgrade Charter, which stresses that the primary source of environmental protection would come from active citizenship in a global civil society. The Charter states, "The goal of environmental education is to develop a world population that is aware of, and concerned about, the environment and its associated problems, and which has the knowledge, skills, attitudes, motivations, and commitment to work individually and collectively toward solutions of current problems and the prevention of new ones."[31]

The Belgrade meeting attempted to balance environmental concerns with differing cultural values. This is a thorny issue because of the differences between humanist and naturalist positions on the environment. It also touches on the concerns of indigenous groups about the impact of environmental changes on their ways of living. Regarding cultural differences, the Belgrade Charter allows "for each nation, according to its culture, to clarify for itself the meaning of such basic concepts as 'quality of life' and 'human happiness' in the context of the total environment."[32] And, anticipating later arguments for sustainable development, the Charter suggests that environmental education should try to balance human needs with environmental protections "to identify which actions will ensure the preservation and improvement of humanity's potentials and develop social and individual well-being in harmony with the biophysical and man-made environment."[33]

The Belgrade Charter calls for shaping global human global behavior toward the environment. It states as a goal, "To create new patterns of behavior of individuals, groups, and society as a whole towards the environment."[34] This goal was restated in the first intergovernmental conference of environmental education, sponsored by UNESCO and held in 1977 in Tbilisi, Georgia. The Tbilisi Report calls for creating "new patterns of behavior of individuals, groups and society as a whole towards the environment."[35] And, as part of helping people to think globally, the Tbilisi Report stresses, "Environmental education should examine major environmental issues from a *world point of view*, while paying due regard to regional differences [emphasis added]."[36] Again reflecting the globalizing force of environmental issues, the Report states, "Environmental education should promote the value and necessity of local, national, and *international cooperation* in the solution of environmental problems [emphasis added]."[37] The Report also foreshadowed the argument for sustainable development: "Environmental education should examine all development and growth from an environmental perspective."[38]

As I discussed in chapter 4, the report of the 1991 Second World Conservation Strategy and the 1992 Rio Earth Summit's *Agenda 21* stressed the importance of sustainable development and ensured the global spread of the idea.[39] As required by *Agenda 21*, UNESCO sponsored the 1997 International Conference on Environment and Society: Education and Public Awareness for Sustainability, held in Thessaloniki, Greece. Federico Mayor, the head of UNESCO, described Conference's purpose in its report *Educating for a Sustainable Future* as being "to highlight the role of education and public awareness for sustainability, to consider the important contribution of environmental education in this context, and to mobilize action to this end."[40]

Similar to the arguments of Bowers and Orr, the Thessaloniki report uses the biosphere paradigm in arguing for a radical change in educational ideas to create schools that are interdisciplinary and wholistic in their approaches. The report declares, "Reorienting education to sustainability requires recognizing that traditional compartments and categories can no longer remain in isolation from each other and that we must work increasingly at the interface of disciplines in order to address the complex problems of today's world."[41] It also requires, according to the report, shifting the schooling away for the industrial paradigm and promoting civic activism. The report claims, "Curricula have tended in the past to reproduce an unsustainable culture with intensified environment and development problems rather than empower citizens to think and work towards their solution."[42]

The Thessaloniki report places citizenship as central to sustainable education. It is important to note that similar to that of other environmental educators, the report's concept of citizenship is *not* linked to support of a nation-state. It does support a global civil society. In fact, there is no mention of the nation-state in the discussion of citizenship. The report states,

> To advance such goals, a curriculum reoriented towards sustainability would place the notion of citizenship among its primary objectives. This would require a revision of many existing curricula and the development of objectives and content themes, and teaching, learning and assessment processes that emphasize moral virtues, ethical motivation and ability to work with others to help build a sustainable future.[43]

Also, similar to the arguments of Bowers and Orr, the report includes in sustainable education issues of social injustice. This reflects the wholistic approach of the biosphere paradigm in which the problem is not just how humans relate to the environment but also how humans relate to each other. "It has to be recognized that many of the world's problems," the report contends, "including environmental problems, are related to our ways of living, and that solutions imply transforming the social conditions of human life .... This draws attention to the economic and political structures which cause poverty and other forms of social injustice and foster unsustainable practices."[44]

The wholistic orientation of the biosphere paradigm is also applied to the curriculum. The report stresses the importance of not isolating environmental education from other subject matter areas and to consider the social and political impact of the sciences. In making a plea for global reform of the curriculum, the report presents these interdisciplinary concerns in the following words:

> This kind of orientation would require, *inter alia*, increased attention to the humanities and social sciences in the curriculum. The natural sciences provide important abstract knowledge of the world but, of themselves, do not contribute to the values and attitudes that must be the foundation of sustainable development. Even increased study of ecology is not sufficient to reorient education towards sustainability. Even though ecology has been described by some as the foundation discipline of environmental education, studies of the biophysical and geophysical work are a necessary—but not sufficient—prerequisite to understanding sustainability. The traditional primacy of nature study, and the often apolitical contexts in which is taught, need to be balanced with the study of social sciences and humanities. Learning about the interactions of ecological processes would then be associated with market forces, cultural values, equitable decision-making, government action and the environmental impacts of human activities in a wholistic interdependent manner.[45]

Finally, the report cited the importance of changing the industrial paradigm so that students interpret the world through a mental framework that gives primary consideration to the sustainability. The curriculum section of this influential report on sustainable education concludes,

> A reaffirmation of the contribution of education to society means that the central goals of education must include helping students learn how to identify elements of unsustainable development that concern them and how to address them. Students need to learn how to reflect critically on their place in the world and to consider what sustainability means to them and their communities. They need to practice envisioning alternative ways of development and living, evaluating alternative visions, learning how to negotiate and justify choices between visions, and making plans for achieving desired ones, and participating in community life to bring such visions into effect.[46]

In the 1990s, Stephen Sterling, who works with international NGOs and developed the Master of Science degree in Environmental and Development Education at the South Bank University in London, began formulating the role of education in promoting sustainable development. Eventually, he coined the term *sustainable education* which, in his words, means "a change in educational culture which both develops and embodies the theory and practice of sustainability in a way which is critically aware."[47] Similar to Bowers and Orr, he rejects the industrial paradigm and current educational goals of promoting economic growth and training global workers. He wants to inculcate in students an ecological paradigm or, in the term used in this book, a biosphere paradigm.

Sterling provided a clear statement on the relationship between the biosphere paradigm, wholistic learning, and sustainability. He divides the biosphere paradigm into "perceptual, conceptual, and practical."[48] A wholistic education will develop each of these three areas of the paradigm. "Perceptual" refers to a widening of the boundaries of human concerns from the personal to the global. "In the age of individualism and materialism," he wrote, "we are not encouraged to include 'the other' in our thinking and transactions, whether this be neighbor, community or minorities, let alone distant environments, peoples, and non-human species."[49] The "conceptual" dimension of the biosphere paradigm involves seeing the interrelationships between all areas of life and culture. And the "practical" refers to a disposition to think about how to have healthy and sustainable relations with all elements of the biosphere. Sterling labeled the perceptual part of the paradigm as "extension," the conceptual as "connection," and the practical as "integration."[50]

Sterling applies this paradigm to education. In other words, what does education look like if interpreted through the biosphere paradigm? He calls this "whole systems thinking" about education. Sterling asserts that the application of biosphere paradigm with its three parts results in thinking about education from the standpoint of "extension," "connection," and "integration." "Extension" leads to considering the purpose of education in reference to the "wider society and biosphere." "Connection" results in thinking about how all aspects of education, including buildings, curriculum, teachers, administrators, textbooks, and instructional methods, are related to the goal of educating students for sustainability. And finally, "integration" leads to thinking about "how whole systems approaches might be reflected in classroom or in community practice, in teaching and learning method, including a systems view of the learner, participative learning and teaching styles."[51] Sterling's example of how the biosphere paradigm results in thinking about education in certain ways illustrates the primary goal of sustainable education, which is to learn to use the biosphere paradigm for all aspects of life.

Sterling provides some examples of what he considers to be sustainable education. One is the Australia's Crystal Waters College founded in 1989 at the initiative of "Sustainable Futures" and the Global Ecovillage Network of the Oceania/Asia Center. Reflecting a wholistic approach, the entire campus of 640 acres is a classroom where students can practice solutions offered in courses which include "productive permaculture gardens and food forest; biological restoration of the soil; integrated animal systems; woodlot establishment ... active reduction of consumption and waste community revitalization; cooperatives; and strengthening of local economic systems."[52] Another example is the United Kingdom's Crispin School. The school's curriculum won an award from the WWF-UK. Officially, the school describes its goals as teaching the principles of sustainable development and developing attitudes that come directly from the biosphere paradigm.[53]

Sustainable education is based on a humanistic approach to the biosphere where human interests are served through protection of other species and the environment. However, naturalists groups, such as PETA and Earth First! work within the same biosphere paradigm but advocate different goals and educational methods. The primary interest of naturalist groups is ending speciesism and removing humans from their dominant position in the biosphere. From a global perspective, the combined actions of advocates of sustainable education and naturalist groups are contributing to the growth of global civil society organized around environmental ethics.

RADICAL PUBLIC EDUCATION: DEMONSTRATIONS, CIVIL DISOBEDIENCE, AND ECOTAGE

An important form of public education conducted by environmental groups involves demonstrations, civil disobedience, and ecotage. This is the curriculum of the public stage where education moves outside of the schoolhouse into the public arena. These forms of education can simply involve changing the content of public literature. For instance, Peter Singer complains that children's books often portray cute little farm animals without ever suggesting the cruel fate that lies ahead for them as they make their journey to the dining tables of humans. Singer suggests an important step in combating speciesism would be changing children's literature. Singer argues, "To alter the stories about animals that we read to our children will not be so easy, since cruelty is not an ideal subject for children's stories. Yet it should be possible to avoid the most gruesome details, and still give children picture books and stories that encourage respect for animals as independent beings, and not as cute little objects that exist for our amusement and table."[54]

A more confrontational form of education involves "monkeywrenching," which is sometimes engaged in by naturalist groups such as Earth First! and PETA. Earth First! advocates direct action, such as tree sitting and blockading logging trucks to save forests. Officially, Earth First! explains the educational value of these acts, "You can't hope to change people's minds or put pressure on politicians without calling attention to the damage [to nature]. Civil disobedience or a clever banner-hanging exposes the issue on the front pages of papers …. Arrests, in particular, sway sentiment by impressing on others the depth of our concern and willingness to sacrifice."[55]

Monkeywrenching refers to attempts to stop environmental changes using methods described by Edward Abbey in his book, *The Monkeywrench Gang*.[56] Monkeywrenching involves tree spiking, destruction of billboards, removal of surveying stakes, pouring sugar or sand into the fuel tanks of earthmoving machinery, and other forms of sabotage or, as it is called, "ecotage." Monkeywrenching, as described by the organization leaders of Earth First!, is a step beyond civil disobedience. It is "nonviolent, aimed only at inanimate objects, and pocketbooks of the industrial despoilers. It is the final defense of the wild … whereby the wilderness defender becomes the wilderness acting in self-defense."[57] While Earth First! denies any organizational support to monkeywrenching, it does admit that some local groups and individuals participate in this dramatic form public education. Also, Earth First! distributes Dave Foreman and Bill Haywood's book *ECODEFENSE: A Field Guide to Monkeywrenching*.[58]

Acts of civil disobedience to protect the biosphere are compared to civil rights movements to end human slavery and discrimination among humans. The new civil rights movement is concerned with the rights of all species of animals and plants along with the Deep Ecology concept of natural beauty. A member of Earth First! proclaimed, "Earth First! shares Dr. King's commitment to individual rights. Today … we publicly extend his vision to include oppressed members of our planetary society."[59] One of the original writers on Deep Ecology, Bill Duvall, described civil disobedience as an important form of public education. Civil disobedience, he asserted, "is aimed at a larger audience, and the action should always be interpreted by the activists. Smart and creative communication of the message is as important as the action itself."[60]

Ecotage as a form of public education is more controversial because it involves potential harm to other humans and the destruction of property. For instance, the spiking of trees could hurt the logger or lumber mill worker. Similar to the arguments supporting civil disobedience, ecotage is compared to the violence used by abolitionists in their efforts to end human slavery. In addition, the intention of an act like spiking trees is to make the cutting of old growth forests unprofitable rather than to harm other humans. The destruction of property, such as the burning of suburban construction sites, is justified according to the property rights of all humans as opposed to the property rights of individuals and corporations. Should corporations and private individuals have the right to change or destroy property that offers beauty to all humans and results in the destruction of the environment? Some Earth First!ers consider ecotage as an essential step in shifting from an industrial to a biosphere paradigm. For instance, Peg Millett, arrested for knocking down an electrical tower in 1989, defined monkeywrenching as "the dismantling of the present industrial system, but I would define it as dismantling the machinery very carefully."[61]

PETA has used a variety of techniques to educate the public about animal rights from throwing acid on fur coats to passing out literature. One of their more interesting projects involved the distribution of packets of 52 cards called *Animal Rights: Weekend Warrior*. Representing each week of the year, the cards carry information and suggestions for civic action. Some of these suggestions are directed at public schools. For instance, the card for "Week 4" is titled "Veganize Your Cafeteria" and calls on schools to offer "a healthier, humane lunch program." It is suggested that the card owner meet with school food services and "request that a vegan entrée be offered at every meal, and suggest that cruelty-free alternatives, like vegan margarine, tofu sour cream ... be made available. Be clear—meat flavorings and vegetables cooked in butter are unacceptable."[62] On another card, "Week 11: Cut Out Dissection," students are urged to write their teacher and principal "to express your feelings about dissection."[63] For "Week 2: Make a Library Display," weekend warriors are told to "educate others in your community about animal rights issues by creating a display for your local library."[64] Other cards suggest weekend warriors go leather-free, hang banners, leaflet fur stores, and protest animal testing of products.

PETA's activities are having a global effect. For instance, PETA members sued the multinational fast food franchise KFC to improve its treatment of chickens and to stop making false claims about its humane handling of animals. KFC slaughters over 700 million chickens a year. In response to criticism from PETA, KFC created an Animal Welfare Advisory Council to establish standards for farms raising chickens for the franchise. In May, 2003, PETA agreed to stop its boycott of KFC after the franchise required breeders to expand the cage size for chickens by 30% and to install cameras to ensure that the animals were killed in the most painless manner possible. However, in July, 2003, PETA filed a legal suit complaining that "the birds raised and killed for the defendant's operations suffer great pain and injuries in massive numbers."[65]

What is important about PETA's actions is the resulting establishment of global standards for the ethical treatment of animals. In the case of KFC, the company officially stated, "As a major purchaser of food products, we have the opportunity, and responsibility, to influence the way animals are treated. We take that responsibility very seriously. We only deal with suppliers who maintain the very highest standards and share our commitment to animal welfare."[66] PETA also won concessions regarding the treatment of animals from the fast food franchises McDonald's, Wendy's, and Burger King. And, of course, their actions, along with those of other environmental groups, are an important form of public education.

MODELS OF ENVIRONMENTAL EDUCATION

Civic Activism and the Global Rivers Environmental Education Network

The Global Rivers Environmental Education Network (GREEN) provides a public school model for educating civic activists. Less confrontational that Earth First! and PETA, its teaching methods provide training for active citizenship within the context of a global civil society. GREEN calls its educational method "Action Research and Community Problem Solving." The method involves using interdisciplinary learning that focuses on environmental problems. The group gives a broad and wholistic definition to the word *environment* by including political, social, economic, and biophysical issues.

Developing a global environmental ethic is the major objective of GREEN's instructional methods. This goal is wholistic and embraces issues of development, peace, human rights, and the rights of other species. Its education manual asserts, "Nobody knows that right ethical lifestyle yet, but we all have to be responsible for seeking a world which is built upon human equality and sustainable sharing of natural resources, not only between members of the Western world, but the world as a whole."[67]

GREEN's educational goals are exemplified by the after-school organization in Freeport, Maine, called Concerns About Kids' Environment (CAKE). At the organization's initial meetings, students discussed the basic threats to the biosphere and identified how they could transform their concerns into action within their local communities. Through group discussion, members decided on one area on which to work. In the case model used by GREEN, the students focused on CFCs (choloroflourocarbons) and the fact that CFCs are contained in polystyrene foam. Through collective research, the students learned that polystyrene foam was made from petroleum, that it was a nonrenewable resource, and that it was not biodegradable. After analyzing the environmental problems posed by polystyrene foam, organization members planned an action program.

Reflecting the goal of educating active citizens, students decided to hold a parade through the center of town demanding a ban on the sale of polystyrene foam in their community. The group collected signatures on a petition calling for the end of the sale of polystyrene products. Through their investigations, the students concluded that the major users of polystyrene products were local fast food franchises. Consequently, the students approached fast food managers asking for a curtailment to their use of polystyrene products. The reaction was mixed. Scott Saucier, manager of the town's Arby's said, "Initially we were opposed. But we didn't want to make a big stink. It's hard to fight kids, especially when they have their teachers behind them."[68] The manager of McDonald's refused to comply, claiming that McDonald's was now using plates and cups with reduced CFCs.

The students then decided to use legal means to stop the use of polystyrene products. They went to town meetings to find out how laws were made. After learning about the operation of the local government, organizational members approached the town council and asked for a public meeting. In response, McDonald's brought in top company executives to explain their elaborate recycling methods. In response, several students left the hearing and returned 20 minutes later with two garbage bags filled with litter. One student said, "If your litter program is so good, how come we were able to collect all this in 20 minutes."[69] It was found that well over 50% of the litter was polystyrene. The city council then passed a law banning the sale of food and beverages in containers using polystyrene foam.

GREEN codified the instructional process followed by CAKE which resulted in the town council's passing a ban on the use of polystyrene food containers. The following is a list of steps in this learning process:

1. Discussion and exploration of ideas
2. Exploration of possibilities, opportunities, and constraints
3. Plan 1
4. Implement Plan 1

5. Plan 2
6. Implement Plan 2
7. Evaluate

Steps 1 and 2 rely on real problems existing in the local community. Initially, students do not use textbooks or other research material. The goal is to educate future citizens who will think about environmental problems and possible solutions. The identification of problems is to be guided by the biosphere paradigm. In Step 2, after identification of the problem, students do research to consider the dimensions of the problem and possible solutions. As preparation for civic activism, students develop in Steps 3 and 4 a plan to solve the problem. Assuming that the plan is not perfect or that other action is required, students reflect on the issues generated by the first plan and develop in Step 5 another plan. Steps 5 and 6 can be repeated if the second plan does not render a solution. The GREEN manual compares the process to a spiral with the evaluation of each plan (Step 7) leading to another plan. The manual states, "As participants begin to generate ideas, they enter the first loop of the spiral. They develop a plan (P) that will help them solve their problem, implement that plan (I), and evaluate its effectiveness (E). Evaluation of the plan leads to the development of another plan, which takes them into the second loop, and the spiral continues …. Loops generate more loops until the problem is resolved to the satisfaction of the participants."[70]

Of course, Action Research and Community Problem Solving is relative to the paradigm guiding the thinking and actions of the participants. In this case, it is assumed that the students have been taught to think within a biosphere paradigm. For instance, an industrial paradigm might lead students to identify economic growth and jobs as community problems with solutions centering on maximizing corporate profits and job training. The biosphere paradigm results in students thinking about the general good of the total environment. In addition, the Action Research and Community Problem Solving assumes that active citizenship is the key to protecting the welfare of the biosphere. However, because of its association with public school instruction, the action part of the learning would probably not include civil disobedience or ecotage.

Cultivating Awareness of Global Problems

Cultivating an awareness of environmental problems without teaching civic activism typifies the educational programs of the WWF. Although their educational programs do not instruct in civic activism, the organization's ties to the World Bank, UNESCO, governments, and other international NGOs make it a key player in the global civil society. The linkages with the global civil society occurred at the birth of the organization. An important figure in the founding of the WWF was the British biologist Julian Huxley, who at the time was acting as the first Director General of UNESCO. In 1960, he traveled to Africa and reported that through hunting and deforestation, much of the continent's wildlife would be destroyed within 20 years. As a result of the interest sparked by Huxley's reports, the WWF was organized in 1961 in Switzerland to provide grants to other environmental NGOs. In 1972, the WWF launched an international Tropical Forest Campaign. By the end of the 1970s, the original concern with wildlife habitat broadened to include the whole range of issues involved in protecting the biosphere. In the 1980s, in cooperation with the United Nations Environment Program, the WWF published a joint *World Conservation Strategy*, which was endorsed by the U.N. Secretary-General. In 1998, the World Bank/WWF Alliance for Forest Conservation and Sustainable use was formed. Officially, the organization stated, "WWF ... maintains links with other non-governmental organizations both national and international. It makes a particular point of responding to local conservation needs, and working with local people. More and more projects involve rural communities in making decisions as to how their environment should be both used and conserved, while providing economic incentives."[71]

The linkages between the WWF and the global civil society are explicitly recognized in their educational programs. A central feature of the WWF's educational campaign is the CyberDodo TV cartoon series, games, toys, and videos. Besides emphasizing environmental issues, the CyberDodo cartoons are supported by the United Nations High Commission for Human Rights because of their promotion of the International Convention on Child Rights. Also, CyberDodo series promotes ecotourism in cooperation with the World Travel and Tourism Council.[72] However, unlike the Cyberschoolbus's Pook game discussed in chapter 3, the CyberDodo series does not teach civic activism. It does develop a consciousness of a world environmental crisis. The first TV and video episode of CyberDodo depicts DODO, the main character who is named after a bird that has been extinct for more that 300 years, returning to his former home in Mauritius to find it overrun by ants. While trying to rid his former house of ants, "DODO learns about *the importance of insects and their complex social structure*."[73] In other episodes, the viewer is instructed on the complexities of sustainable development and its relationship to the biosphere. In episode 12, DODO decides to start a banana plantation and is frustrated at the slow growth of his profits by the time taken to grow the bananas. As a result, he overuses fertilizers to the discomfort of a colony of moles. The moles complain and instruct DODO on "*the importance of soil conservation as well as the dangers of fertilizer abuse*."[74] In the next episode, DODO is distressed that his bananas are being eaten by monkeys. He meets monkeys who tell him about their species and their liking of bananas. DODO negotiates with the monkeys—this I would argue is a very misleading episode—and for the bananas they eat they agree to help harvest the others.[75] In the next episode, DODO, driven by greed, tries to pack as many bananas as possible into a crate resulting in their becoming liquid. DODO's companion the "ant explains to DODO that greed is the enemy of profit, then an irate spider emerges from the crates and explains to DODO that bananas are not the only things to suffer from inappropriate conditions of transport. He advises DODO about traffic in exotic species and the transport of farm animals."[76]

Other educational material, including fact sheets, guides to animals and environmental settings, and quizzes, distributed by the WWF also emphasize raising the level of awareness of environmental problems. Although this awareness is not tied to civic action, it does make the student conscious of environmental problems and sustainability issues. Most importantly, it teaches the student to think globally about environmental issues. Awareness of global environmental problems could result in the student taking civic action and participating in the global civil society. Because of the WWF's active role in the global civil society, the user of the WWF's educational material is consciously or unconsciously participating in that global civil society.

Some forms of education simply support citizen awareness as a means of supporting the work of environmental experts. For instance, sustainability requires experts with backgrounds in science and engineering to analyze the effects of development and to correct environmental problems. In 1983, the North American Association for Environmental Education placed importance on educating environmental experts while calling on all citizens to support the work of experts. This organization publicly declared, "The purpose of environmental education is to foster the education of skilled individuals able to understand environmental problems and possessing the expertise to devise effective solutions to them."[77] This organization places less emphasis than other organizations on an active citizenry involved in environmental issues. In this context, the public is given a passive and supporting role to environmental experts. The organization calls for the "development of a citizenry *conscious* of the scope and complexity of current and emerging environmental problems and *supportive* of solutions and policies which are ecologically sound [emphasis added]."[78]

Cultivating Awareness Through Consumption

Wearing a WWF T-shirt and carrying a tote bag with the WWF panda logo could be considered a form of public education for both the wearer and the viewer. Also, a person's consumerism can support environmental protection through shopping with a WWF Visa credit card.[79] The WWF promotes a consumerist ideology similar to that of a multinational corporation through its sale of toys and dolls. As discussed previously, organizations supporting sustainable development tend to accept consumerist ideology but differentiate between good and bad consumerism.

Many other organizations participate in eco-friendly consumerism. For instance, the Earth Day Network offers products through its online Earth Day Store with the entreaty "Shop & Support Earth Day Network." These products are classified as "Earth Day," "Internationally Available Products," and "Natural Products."[80] Products offered for sale include Earth Day T-shirts and sweatshirts; hemp bags; Ethiopian, Sumatran, and Guatemalan coffee; various teas; a woven bag with jungle chocolates; and a Tagua nut necklace kit. The recent crop of organic food stores turn food consumption into an environmentally friendly action. In my community, I shop at Mrs. Green's Natural Market. Its Web site opens a photo connecting organic food with environmental preservation. It shows three backpackers hiking through an evergreen forest. Across the scene is emblazoned, "Shop, Learn … Be Healthy."[81]

In 2000, a natural business communications company in Broomfield, Colorado, was credited with introducing the marketing term LOHAS (Lifestyles of Health and Sustainability) with the publication of the marketing magazine *LOHAS Journal*. The *New York Times* reported in an article with the descriptive title, "They Care About the World (and They Shop, Too)," that LOHAS is now a popular marketing term for "consumers who worry about the environment, want products to be produced in a sustainable way and spend money to advance what they see as their personal development and potential."[82] In the language of sustainable development, these are people interested in "sustainable consumption." The Natural Marketing Institute estimates 68 million American adults or about a third of the U.S. population are LOHAS, who are interested in buying natural foods, garments and household products made from organic fibers, solar heating, hybrid car engines, and, of course, ecotourism. Companies, such as Ford Motors, are pitching sales to this market through the development of a hybrid engine SUV which, I think, is the equivalent to the incongruity of an ecotourist lodge maintaining a golf course.

The potential educating power of advertising should never be underestimated. It could be that advertising to attract LOHAS to a product will result in educating the general public about the concept of sustainable consumption. Such an advertising campaign could make sustainable consumption an important element in a global environmental ethic.

In these examples, consumption is turned into a form of environmental education. The hidden message in these so-called environmentally friendly consumer items is that consumerist ideology is okay as long as it involves the right products. There is no critique of the image of the good society being one of continuous industrial growth and shopping. The reliance on consumerist ideology to educate about and sell environmentalism could be the Trojan Horse of the international green movement.

National Parks

Originating with the 1872 founding of Yellowstone National Park in the United States, national parks are now a global phenomenon, with nation-states protecting wilderness areas for preservation, recreation, and public education. The first World Conference on National Parks was held in Seattle in 1962, followed by several other global conferences leading to the 1982 meeting in Bali. The Bali conference was officially called World National Parks Congress. These meetings were co-sponsored by the World Conservation Union (originally known as the International Union for the Conservation of Nature and Natural Resources or IUCN) and UNESCO.[83] The World Conservation Union's mission statement reflects the globalizing influence of the environmental movement: "To promote the establishment and effective management of a world-wide representative network of terrestrial and marine protected areas." In 2003, the World Parks Congress (also known as the World Congress on Protected Areas) met in Durban, South Africa. The agenda plan for the conference reflected a wholistic approach to environmental problems.

> The World Parks Congress is the premier global event where the big issues for the protected area profession will be drawn out and debated. The Congress programme seeks to balance vigorous debate on these issues with a technical focus, that will deliver useful outputs for those working in the profession. Issues on center stage in Durban will be the role of protected areas in alleviating poverty; how protected areas adapt and anticipate global change—biophysical, economic, and social; the place of protected areas as part of our sustainable future; and the contribution of protected areas to security.[84]

The wholistic approach of this agenda was reflected in the inclusion of economic and social issues. National parks exist to both protect nature and human conditions through promoting sustainable development and alleviating poverty.

National Parks play an important role in environmental education. As part of the research for this book, I made two trips to explore methods of environmental education, in national parks and ecotourist areas. For examples of national parks education I visited Banff and Jasper National Parks in Canada. For examples of education and ecotourism, which I discuss in the next section, I visited the Acajatuba and Uakari Lodges in the Brazilian Amazon. Parks Canada, as the system of parks in Canada are called, offers a wide selection of material for classroom use as attested to by its Web site's claim, "Parks Canada is committed to providing educators with quality educational materials that can enhance their students' learning experiences about Canada's national heritage places."[85]

After three Canadian Pacific Railway workers in 1883 found hot springs in the Canadian Rockies, Banff National Park was created as the world's third and Canada's first national park. In 1907, Jasper National Park was established as the largest of Canada's Rocky Mountain Parks. Both Banff and Jasper are designated as UNESCO World Heritage Sites. The opening of these two parks occurred at a time when vacationing was primarily limited to the upper class. Nature tourism was encouraged by the Canadian Pacific Railway when it completed Banff Springs Hotel in 1888. Built for the luxury tourist, the hotel is called Canada's Castle in the Rockies. In 1890, the railroad opened the Chateau Lake Louise, and in 1915 the Jasper Lodge was opened by the Grand Trunk Pacific Railway.

In May and June of 2003, I visited these three original nature tourist spots, which are now owned by the international Fairmont Hotels and Resorts Corporation. Unlike the past when visitors would spend weeks at one of these resorts hiking trails and climbing mountains, at least 40% of current visitors, I was informed, arrive on packaged tours for one-night stays. These short visits hardly leave much time for appreciating nature beyond looking at the scenery from bus and train windows. Most of the foreign tourists, according to my interviews with hotel officials, are from the United States, Great Britain, Germany, and Japan. In other words, the globalization effect of nature tourism primarily affects people from rich countries. For instance, a popular tour is the seven-day Rocky Mountaineer rail package which starts with a one-day tour of Vancouver. On the next day, the group travels by train for an overnight stay in Kamloops, British Columbia. The third night is spent at the Banff Springs Hotel, followed the next day by a motorcoach trip to Lake Louise with an overnight at the Chateau Lake Louise and then by motorcoach for a one-night stay at the Jasper Lodge. Tour members leave Jasper by train with another overnight in Kamloops before returning to Vancouver. The total seven-day package for a single person costs U.S. $5,099.[86]

In their rooms, nature tourists are provided with information on the Fairmont Corporation's efforts to protect the environment. For instance, at the Banff Springs' hotel I found several pages in their guest information book devoted to *Environmental Stewardship*. If the international traveler reads the guest books in their rooms, they will learn about "sustainable tourism." The pages on *Environmental Stewardship* describe sustainable tourism.

> Known as the "Castle in the Rockies" ... The Fairmont Banff Springs Hotel has been located in the breathtaking Rocky Mountains for over 100 years and

one can't help being reminded of the importance of maintaining this natural environment. The Fairmont Banff Springs invites you to join us in our efforts to reuse and recycle. In every aspect of the management of The Fairmont Banff Springs we will encourage environmental stewardship upon which *sustainable tourism depends* [emphasis added].[87]

The guest book lists the efforts made by the hotel to achieve sustainable tourism, such as optional daily towel and linen replacement (the more cynical might consider this a cost-cutting measure because it saves on hotel laundry expenses), changes to reduce the use of electricity and natural gas, recycling, and water conservation.

The Fairmont Corporation has also established a "Green Partnership Program" which the *National Geographic Traveller* called the "most comprehensive environmental program in the North American hotel industry."[88] In addition, the corporation has a Department of Environmental Affairs, which operates an environmental Web site (environment@fairmont.com) and distributes a comprehensive guide for employees called "The Green Partnership Guide." The corporation quotes Dr. David Suzuki, whom the booklet describes as "the foremost environmentalist in North America," that the guide "is a concrete example of how businesses can involve employees in something everyone can feel good about. It's good for business, it's good for morale, it's good for the planet."[89]

The Fairmont Corporation also attempts to abide by the broader definition of sustainable tourism, which includes the protection of culture. Unfortunately, this cultural protection does not extend to indigenous peoples. It neglects the fact that the extension of the Canadian railroad system resulted in European Canadians displacing indigenous peoples from their lands. Railroad construction in western Canada was a form of imperialism. The Banff Springs' guest book is explicit about its role in nation-building:

> Heritage Tourism: The Fairmont Banff Springs is a symbol of Canada and a National Historic Site. The history of the hotel is *associated with the building of the nation* and the creation of Canada's oldest National Park system.
>
> Our principal goal in the Mountain Heritage Program is to demonstrate our responsibility for protecting and sharing the natural and cultural heritage of Banff National Park for the benefit and preservation of future generations. In every aspect of the management of The Fairmont Banff Springs, we will encourage *environmental stewardship upon which sustainable tourism depends* [emphasis added].[90]

As mentioned in chapter 4, ecotourism requires a respect and recognition of local indigenous cultures. This aspect of ecotourism is neglected in the Fairmont Corporation's program of environmental stewardship. In fact, the only recognition of indigenous cultures is at the shopping mall near the Fairmont Chateau Lake Louise. Called the Samson Mall, a small plaque indicates that it is owned by the Samson Cree Nation. The culture of the tribe is neglected while its economic interests are promoted.

Reflecting the importance of pressure from international NGOs, the Fairmont Corporation cooperates with Audubon International in the operation of its golf courses. As world class golf courses, both the Banff Springs and Jasper Lodge are accredited members of the Audubon Cooperative Sanctuary System. As stated in the hotels' literature, this means enhancing "habitat for wildlife on the Golf Course and preserv[ing] natural resources as well as promoting research, education and stewardship action."[91]

The cooperation with the Fairmont Hotel chain highlights the effectiveness of the educational program of the Audubon International. The organization developed out of the original New York State Audubon Society founded in the 1880s. This was one of the first environmentally concerned NGOs. Today, the Audubon International promotes the protection of wildlife habitats on private and public lands. Officially, the organization describes its efforts as such:

> Audubon International spearheads education and conservation assistance programs that promote environmental stewardship and sustainability. Programs encourage pro-active, cooperative partnerships among Audubon International, landowners or managers enrolled in the program, and local community organizations. Audubon International believes that such positive relationships form the foundation for sustained conservation action.[92]

The organization considers its Cooperative Sanctuary System to be its "premiere education program," because it "educates people about environmental stewardship and motivates them to take action in their daily lives that will enhance and protect wildlife and their habitats and conserve natural resources. Programs for homeowners, businesses, schools, and golf courses tailor information to the unique setting and needs of each member."[93] The International Audubon's efforts appear to be working, as I witnessed golfers at the Jasper Lodge lobbing balls over elk eating the course's grass and over freely roaming gaggles of Canadian geese.

While nature tourism for some might be reduced to looking from bus and train windows with quick one-night stays in luxury resorts, international environmental NGOs appear to be effective in their global educational programs. They are, as exemplified by the educational programs of the Audubon International, creating global standards for hotels and resorts. Tourists are also educated about environmental issues as they read the promotional literature provided by hotels. Unfortunately, as represented by nature tourism to the Canadian Rockies, this form of global learning appears to be limited to those with enough money to travel. Also, nature tourism as promoted by the Fairmont Hotels and Resorts neglects the cultures of indigenous peoples.

There is no evidence at Banff and Jasper that Parks Canada is interested in trying to fulfill the previously mentioned concern of the World Parks Congress with the "role of protected areas in alleviating poverty." The Fairmont Corporation's Green Partnership Program does claim to redistribute leftover food to the needy. The statement of "Food Redistribution" is given in their brochure.

> Ever wonder what happens to the leftover food on the buffet table after the guests have finished? The thought of adding to our growing landfill woes by throwing away untouched food, when at the same time so many in our communities go hungry, seemed a double tragedy. Through partnerships established with local shelters, food banks and soup kitchens, Fairmont continues to successfully divert thousand of meals to people in need.[94]

For those who spend more time at Banff and Jasper, there are naturalist education centers and information. A very active role is played by the NGO Friends of Banff, which provides a speaker series at Banff and Lake Louise and educational kits on bears, wolves, and elk. At roadside pullouts, the Friends of Banff provide naturalist interpreters to discuss the park's wildlife to passing motorists. They also conduct naturalist tours for schools and a training session for teachers.[95] Parks Canada Web site offers 60 downloadable curricula for school teachers. One example is "Forest Connections: Food Web" for Grades 3, 4, and 7. Its description is: "This hands-on interactive classroom activity allows students to learn about the importance and complexity of food webs. National Parks contain different types of habitats and ecosystems, which consist of plant and animal species that are dependent on one another and their natural surroundings (habitats)."[96]

In conclusion, the meetings of the World Parks Congress provide another instance of the globalizing effect of environmental concerns. Despite the neglect of indigenous cultures and concerns about poverty, Banff and Jasper Parks as world heritage sites play an international role in promoting environmental education. The relationship between the Fairmont Corporation and Audubon International demonstrates the effect of international NGOs and the development of global standards for the interaction of multinational corporations with the environment. These relationships reflect the globalizing effect of tourism and the fact that much of this tourism originates from richer countries.

Acajatuba and Uakari Lodges

At Acajatuba and Uakari lodges, I experienced Brazil's efforts at promoting ecotourism and environmental education. In fact, ecotourism as a trendy way to make money was evident when arriving at the Manaus airport as tour guides waved signs with *eco* as a prefix to words ranging from *site* to *scene*. The Brazilian government's educational efforts were manifested one day at the Acajatuba lodge with the arrival of 30 students on a field trip as part of their four-year Tourism curriculum. They were being prepared for jobs in government, managing tour groups and hotels, and in travel offices. An important part of their curriculum, besides languages, was studying the principles of ecotourism and sustainable development. A guide took the group out to study the local waters and jungle, and experience the life of the tourist. The manager of the Uakari lodge was a graduate of a similar four-year curriculum; he knew multiple languages, knew the theory of sustainable development and ecotourism, and sometimes acted as a nature guide.

My first visit was to the Acajatuba Lodge, which was a 5½-hour boat ride up the Rio Negro river from Manaus. At Manaus the black waters of the Rio Negro and the white or yellow waters of the Amazon flow together in a visual display referred to as the meeting of the waters. The accommodations at the small lodge were in two-room, palm-leaf-covered huts spread through the jungle and connected by an elevated walkway. At the lodge, unlike at the Uakari Lodge, there was no formal educational introduction to the theory of ecotourism or the environment of the surrounding jungle. However, the lodge did provide a very knowledgeable local guide who led groups on nature tours. The guide's name was Eliaquim Soares, and his business card said he was available to lead Ecological Safaris and that he speaks English, Portugese, French, Italian, and Spanish. He also told me he speaks Japanese. He has European and Native American ancestry and gained firsthand knowledge of the area while growing up there and learning from his father who had been a hunter and fisherman. His naturalist descriptions were often laced with native lore along with scientific data. For instance, on one guided tour I asked about the source of a loud noise coming from the edge of the river. He replied, "Those are the frogs announcing that the water is leaving." At the time of my June arrival, the rivers had reached their peak flooded period and were beginning to recede. Consequently, at this time of the year most of the jungle is flooded and tours are conducted in canoes. When the flood crests, a new generation of frogs are born and their voices tell locals that the waters will be receding.

Soares was very serious about his work as a nature guide. He imparted a great deal of knowledge to members of the tour, particularly about trees and their various uses. Most of the nature trips took place in boats with many sightings of grey and pink river dolphins and one view of monkeys. As he explained, the Rio Negro is slightly acidic because of decaying plant life. Consequently, there are few mosquitos since the larvae cannot survive in the water. In some highland places, we hiked through the jungle learning about various plants, ants, and other insects. In keeping with the principles of ecotourism, the group was taken to a local village to buy folk crafts. I considered Eliaquim Soares an excellent teacher who displayed a great deal of sensitivity about the destruction of the environment. In one area, he mentioned that there had been over 200 ducks until they were killed by wealthy hunters.

While the Acajatuba Lodge is a purely commercial venture embodying the principles of ecotourism, the Uakari Lodge in the Mamirauá Reserve represents the educational aspects of globalization. Biologist Eduardo Martins claimed, "Mamirauá was the first to apply the concept of sustainability (in which protected natural resources are used in a renewable way). While this concept has been widely discussed around the world, it has rarely been applied in real-life situations."[97] As an example of globalization, work at the Reserve is funded by European Union, the Wildlife Conservation Society, the government of the State of the Amazon, Brazil's Ministry of Culture, and the Institute of Sustainable Development of Mamirauá. The WWF trained the first guides for the Uakari Lodge.

Only 1,000 tourists a year are allowed into the Reserve, which is reached by a one-hour plane ride from Manaus to the small river town of Tefé, where the ecotourist is met by a Mamirauá Reserve speedboat which then travels one and a half hours to the Lodge. The Uakari Lodge is a group of floating modules attached by walkways. At night, sleeping under mosquito netting, I could feel my room bobbing up and down to the river's motion and I could hear what I thought were Caimans hauling themselves out of the river onto the logs supporting the room.

Shortly after my arrival, the Lodge's manager presented a slide show and lecture on the concept of sustainable development and the Mamirauá Reserve. His lecture was supplemented by two books, available in the Lodge's library, published by groups associated with the Mamirauá Reserve. The books were *Mamirauá* published by the Sociedade Civil Mamirauá and *Mamirauá: A Guide to the Natural History of the Amazon Flooded Forest* published by Instituto de Desenvolvimento Sustentável Mamirauá.[98] Money from purchases of the books went to support research endeavors in the Reserve. Sustainable development in the Mamirauá Reserve involves protection of the environment, research on plants, wildlife, and fish, and economic and medical assistance to people living within the Reserve. Local communities through elected representatives participate in the management of the Reserve. Local associations produce crafts to be sold to tourists. Medical and environmental education is provided to local communities.

According to the manager's lecture, the Reserve is divided into several zones. Tourists are restricted to a small area of the Reserve. In fact, after several canoe trips into the flooded forest, I began to recognize trail markers indicating established tourist routes. Local communities are allowed to fish in some areas, whereas other areas are only open to researchers. Brazil has very strict laws regarding the export of plants, insects, and wildlife. We heard many tales of foreigners being arrested at airports while trying to smuggle spiders and butterflies out of the country. According to the manager, a major project in the Reserve is the study of pink river dolphins. The Mamirauá Reserve has the largest concentration of gray and pink river dolphins and manatees in the Amazon.

In the book *Mamirauá*, biologist Martins, in a chapter on "Sustainability in Mamirauá: Construction of a New Vision for Humanity," expresses the educational value of the Reserve, "I realize that work in the forest is actually a learning process in which we come face to face with our own limitations while simultaneously seeking to explain and mange the wealthiest biodiversity on Earth."[99] He describes sustainable development in the context of the Amazon: "The concept of sustainability, when applied in the Amazon, must consider certain basic principles: national versus international interests; economic needs versus international interests; economic needs versus preservation of the forest; and the interests of the local population versus that of Brazilian society at-large."[100]

The ecotourism aspect of sustainable development is explained in *Mamirauá: A Guide to the Natural History of the Amazon Flooded Forest*: "In its zoning, the Mamirauá Reserve management plan designated a special zone for the development of an ecotourism program, to exploit the scenic beauty of this protected area. The Mamirauá ecotourism program was developed as one of the strategies to ensure the future funding of the Mamirauá Institute, as well as a source of alternative income to local residents."[101]

Alternative income for local residents is provided through the employment of guides and lodge staff. As mentioned previously, the WWF trained the first group of local residents to serve as guides for ecotourists staying at the Uakari Lodge. Unfortunately for foreigners these guides are not multilingual. However, I did not find this a particular disadvantage since it was recommended that no talking take place during the tour to avoid frightening away animals. Travel through the flooded forest takes place in a canoe with a guide and one or two ecotourists. During the tour, the guide silently points in directions where he sees animals and birds. The ecotourist usually sees a number of species of monkeys, sloths, and birds along with river mammals.

As a globalizing educational experience, Acajatuba and Mamirauá primarily serve ecotourists from wealthy nations, particularly Americans and Europeans. During my stay at the Acajatuba Lodge, there was only one Brazilian tourist. At the Uakari Lodge, there were Americans and a group of Finnish ecotourists. The manager of Uakari Lodge indicated that only about 30% of their visitors are Brazilian.

In summary, national parks and ecotourism provide an educational experience in nature appreciation for the wealthier world traveler. This form of global environmental education should not be dismissed as play time for the rich and middle class. First, it does provide a common global experience for part of the world's population. Second, many of these world travelers probably develop a deeper appreciation for nature and could become advocates for environmental protection when returning to homelands. It could develop Deep Ecology. But it is a passive form of education that does not provide the traveler with the knowledge and tools for influencing governments and multinational corporations. However, it must be recognized as an important contribution to forming a global ethic for protection of the biosphere.

CONCLUSION: THE PARADIGM SHIFT AND GLOBAL CIVIL SOCIETY

Environmental education runs counter to the educational efforts of nation-states, such as the United States and Singapore, and to the neoliberal policies of organizations like the World Bank. The radical characteristics of the movement are in its efforts to change the world's thinking from an industrial to a biosphere paradigm and to eradicate speciesism and anthropocentrism. Environmental education attempts to transform human thinking by displacing humans as the central and dominant form of life. Humans become just one species existing among other animal and plant species. In addition, environmental education teaches that the meaning and pleasure of life is dependent on the quality of human interaction with nature. The biosphere paradigm is a mental filter which interprets human experience in the context of a web of relations with the land, air, water, and other plant and animal species. It also results in seeing human knowledge as dependent on the same web of relationships. Consequently, environmental education is considered as something that must be wholistic and interdisciplinary.

There are important differences between sustainable education, the public education acts of Earth First! and PETA, education for sustainable consumption, and education through ecotourism. But, taken as a whole, all of these forms of education are playing a role in building a global ethic centered on concerns about life in the biosphere. Admittedly, some of these are economically exploitive such as sustainable consumerism and ecotourism. However, they all contain some element of Deep Ecology.

Also, most environmental education programs promote the idea of global citizenship and a global civil society. In this context, citizenship means actively working to ensure the quality of the biosphere as opposed to traditional concepts of citizenship that support the nation-state. This approach to citizenship education undermines the strength of the nation-state and supports the evolution of a global civil society. The environmental concept of citizenship supports a Deep Ecology approach to patriotism. Environmental patriotism involves love of the biosphere in contrast to love of the nation.

Some environmental educators, such as Chet Bowers, worry that global citizenship will lead to cultural uniformity. Bowers argues that the paradigm change includes valuing traditional knowledge. In the 19th and 20th centuries, particularly in the writings of such educators as John Dewey, it was assumed that the best approach to solving social problems is the application of scientific methods. Often this approach discounts the importance of traditional knowledge. As Bowers demonstrates, embedded in traditional knowledge are methods by which people have learned to preserve their communities and, in some cases, maintain sustainable ways of living.[102] Of course, traditional knowledge is sometimes faulty and can be improved. But cultures are a source for understanding how human communities can exist in peace and in relationship to the environment. Support of traditional knowledge leads to support of cultural diversity. All cultures have developed ways of living within the biosphere. Of course, some cultures are more destructive of the biosphere than others. But what is important is to allow all cultures to evolve and adapt to the needs of the biosphere. In the process of adaptation to the biosphere's needs, the best of cultural traditions for maintaining human life and sustainability are shared and preserved.

I certainly do not want to give the impression that environmental education is quickly winning adherents and replacing industrial forms of education. Nation-states, such as the United States and Singapore, are still championing industrial forms of schooling and promoting loyalty to the nation. There appears to be little happening in their school systems to suggest a shift from an industrial to a biosphere paradigm. In addition, the World Bank and multinational corporations are still promoting education as a means of economic growth and equality of consumption. There is little in their efforts to suggest a change in paradigms or the creation of an appreciation of Deep Ecology. In the end, the major challenge for environmental educators will be enhancing the power of global civil society against the power of nation-states and international corporations.

The Future of Education in Global Society

The assumption of previous chapters is that educational ideologies are helping to create a global civil society that will share certain common ethical standards. But is a global society really being formed? The most cogent critic of this idea is Samuel P. Huntington who argues that since the end of the Cold War in the 1990s, the world has been splintering into conflicting factions based on differences in religious and cultural values.[1] Also, there are conflicting goals between global educational ideologies. In this chapter, I begin my discussion of these issues by first analyzing the differences between global educational ideologies. Second, I consider Huntington's prediction that the world will be plagued by increasing clashes between civilizations by exploring the issues of global languages, and religious and cultural differences. Huntington might be right that the world is rapidly moving away from sharing a common culture and ethical standards.

THE CLASH OF EDUCATIONAL IDEOLOGIES

There are fundamental differences in goals, content, and methods between the educational interests of the nation-state, neoliberal ideas, and human rights and environmental educational agendas. First is the concept of citizenship and the role of the nation-state in a global society. Nationalist forms of education, as represented by Singapore and the United States, stress loyalty to the nation-state and national citizenship. In the context of a global society, nation-states want to educate citizens who can work in a global economy for the good of their countries, or as I portrayed in chapter 1, global workers who carry their nations in their hearts. However, neoliberal ideas are changing the role of governments in nation-states by shifting the provision of public

164

services, such as schools to the private sector and focusing government action on the regulation of privately provided services. For instance, Singapore's government is retaining its control over provision of public services, while advocates of neoliberalism in the United States are trying to reduce the role of government in the provision of schools and strengthen its role through management of testing and curriculum standards.

Neoliberalism, and human rights and environmental education are stressing new forms non-nationalistic forms of patriotism and citizenship. World Bank educational policies reinforce loyalty to national economies in contrast to loyalty to the political symbols of nation-states. World Bank policies support an identification with a global economy, which weakens a sense of loyalty to the nation-state. Advocates of human rights and environmental education are sometimes openly hostile to the concept of the nation-state. These educational ideologies promote a global citizenship based on ethical standards for the whole world. A global civil society, for many of the supporters of these educational ideologies, is an antidote or countervailing power to the actions of nation-states. Among environmentalists, and some human rights educators, patriotism involves love for all people and species as opposed to love of nation. Loyalty becomes loyalty to the good of all.

These dramatic differences in ideas of citizenship and loyalty directly affect educational methods and content. Strong nation-states want to instill discipline in their students. One method is the use of national testing to determine students' advancement through the school system and, as a result, their place in the nation's occupational structure. National testing requires that students submit to the power of the state to determine their futures. Also, strong states tend to centralize control of the content of instruction by establishing strict curriculum standards. Indirectly, the student learns that the just arbiter of what knowledge is of most worth is the government and, consequently, it is wise to submit to the state's authority. In addition, the content of history and civic courses are organized to teach loyalty and national citizenship.

Nation-states and global institutions such as the World Bank share an interest in creating an industrial and consumerist paradigm in students' minds for interpreting world events. When, in strong nation-states like Singapore and the United States, government officials refer to attacks on the nation's "way of life," they are usually referring to attacks on the ability of people to work for the consumption of goods. The industrial and consumerist paradigm results in students' evaluating world events according to their effect on economic growth and the equal opportunity to consume. The hidden curriculum of schools is the imparting to students an industrial and consumerist paradigm.

In contrast, most human rights and environmental educators advocate activist citizenship and shun the political discipline required by the nation-state. Consequently, government testing of students and curriculum standards find no place in these educational ideologies. In fact, government testing and curriculum standards could be considered violations of children's rights to free access to educational materials and ideas. Consequently, both human rights and environmental educators emphasize problem-solving methods. Simply stated, students are given human rights violations or environmental problems and they are asked to solve them. All subject areas are integrated into a curriculum designed to improve the human condition within the biosphere.

The hidden curriculum of human rights education is a paradigm that interprets world events according to their effect on human rights rather than economic growth and consumption. Human rights doctrines cover issues of social and economic justice including the ability of people to eat, and have shelter and medical care. Consequently, those thinking within the human rights paradigm wonder how an event affects people's freedom, and social and economic conditions. The hidden curriculum of environmental educators is the biosphere paradigm. Students learn to interpret the world through a lens that judges events according to their effect on the entire biosphere.

Human rights and environmental educators give more importance to traditional knowledge than nationalist and neoliberal forms of education. Nationalist educators teach history and cultural traditions for patriotism and to reduce racial and ethnic tensions rather than as a source of knowledge about how to live with nature and other people. Neoliberal ideologists utilize local cultures to develop educational programs that will create an industrial and consumer society. In this context, local cultures are seen as a means to an end rather than being of value in themselves. Human rights educators tend to emphasize the protection of local cultures and languages. Human rights doctrines include the right to one's own culture and language. Environmental educators consider traditional knowledge as a source for understanding sustainable patterns of living and community organization.

The preceding are fundamental differences in educational ideologies. Where do I stand on these issues? First, I doubt the ability of the industrial and consumer paradigm to maximize the quality of life for all people. Evidence suggests that the industrial paradigm coupled with neoliberal arguments for free markets is not contributing to greater global economic and social justice. The Human Development Report 2003 of the United Nations Development Program claims that since 1990, 54 countries are poorer, the rate of hunger has increased in 21 nations, and the percentage of children below the age of 5 has risen in 14 nations. In some countries, conditions have improved, particularly in China, India, and Vietnam. It should be noted that officially India is a socialist country while China and Vietnam are communist, which might raise doubts about the claim that free market economics are the panacea for global ills.[2] The Human Development Program summarized what it considers to be the three most important aspects of a quality life: "living a long and healthy life, being educated and having a decent standard of living." During the 1990s, the human development index declined in 21 countries.[3]

There continues to be a sharp contrast between the richest and poorest countries. The top 20 countries on the human development index are European and North American countries along with Australia and New Zealand.[4] The bottom 20 are all in sub-Saharan Africa and they are all former colonies of European countries.[5] All but 1 of the 33 countries listed as having low human development are former European colonies.[6] These statistics undermine any claims about the beneficent effect of European rule and attempts to introduce Western ways of thinking.

These global disparities are highlighted by a comparison of the top and bottom countries on the development index. At the top of the human development index is Norway, where people in 2001 had a life expectancy at birth of 78.7 years, shared a combined primary and secondary school enrollment of 98%, and enjoyed a gross domestic product per capita of U.S. $29,620.[7] At the bottom of the index is Sierra Leone, where in 2001 citizens had a life expectancy at birth of 34.5 years, there was a combined primary and secondary school enrollment of 64%, and the country had a gross domestic product per capita of U.S. $7,376.[8]

Of course, neoliberal ideology and the effects of colonialism may not be the only causes of the increasing disparities between rich and poor countries. Besides their superior economic and military power, rich nations might be maintaining their top places on the human development index by exploiting poorer countries. Socialism and communism seem to have helped India, China, and Vietnam. However, from an environmentalist perspective, a major problem with these countries is that they still operate within the industrial and consumer paradigm. In my mind, given differences in military power, the limits on natural resources and the inability of the Earth to handle industrial wastes, it is futile to debate about whether or not capitalism and communism are the best economic systems. The industrial and consumerist paradigm will not and cannot provide the best life for all the world's peoples.

Consequently, I am persuaded we need schools that educate for active global citizenship within the biosphere paradigm. As a citizen of the United States, I could, from a purely selfish standpoint, support a nationalist form of education that has the goals of economic growth and equality of consumption. After all, I am personally benefitting from the United States' rank of seven on the human development index (the first six in rank order are Norway, Iceland, Sweden, Australia, Netherlands, and Belgium).[9] I point out to my American students that they benefit from the United States' economic and military power over poorer nations.

THE LANGUAGE OF EARTH

A shared world language would be a major step in creating a global civil society. And, of course, schools would have a major role in teaching this universal language. However, the language issue is complex. First, a common global language might foster peace by breaking down walls of misunderstanding between cultures and by promoting a global civil society. However, there was a common language between combatants during the American Civil War and it did not stop the killing of nearly a million soldiers. Second, a common global language might threaten the existence of minority languages which in turn, since culture and language depend on each other, might eradicate minority cultures. Third, a common global language might divide people economically and socially because only elite groups might have access to extensive language training.

These factors create a dilemma for educators. Should all the world's schools teach a language that makes it possible for all of humanity to communicate? Will a global language enhance the power of a global civil society? What should be the global language? Should the global language be Mandarin, Arabic, English, or Esperanto? If all schools teach a global language then what happens to minority languages and cultures? What will be the economic and social consequences of teaching a global language? Will there be economic and social *disadvantages* for those whose mother tongue is not the global language and for whom the global language is a second language? What will be the consequences for those who do not learn the global language?

The issues surrounding the use of a global language are exemplified in the history and justification for Esperanto. Searching for a language that would unite humanity without causing social class conflicts and political strife, Lazar Ludwik Zamenhof published his first booklet on *International Language* in 1887 under the pseudonym Dr. Esperanto. Growing up in the city of Bialystok, which sometimes was claimed by Poland and other times by Lithuania, he experienced a city divided religiously, economically, and politically by four different languages—German, Russian, Polish, and Yiddish. Zamenhof claimed,

> Had I not been a Jew from the ghetto, the idea of uniting humanity would either never have come into my head or, if it did, would never have become a lifetime preoccupation .... No one can feel the need for a language free of a sense of nationality as strongly as the Jew who obliged to pray to God in a language long dead, receives his upbringing and education in the language of a

people that rejects him, and has fellow-sufferers throughout the world with whom he cannot communicate.[10]

While not the first to invent a language, Zamenhof was more attuned than others to the possible social and political impact of a global language. Consequently, valuable lessons about the effect of global languages can be learned from his efforts. From the 16th to the 20th century, there were more than 50 attempts to launch planned global languages for ideological, nationalistic, and political purposes.[11]

Zamenhof wanted to create an artificial language that would not offend the chauvinistic supporters of national languages. He advocated equality for all ethnic languages. The goal was for students to be educated in both their mother tongue and the global language of Esperanto. Regarding language equality, he hoped that there would be "neither strong nations nor weak, neither privileged nor underprivileged; no one is humiliated, no one is made uneasy. We all stand on the same neutral footing, the rights of all are fully equal, we feel ourselves members ... of a single family."[12]

He believed that a global language should be simple to learn so that it would not result in social class divisions. From his perspective, a linguistically difficult global language would favor those with the time and money to take extensive language training. For instance, he felt that if a natural language such as English, Mandarin, or Russian became global, "we would not have an international language in the true meaning of the word, but simply an international language for the higher social classes."[13] In contrast, an artificial language planned for ease of learning would avoid the social class divisions resulting from a natural language becoming global. He claimed that "with an artificial language, everyone, not just the intelligent and the rich, but all spheres of human society, even the poorest and least educated of villagers, would be able to master it within a few months."[14]

In *Esperanto: Language, Literature, and Community*, Pierre Janton provided the following summary of the objectives of Esperanto:

> Only a language that can be acquired by the poor and the uneducated will serve to democratize culture and communication. The goal of an international planned language is to allow direct communication among the masses without the required mediation of the elite and the ruling classes—in sum, to allow the masses to free themselves, at least as far as language is concerned, from their dependence on the privileged classes.[15]

While Esperantists, as advocates are called, want an artificial language that is not tied to any particular economic or political ideology, such as fascism, communism, or capitalism, they do believe that a common language is the key to world peace, and sisterhood and brotherhood. One could call this a language ideology in which the heart of the political goal (peace) is

achieved through universal language training in a supposedly neutral artificial language. Of course, it is not neutral because it advocates world
unity—a goal not subscribed to by fervent nationalists. This language ideology is expressed in the "Declaration on the Essence of Esperantism," issued
at the first World Congress of Esperanto in 1905.

> Esperantism is an effort to disseminate throughout the world the use of a neu-
> trally human language, which, "without interfering in the internal affairs of
> individual peoples and in no way seeking to dislodge the existing national lan-
> guages," would afford people of different nations the possibility of mutual un-
> derstanding; which would also serve as a pacifying language for public
> institutions in those countries where various nations quarrel among them-
> selves about language, and in which there might be published those works of
> common interest to all people. All other ideas or aspirations which the indi-
> vidual Esperantist may attach to Esperantism are purely a private matter, for
> which Esperantism is not responsible.[16]

The problem for Esperantists is convincing people to adopt Esperanto as
the global language. By the very nature of their goal of world peace and the
lack of support from nation-states, Esperantists do not have available, unlike colonial powers, the use of military strength to impose their language
agenda. Consequently, Esperantism is spread primarily through voluntary
associations. The Universal Esperanto Association located in Rotterdam
claims representatives in 72 countries and 47 affiliated national associations, including the Chinese Esperanto League and the Polish Esperanto
Association. There are over 50 international Esperanto organizations that
focus on particular interests ranging from agriculture to yoga. At the global
level, the Universal Esperanto Association works with UNESCO to promote
the spread of the language. What is striking about the movement is its reliance on a global civil society to spread the usage of Esperanto.[17]

Despite the efforts of Esperantists, there is little sign of its triumphing as
the global language. Today, some claim English is rapidly becoming the
global language and people around the world are rushing to learn the language so that they participate in the global economy.[18] Consequently,
knowledge of English might be one key to economic success in the global
economy which means that non-English speakers are at a disadvantage. On
the other hand, Samuel Huntington presents evidence of the declining
global usage of English. For instance, according to his figures the percentage of the world's population speaking English declined from 9.8 in 1958 to
7.6 in 1992. In contrast, Hindi language speakers as a percentage of the
world's population increased from 5.2 in 1958 to 6.4 in 1992, and speakers
of Mandarin as a percentage of the world's population during this time period declined slightly from 15.6 to 15.2.[19]

Mandarin is spoken by the largest percentage of the world's population. As mentioned in chapter 1, Singapore is now stressing the teaching of Mandarin in its schools because of the economic opportunities in China and Singapore's large ethnic Chinese population. According to Huntington, other Asian nations are adopting similar policies to take advantage of Chinese markets. However, there is no evidence that Mandarin, or any other Chinese languages are becoming a global language. Between 1958 and 1992 the percentage of the world's population speaking Chinese languages (Mandarin, Cantonese, Wu, Min, and Hakka) declined from 20.5 to 18.8. Nor is there any evidence that European languages are growing in importance with the world's percentage of speakers of these languages, declining 24.1 in 1958 to 20.8 in 1992. It is an interesting fact that in 1958 almost half (44%) the world's population spoke either Chinese or European languages. By 1992 this percentage had declined to 39.4.[20]

According to Huntington, these figures should not discount the importance of English as a form of *intercultural* communication between diplomats, airline pilots, scientists, business people, and tourists. As an intercultural form of communication it presupposes, he argues, the existence of separate cultures. Used as intercultural communication, English becomes "de-ethnicized." The same thing can be said about Spanish. The intercultural and de-ethnicized use of English and Spanish occurred, according to Huntington, after the collapse of European colonial empires. During the period of colonialism, there was an attempt to destroy local cultures by requiring the use of European languages. The most successful of what might be called language imperialists were England, the United States, and Spain, with France and Portugal close behind. England successfully spread English usage into parts of Africa, India, North America, Australia, New Zealand, and the Carribean. Spanish was the linguistic rival of English spreading through conquest and missionary work in Central and South America, and in the Philippines. The English firmly believed that learning to speak English introduced people to a superior Anglo-Saxon culture. The United States aided England by including teaching English in the concept of the country's manifest destiny to spread democracy and Protestantism. A primary goal of American policies was to force Native Americans and Spaniards in the conquered areas of the Western part of the United States to speak English. Similar attempts were made by the U.S. government in Puerto Rico and the Philippines after the Spanish–American war.

Today, the use of English is not necessarily tied to Anglo-Saxon culture and the use of Spanish is not necessarily linked to Iberian culture. We now live in a world of "Englishes" and "Spanishes" where residents in former colonies continue to speak a form of English or Spanish that reflects their local cultures.[21] As Huntington observes regarding the English legacy in India, "Indian English is taking on many distinctive characteristics of its own: it is being Indianized, or rather it is being localized as differences develop among the various speakers of English with different local tongues. English is being absorbed into Indian culture just as Sanskrit and Persian were earlier."[22] Similar arguments can be made about the difference between the Spanishes spoken in Argentina and Mexico. While residents of these countries can communicate in Spanish, their cultures are quite distinct.

Esperanto's analytical framework helps in considering the possible consequences of English, Mandarin, Arabic, and Spanish as common global languages. First, contrary to Huntington's claim that these languages are de-ethnicized, some argue that they continue to carry imperial cultural values.[23] Unlike Esperanto, the global use of these languages can contain the hidden message that their cultures of origin are superior. In fact, many English speakers in the United States and England consider their culture superior to other world cultures. Followers of Islam believe in the inevitable triumph of their religion. And the Chinese have a long history of considering outsiders as barbarians.[24] In other words, all of these languages have a chauvinistic foundation.

Second, none of these languages are easy to learn by people whose mother tongue is another language unless they receive extensive language training. Extensive language training requires time and money. Consequently, English or Mandarin as the global language would contribute to strengthening social class differences. This is exactly the problem identified by Esperantists. If English becomes the global language, which some people claim it already is, then access to global political power and participation in leadership in the global economy, particularly in management of multinational corporations, would depend on a person's ability to receive instruction in English. Those having English as a mother tongue would have an advantage in accessing global political and economic power. There is a clear disadvantage for those not having English as their mother tongue. It is primarily the upper class in non-English-speaking nations that have access to the extensive training required to learn the amount of English necessary for participation in global leadership in politics and economic affairs. The same thing would be true if Mandarin were to become the common global language as exemplified by the much publicized Princeton University's Princeton-in-Beijing Chinese language immersion program that has been operating since 1994. How many English speakers in the United States can afford or gain admission to this program at one of America's elite institutions or can afford travel and residency in Beijing?[25]

If culture is embedded in language, then consider the potential consequences of English as the global language. English as the global language might ensure the continued influence of Anglo-Saxon culture on global culture, including the spread of American consumerist culture. Also, the triumph of English as the global language might contain the message that English-speaking cultures are superior to non-English-speaking cultures. English as the global language might, therefore, complete England's colonialist project of spreading Anglo-Saxon culture and the fulfillment of America's manifest destiny to civilize the world. Of course, Huntington and others might be correct that Englishes and Spanishes may no longer reflect the culture of their imperialist origins.

Culture and language issues are highlighted by the debates about language policies in the United States. Today, large numbers of immigrants from Central America, South America, and the Dominican Republic have added to the already large number of U.S. Spanish speakers who became part of the population as a result of U.S. conquest of Mexican lands extending from Texas to California in the 19th century. Some Spanish speakers resist attempts by schools to erode their cultural and language traditions. However, it is important to recognize that Spanish, like English, is an imperialist language that was forced on Native Americans and Africans. However, within the context of Spanishes, the continued speaking of Spanish by immigrant groups symbolizes maintenance of their particular cultures. Therefore, although both Puerto Rican and Dominican immigrants to the United States speak Spanish, their cultures are quite distinct, and there is a certain amount of cultural friction between the two groups. The struggle to maintain the use of Spanish in the United States is an attempt to protect minority cultures. Still, the reality is that knowledge of English in the United States is important for gaining economic and political power. And it is possible that children raised in Spanish-speaking homes might be at an economic disadvantage in competing with children raised in English-speaking households. Also, Spanish-speaking immigrants might be at a disadvantage if they cannot afford the money and time for extensive language training.

Esperantists would respond to the American situation with the argument that all people should retain their mother tongues, including using these languages in school instruction, while being taught the universal language of Esperanto. This would ensure that a speaker of Spanish or English would not have an economic or political advantage. Cross-ethnic communications would be in Esperanto. The retention and maintenance of ethnic languages would help to preserve a variety of cultures. This is important from the perspective of Deep Ecology and its concern with preserving traditional cultures. In her famous book, *Linguistic Genocide in Education or Worldwide Diversity and Human Rights?*, Tove Skutnabb-Kangas compared the loss of languages to the loss of animal and plant species. Preservation of languages is important for preservation of culture which in turn is important for learning how societies are maintained and how sustainable development is possible. Skuttnabb-Kangas advocates that everyone become bilingual in the official language of their country and in their mother tongue.[26] Esperantists would consider bilingualism in one's mother tongue and Esperanto a more satisfactory solution because it would promote social equality and global unity.

The triumph of English, Mandarin, or some other natural language as a global language might do great harm to the cause of human rights, social equality, and economic justice. Even within the framework of Huntington's notion of intercultural communication, the triumph of one of these languages might ensure the global power of an international elite who have the time and money for extensive language studies. I believe that Esperantists might be correct that only a global language that is artificial and simple to learn will be able to overcome the power of language to be used as an instrument of political and economic domination in a global society.

RELIGION AND THE CLASH OF CIVILIZATIONS

As I am writing this book the world is embroiled in violent religious struggles between Christians, Moslems, Hindus, and Jews. The two major evangelical religions, Christianity and Islam, are locked in a struggle to win the hearts and minds of the world's peoples. As two exclusive religions, both Hinduism and Judaism are engaged in violent struggles with Islam. Between 1900 and 2000, the percentage of the world's people belonging to the Western Christian religion (as distinct from Eastern Orthodox Christianity) increased from 26.9 to 29.9. During the same period, the percentage of the world's people belonging to Islam increased from 12.4 to 19.2. In 2000, Hinduism was the world's third largest religion with the participation of 17.1% of the world's population. Huntington predicts that by 2025, Islam will be the world's largest religion with membership of 30% of the world's population.[27]

I agree with Huntington that these religious differences support differences in civilizational values. But do the differences in religious and civilizational values deter the evolution of a global civil society based on human rights and environmental ethics? Huntington's answer is yes! My answer is not necessarily. Let's consider Huntington's arguments on the clash of civilizations. He argues that there were three distinct periods in the world's organization in the 20th century. Around 1920, he argues, the world was divided by areas ruled by Western countries and those independent of Western rule. Western domination extended over Southern and Southeast Asia, Australia and New Zealand, North America, scattered areas through the Carribean and Central and South America, most of Africa, and, of course, Europe.[28]

This sweeping world empire convinced Westerners, Huntington argues, that a global civilization was possible. As colonial empires collapsed, non-Westerners rebelled against the idea of a global society because the notion appeared to be a justification for Western imperialism. In Huntingdon's words, "The non-Wests see as Western what the West sees as universal. What Westerners herald as benign global integration, such as the proliferation of worldwide media, non-Westerners denounce as nefarious Western imperialism. To the extent that non-Westerners see the World as one, they see it as a threat."[29]

After World War II, the Cold War divided the world between the so-called Free World, the Communist Bloc, and unaligned nations. The Cold War strengthened the role of nation-states in determining world events. In the 1990s, the end of the Cold War, along with the earlier demise of colonialism, set the stage for the world's peoples to celebrate their cultural, language, and religious diversity. As a result, he argues, the world is currently divided into eight conflicting civilizational groups. The following outline is my approximate compilation of maps and tables Huntington used to create these civilizational categories. Next to each civilizational category are the 1993 figures for the approximate territory occupied by each group and the estimated population. These eight civilizations occupy approximately 94.9% of the world's land mass, and, according to Huntington's figures, will encompass about 97% of the world's population by 2025.[30]

World's Eight Major Civilizations

1. Western (24.2% of the world's territory, encompassing a population of 805,400,000 in 1993)
   a. North America
   b. Europe
   c. Australia
   d. New Zealand
2. Latin American (14.9% of the world's territory, encompassing a population of 507,500,000 in 1993)
   a. Central and South America
   b. Caribbean
3. African (10.8% of the world's territory, encompassing a population of 392,100,000 in 1993)
   a. sub-Saharan Africa
4. Islamic (21.1% of the world's territory, encompassing a population of 927,600,000 in 1993)
   a. North Africa
   b. Arab Peninsula
   c. Middle East (from Turkey east to Pakistan and Bangladesh)

    d. Malaysia
    e. Indonesia
5. Sinic (7.5% of the world's territory, encompassing a population of
   1,340,900,000 in 1993)
    a. China
    b. Korea (North and South)
    c. Vietnam
6. Hindu (2.4% of the world's territory, encompassing a population of
   915,800,000 in 1993)
    a. India
7. Orthodox (13.7% of the world's territory, encompassing a population of 261,300,000 in 1993)
    a. Russia
    b. Georgia
    c. Bulgaria
    d. Serbia
    e. Lands extending east from Russia to the Pacific Ocean
8. Japanese (0.3% of the world's territory, encompassing a population
   of 124,700,000 in 1993) [31]

Huntington's vision is of a world divided by religious, cultural, and economic differences. Similar to others, he believes that the importance of the
nation-state will diminish. Civilizational linkages, Huntington contends,
will be of greater importance than the nation-state. Of striking importance
for the future is the declining influence of Western civilization and the increasing influence of Islamic and Sinic civilizations. For instance, he cites
figures that the percentage of the world's population under Western political control will decrease from 44.3% in 1900 to 10.1% in 2025. During the
same period, Islamic control over the world's population will increase from
4.2% to 19.2% and African control from 0.4% to 14.4% of the world's population. Huntington predicts that by 2025, the largest civilizations by percentage of the world's population will be Sinic (21.0%), Islamic (19.2%),
Hindu (16.9%), and African (14.4%).[32]

From Huntington's perspective, the clash between civilizations will determine the future history of the world. His prophetic book was published
in 1996. In the early 21st century, his analysis seemed right on target after
the destruction of the twin towers of the World Trade Center in the United
States and the U.S. invasion of Iraq. According to U.S. government officials,
a major reason for the invasion of Iraq was to create a model of a Western-style democracy, free trade economy, and a school system that would
influence the economic and political organization of other Islamic governments. These goals were originally advocated as early as 1997 with the establishment of the Project for the New American Century, whose founders

included the future Secretary of Defense Donald Rumsfeld and Assistant Secretary of Defense Paul Wolfowitz in the administration of President George W. Bush.[33]

After the 2003 invasion of Iraq, the U.S. government moved quickly to try an install in Iraq a U.S.-based educational program. The U.S. Agency for International Development contracted with the private educational firm Creative Associates International Inc. "to address immediate educational needs and promote participation of the Iraqi people in a sustainable, decentralized educational system. The U.S. government's goal is to ensure that children are prepared for the new school year beginning in September 2003."[34] By September 2003 there appeared to be little chance that the U.S. government could carry out this plan. One could argue that American leaders should have read Huntington to understand the fundamental differences in civilizational values between the West and Islam and the difficulty of overcoming these differences in religious and cultural values.

Huntington contends that world leaders should accept the idea of a multipolar and multicivilizational world. World peace will require learning to work within the framework of religious and cultural differences. For the West and the world, he offers the following advice, "The survival of the West depends on Americans reaffirming their Western identity and Westerners accepting their civilization *as unique not universal* and uniting to renew and preserve it against challenges from non-Western societies. Avoidance of global war of civilizations depends on world leaders *accepting and cooperating to maintain the multicivilizational character of global politics* [emphasis added]."[35]

The major flaw in Huntington's futuristic clash of civilizations is Michael Hardt and Antonio Negri's previously quoted observation that, "A specter haunts the world and it is the specter of migration."[36] It is possible that the sheer magnitude of the world's migration of peoples will overwhelm civilizational claims to particular areas of the world's territories. However, migration might increase multicivilizational conflicts within nation-states and undermine the cultural cohesion of these political organizations.

My concern is what Huntington's arguments mean for global educational ideologies. If Huntington is correct and global migration continues, then nation-states will increasingly have to grapple with the issue of multicultural education. Similar to Singapore, nation-states will have to develop educational programs that recognize civilizational differences in student populations. If these differences are not accommodated in educational programs, then there is the possibility of continuing educational conflicts over language, religion, and culture. Consequently, the idea of cultural unity as the backbone of patriotic education in the nation-state will change to an emphasis on unity through shared economic and political goals. In the future, love of country might be focused on what the country can provide economically. This could be happening in strong nation-states like the United States, where ethnic differences are being celebrated while the population is united in a belief that the U.S. economic system is the best in the world.

If Huntington is correct, then neoliberal dreams of a globe organized around free markets and economic individualism will give way to civilizational values. Islamic and Sinic civilizations have a long tradition of economic cooperation in contrast to the economic individualism of the West. Islamic education emphasizes the importance of community sharing of wealth. In Islamic schools, students read the collected sayings of Mohammed in the *Hadith*. The *Hadith* states,

> The *Qur'an* teaches that the poor and needy have a right to a share of other people's wealth.
> Avoid Hell by giving charity, even if it means sharing your last date, and, if you have nothing at all, by speaking a kind word.
> God will have no sympathy for the person who showed no sympathy for men.[37]

Confucianism, the educational foundation of Sinic civilization, also rejects the Western concept of economic individualism for belief in the shared responsibility of humans to protect each other. The interrelationship of self, community, and government is emphasized in the following famous passage from Confucius' *The Great Learning*:

> The ancients who wished to manifest their clear character to the world would first bring order to their states. Those who wished to bring order to their states would first regulate their families. Those who wished to regulate their families would first cultivate their personal lives. Those who wished to cultivate their personal lives would first rectify their minds. Those who wished to rectify their minds would first make their wills sincere. Those who wished to make their wills sincere would first extend their knowledge. The extension of knowledge consists in the investigation of things. When things are investigated, knowledge is extended; when knowledge is extended, the will becomes sincere; when the will is sincere, the mind is rectified; when the mind is rectified, the personal life is cultivated; when the personal life is cultivated, the family will be regulated; when the family is regulated, the state will be in order; and when the state is in order, there will be peace throughout the world. From the son of Heaven down to the common people, all must regard cultivation of the personal life as the root or foundation.[38]

Again, if Huntington is correct, the neoliberal goals of using schools to primarily train workers for free markets based on individual competition will not prevail around the globe. It is hard to imagine that schools under Islamic control would abandon the teachings of Islamic morality for a secular economic doctrine and that they would prepare students to participate in a Western consumer culture.

What about human rights and peace education in the context of clashes of civilization? This is a difficult question which I have already explored in two books.[39] I have proposed specific guidelines for the universal right to education that attempt to recognize and incorporate civilizational differences. However, it must be recognized that there are some serious incongruities within human rights doctrines that make it difficult for them to become standards of behavior in a global society. The major problem area are those human rights doctrines supporting freedom of speech and consciousness and those supporting freedom of religion and culture. Many religions and cultures do not believe in freedom of speech and consciousness, particularly regarding the education of children. In fact, most major religions want schooling to instill a belief in their religious doctrines and morality, and most cultures want to protect their traditions and languages. In this context, education becomes a form of indoctrination rather than a conscious effort to expose children to a wide variety of beliefs and moral standards so that they can make personal choices.

The issue of religion and freedom of thought is very difficult to resolve and, in fact, it may never be adequately resolved given the growing fervor of Christian, Hindu, and Islamic religions. My own preference is clearly stated in my book, *The Universal Right to Education*.

Liberty and Education Rights

The right of children to free access to information and freedom of thought is necessary for an education that provides an understanding of the advantages and disadvantages of the global economy and culture, and of human rights. Since human rights protect freedom of thought and access to information, then an education in human rights requires recognition of these principles. Currently, these principles are being violated by the national and state examinations that control the content of the curriculum and methods of instruction, and by human capital theories that define the major purpose of schooling as educating better workers to increase economic growth. Therefore the right to education includes:

> Universal liberty rights for children, such as freedom of expression; freedom to seek, receive and impart information and ideas; and freedom of thought.
> The universal right to an education that *does not* serve nationalistic or particular political ends by indoctrination, propaganda or the use of national examinations to control teacher and student learning.[40]

It is important to point out that all human rights doctrines support cultural and linguistic diversity. However, some cultural practices, such as female circumcision and abortion, are highly controversial. My approach is to suggest that they become topics for discussion regarding human rights. I suggested the following in my book, *The Universal Right to Education*.

Culture, Language, and Education Rights

A universal right to education requires recognition of cultural and language differences. Since human rights doctrines are now the major source of protection of minority and indigenous cultures and languages, the exercise of cultural rights must be in accordance with human rights. As I discussed earlier, education can serve as a vehicle for moral discourses about potential conflicts over cultural and human rights, such as abortion and female circumcision. The right to education includes the following cultural and language rights:

All people have a right to an education in their own language and in methods of teaching and learning appropriate to their own culture.

All people have the right to an education that teaches:

1. An understanding of their own culture and their relation to it
2. Their mother tongue
3. The dominant or official language of the nation
4. An understanding of the effect of the world culture and economy on their own culture and economy[41]

In order to achieve some compromise over a secular versus religious education, which is a key element in clashes between Christianity, Hinduism, and Islam, I have proposed the right to a religious education for all students. As stated in *Globalization and Educational Rights*, my proposal is that for every child, "the duty and right to an education includes the right to a secular or religious education financed by the government. *No student will be forced to receive a religious education*."[42]

I realize that this proposal really hedges the issue of intellectual freedom. Most religious education does not practice freedom of ideas. However, as I have worded this statement, students are simply exercising their intellectual freedom by choosing a religious education. Given the global religious clashes, I think this compromise is warranted.

Therefore, I do believe that with minimum compromises and adjustments, human rights education can be adapted to a multicivilizational world and serve to establish a standard of ethical behavior among the world's peoples that includes respect for religious, cultural, and linguistic differences.

CONCLUSION: ENVIRONMENTALISM AS THE CRITICAL GLOBAL EDUCATIONAL IDEOLOGY

I am convinced that environmental education can create global standards for interacting with the biosphere. As I discussed, all major world religions incorporate deep spiritual ties to nature and, according to Deep Ecology, most humans receive meaning and satisfaction from interacting with nature. The destruction of air, water, and animal and plant species seriously detracts from the quality of life for all people, and it violates the norms for most religions and cultures. The human attachment to preservation of the biosphere for both survival and quality of life might be the ethic that will bind the world together. This makes environmental education the central order of business for global schooling. In *The Universal Right to Education*, I suggested the adoption of the following human right:

Environmental Destruction and the Right to Education

Since the right to life is the most fundamental right, protecting the planet from environmental destruction provides another justification for the right to education. The following provides a summary of the relationship between the right to education and environmental education.

1. Environmental destruction threatens the basic human right of the right to life
2. The right to education, which includes environmental education, might safeguard the planet
3. The preservation and growth of the wholistic knowledge of nature of indigenous peoples could be a safeguard against planetary devastation
4. In order to protect the earth, indigenous peoples' education should include their cultural and scientific traditions and should be according to their cultural practices with instruction in their mother tongues and the official or dominant languages of their nations
5. Therefore, the right to education, which includes environmental education and respect for the wholistic knowledge of indigenous peoples, is necessary for protection of the basic human right of right to life[43]

Like many environmentalists, I believe that the quality of my life is dependent on the quality of the environment and that this is a global issue that can only be solved through the active citizenship in a global civil society. I accept the arguments of Deep Ecology and affirm the pleasure I have in smelling fresh air, seeing and swimming in clean water, hiking through forests and countrysides filled with many plant and animal species, and listening to and watching the beauty of birds and insects. I also believe that we need to shift from an industrial to a biosphere paradigm, which prizes the quality of human life over economic growth and consumption. I believe that part of the paradigm shift includes educating people to have an ethical responsibility to protect the rights of others and to protect the biosphere. I believe that the nation-state has outlived its usefulness and that democracy has become a sham with the real political power being in the hands of mass media owned by multinational corporations. Solving the Earth's ecological, social, and economic problems requires a problem-solving and activist education for global citizenship and a disbanding of educational systems that discipline students through government testing, promote patriotism to the nation-state, and instill an industrial and consumerist paradigm.

Despite my personal preferences, there are multiple forces at work in shaping the future of global school systems. First, multinational corporations will continue to want schools to educate workers and to implant an ideology supportive of economic growth. Second, NGOs will force corpor- ations to make some compromises regarding working conditions and the environment. A corporate green policy, as highlighted by my discussion of the Fairmont Hotel chain, will probably spill over into the schools. But it does not seem likely that this corporate green policy will include a desire to shift the curriculum from an industrial to a biosphere curriculum. Nation-states will probably continue struggling to maintain their power but will eventually have to succumb to the power of the global economy and civil society by reducing their emphasis on nationalistic forms of education. National testing programs that exist to control the curriculum and discipline students will continue to be a focus of controversy. As I mentioned, Singapore's educational leaders are now worrying that the discipline of the test is stifling the initiative and creativity required for economic growth. Probably increasing numbers of people will recognize the damage the nation-state and corporate media have done to the idea of democracy. Using school systems, the nation-state has attempted to control the minds of citizens and reduce freedom of thought. Using media, corporations have served their own interests by trying to manipulate the public mind and actions at the voting booth.

The global civil society with its web of NGOs will probably continue to grow and extend its influence over school systems and act as a countervailing force to multinational corporations. Even organizations such as the World Bank recognize the importance of the global civil society and are trying to harness its energies to serve its needs. However, the process is a two-way road. The World Bank's work with human rights and environmental groups is resulting in development plans that reflect the pressures of these organizations. There seems to be a major support among government and NGOs for sustainable development with its broad concern for human rights and environmental protections. The major block to these ideas entering school curricula is corporate power. I cannot predict the outcome of all these forces affecting global educational policy, but I do hope that the result is a happier world.

Notes

PREFACE

1. Michael Hardt and Antonio Negri, *Empire* (Cambridge: Harvard University Press, 2000), p. 213.

CHAPTER 1

1. Bassam Tibi, *Arab Nationalism: Between Islam and the Nation-state* (New York: St. Martin's Press, 1997), p. 148.
2. Ibid., p. 148.
3. "Syria-Constitution," *http://www.oefre.unibe.ch/law/icl/sy00000_.html.*
4. *The Emile of Jean Jacques Rousseau: Selections* translated and edited by William Boyd (New York: Teachers College Press, 1956), p. 189.
5. Jean Jacques Rousseau, *Emile* translated by Barbara Foxley (London: Everyman, 1993), p. 508.
6. Ibid., pp. 509–510.
7. Ibid., p. 525.
8. *The Emile of Jean Jacques Rousseau ...*, p. 184.
9. Ibid., p. 191.
10. Ibid., p. 185.
11. Ibid., p. 184.
12. Ibid., p. 191.
13. George Mosse, *The Nationalization of the Masses: Political Symbolism and Mass Movements in Germany from the Napoleonic Wars through the Third Reich* (New York: New American Library, 1975), p. 2.
14. Ibid., p. 2.
15. "Imperial Rescript: The Great Principles of Education, 1879," in Herbert Passim, *Society and Education in Japan* (New York: Teachers College Press, 1965), p. 227.
16. Teruhisa Horio, *Educational Thought and Ideology in Modern Japan: State Authority and Intellectual Freedom* edited and translated by Steven Platzer (Tokyo: University of Tokyo Press, 1988), p. 68.
17. Ibid., p. 68.

18. A. S. Makarenko, *A Book for Parents* (Amsterdam: Fredonia Books, 2002), p. 22.

19. Anna Quindlen, "Indivisible? Wanna Bet?" *Newsweek* (15 July 2002), p. 64. Also see Rhea Borja, "Pledge of Allegiance in the Legal Spotlight," *Education Week* (10 July 2002).

20. Ibid.

21. "Scalia Attacks Church-State Court Rulings," *The New York Times* (13 January 2003), p. 19.

22. "State of the Union Address," *New York Times on the Web, http://www.nytimes.com* (29 January 2003).

23. Ibid.

24. Michael Hardt and Antonio Negri, *Empire* (Cambridge: Harvard University Press, 2000), p. 213.

25. Joel Spring, *Education and the Rise of the Global Economy* (Mahwah, New Jersey: Lawrence Erlbaum Associates, 1998).

26. Jon Woronoff, *Asia's 'Miracle' Economies, Second Edition* (Armonk, New York: M.E. Sharpe Inc.), pp. 121–142.

27. Ministry of Education, "The Singapore Education Service: Our Mission Molding the Future of Our Nation," *http://www.moe.edu.sg*, p. 1.

28. Teo Chee Hean, "Addenda to President's Address at Opening of Parliament, 27 May 1997, Ministry of Education," *http://www.moe.edu.sg*, p. 1.

29. "Speech by Bg Lee Hsien Loong, Deputy Prime Minister at the Launch of National Education on Saturday 17 May 1997 at TCS TV Theater at 9:30 AM," *Ministry of Education, Singapore, http://www.moe.edu.sg*, p. 1.

30. Ibid., p. 3.

31. Ibid., p. 8.

32. "Key Indicators of the Resident Population," *http://www.singstat.gov.sg/keystats/people.html#demo*.

33. Singapore's Constitution can be found at *http://www.oefre.unibe.ch/law/icl/sn00000_.html*.

34. Ibid.

35. Ibid.

36. Ministry of Education, "The Education System in Singapore—Primary Education: An Information Guide for Parents," *http://www.moe.edu.sg*, p. 5.

37. "Activity: Away from Home," *http:www1.moe.edu.sg/etv/webbit/counry/activity.htm*.

38. Ibid.

39. Mosse, p. 8.

40. "Activity: Made in Singapore!" *http:www1.moe.edu.sg/etv/webbit/country/activity.htm*.

41. Ibid.

42. Ibid.

43. "Activity: I can make a difference!," *http:www1.moe.edu.sg/etv/webbit/country/activity.htm*.

44. Ibid.

45. Ministry of Education Singapore, "Desired Outcomes of Education," *http://www1.moe.edu.sg/desired.htm*.

46. Ibid.

47. Ibid.

48. NEXUS (formerly Central National Education Office), *Engaging Hearts & Minds* (Singapore: NEXUS, 2003), p. 6.

49. Ibid., p. 13.
50. Ibid., p. 13.
51. Ibid., p. 16.
52. Ibid., p. 30.
53. Ibid., p. 31.
54. Ibid., p. 24.
55. Chua Lee Hoong, "This National Day, celebrate the joy of work," *The Straits Times Interactive* (10 July 2002), *http://straitstimes.asia1.com.sg/columnist/0, 1886,16-131034,00.html.*
56. Ibid.
57. Ibid.
58. "Speech by Bg Lee Hsien Loong, Deputy Prime Minister at the Launch of National Education on Saturday 17 May 1997 at TCS TV Theater at 9:30 AM," *Ministry of Education, Singapore, http://www.moe.edu.sg.*
59. Ministry of Education, "The Singapore Education Service: Our Mission Molding the Future of Our Nation," *http://www.moe.edu.sg,* p. 2.
60. Ibid., p. 8.
61. Quoted in Ibid., p. 98.
62. I had a series of conversations with Allan Luke about his work in Singapore in 2002 and 2003.
63. "Speech By Mr. Lim Swee Say, Minister for the Environment, at Biopolis Topping Out Ceremony, 15 January 2003, 1 PM, Biopolis Event Site," *http://app.sprinter.gov.sg/data/pr/2003011501.htm.*
64. "English Text of Prime Minister's National Day Rally 2002 Speech in Chinese, Sunday, 18 August 2002," *http://www.gov.sg/singov/announce/ 180802pm2.htm.*
65. Ibid.
66. Ibid.
67. "Indians feel left out in PM's National Day Rally speech, Tuesday, August 27, 2002," *http://app.internet.gov.sg/data/mcds/mcdsfeedback/media/media186.htm.*
68. Ibid.
69. Ibid.
70. Ibid.
71. "Learn Chinese for culture or for economics?, Wednesday, August 28, 2002," *http://app.internet.gov.sg/data/mcds/mcdsfeedback/media/media189.htm.*
72. Ibid.
73. Ibid.
74. Ministry of Education, "National Heritage Tours for Schools," *http://www1.moe.edu.sg/nht.*
75. Ibid.
76. Ibid.
77. Descriptions of these ethnic conservation areas are taken from the Singapore Web site *http://www.ura.gov.sg/conservation/glam.htm.*
78. Ministry of Education, "National Heritage Tours ...."
79. Ibid.
80. "Museum Planning Report, 1997," *http://www.ura.gov.sg/dgp_reorts/museum/ int-hist.html.*

81. "MUSEUM PLANNING AREA—AN INSTITUTIONAL HUB 13 MARCH 1997," *http://www.ura.gov.sg/pr/text/pr97-17.html*.
82. Ibid.
83. Ministry of Education, "National Heritage Tours ...."
84. Ibid.

CHAPTER 2

1. The World Bank, *Education and Development*, (Washington, DC: The World Bank, 2002), p. 2.
2. John Boli and George M. Thomas, "INGOs and the Organization of World Culture," in *Constructing World Culture: International Nongovernmental Organizations Since 1875* edited by John Boli and George M. Thomas (Stanford: Stanford University Press, 1999), p. 14.
3. The United Nations Web site is *www.cyberschoolbus.un.org*.
4. "The African Virtual University and Growth in Africa: A Knowledge and Learning Challenge," *Findings* (February 2003): *http://www.worldbank.org/afr/findings*, p. 1.
5. "Early Child Development: The First Step to Education for All," *http://www.worldbank.org*.
6. *World Bank Education: Education Sector Strategy* (Washington, DC: The International Bank for Reconstruction and Development/ The World Bank, 1999), p. vii.
7. On the Educational for All conference and initiative, see Joel Spring, *Education and the Rise of the Global Economy* (Mahwah, New Jersey: Lawrence Erlbaum Associates, 1998), pp. 190–201.
8. Ibid., pp. 159–178.
9. Akira Iriye, *Global Community: The Role of International Organizations in the Making of the Contemporary World* (Berkeley: University of California Press, 2002).
10. "Overview of World Bank Collaboration with Civil Society," *http://wbln0018.worldbank.org/essd/essd.nsf/NGOs/home*.
11. "The World Bank and Civil Society," *http://wbln0018.Worldbank.org/essd/essd.nsf/NGOs/home*.
12. Kumi Naidoo, "Civil Society, Governance and Globalization: World Bank Presidential Fellow Lecture," *http://lnweb18.worldbank.org/essd/essd.nsf/All/943999D14D69CEB585256CC900838324?OpenDocument*.
13. Richard Holloway, *Using the Civil Society Index: Assessing the Health of Civil Society* (Canada: Civicus, 2001), p. 2.
14. "About Us," *http://www.civicus.org/cc/portal/index2.cfm?Navigation_ID=168&NavLevel=1&contentid=111&link_url=*.
15. Kumi Naidoo, p. 5.
16. "Public Advocacy: A Cornerstone of Democratic Society," *Civicus World: Newsletter of CIVICUS: World Alliance for Citizen Participation* (May–June 1998), p. 1.
17. Michael Hardt and Antonio Negri, *Empire* (Cambridge: Harvard University Press, 2000), pp. 102–103.

18. Iriye, p. 3.
19. Ibid., p. 14.
20. Boli and Thomas, p. 23.
21. Margaret E. Keck and Kathryn Sikkink, *Activists Beyond Borders* (Ithaca: Cornell University Press, 1998), p. 11.
22. Ibid., p. 33.
23. Ibid., p. 35.
24. Ibid., p. 36.
25. John Boli, Thomas A. Loya, and Teresa Loftin, "National Participation in World-Polity Organization," *Constructing World Culture* ..., p. 53.
26. Ibid., p. 56.
27. Ibid., pp. 74–75.
28. Lynton Keith Caldwell, *International Environmental Policy: From the Twentieth to the Twenty-First Century, Third Edition* (Durham: Duke University Press, 1996), p. 15.
29. Kevin Danaher, ed., *Democratizing the Global Economy: The Battle Against the World Bank and the International Monetary Fund* (Monroe, Maine: Common Courage Press, 2001), p. 8.
30. Ibid., p. 10.
31. Ibid., p. 11.
32. Network Platform & Demands to the IMF and World Bank, *http://www.50years.org/about/*.
33. Danaher, p. 11.
34. "House Vote Opposes IMF & World Bank on 'User Fees' for Education and Health in Poorest Countries," *http://www.50years.org/update/userfees.html*.
35. "Greenpeace: About Us," *http://www.greenpeace.org/aboutus/*.
36. Iriye, p. 161.
37. "World Bank," *http://archives.greenpeace.org/search.shtml*.
38. Ibid.
39. Ibid.
40. The World Bank Group, "Best Practices in Dealing with the Social Impacts of Hydrocarbon Operations: Governance and Human Rights: Key Reference Documents," *http://www.worldbank.org/html/fpd/enrgy/oil&gas/Bestpractices/3/33.html*.
41. *Development and Human Rights: The Role of the World Bank* (Washington, DC: The International Bank for Reconstruction and Development/The World Bank, 1998), p. vii.
42. Ibid., p. 3.
43. Ibid., p. 29.
44. Ibid., p. 29.
45. Iriye, 15.
46. Ibid., p. 34.
47. Spring, *Education and the Rise* ..., pp. 51–54.
48. Teruhisa Horio, *Educational Thought and Ideology in Modern Japan: State Authority and Intellectual Freedom* (Tokyo: University of Tokyo Press, 1988) edited and translated by Steven Platzer, p. 147.
49. Akira, p. 52.

50. "Oxfam International's Mission Statement," *http://www.oxfam.org/eng/about_strat_mission.htm*.

51. Towards Global Equity, Oxfam International's Strategic Plan for 2001–2004, *http://www.oxfam.org/eng/about_strat.htm*.

52. "About Us," *http://www.oxfam.org/eng/about.htm*.

53. Oxfam International News Release, "Oxfam International's call to World Bank's James Wolfensohn: 'Breathe new life into poor country debt plan', (17 April 1997)," *http://www.oxfam.org.uk/whatnew/press/prdawn.htm*.

54. The World Bank Group DevNews Center, "World Bank, Oxfam Push for Education Aid (13 June 2002)," *http://web.worldbank.org/WBSITE/EXTERAL/NEWS/0,,date:06-13-2002~menuPK:34461~pagePK:34392~piPK:34427,00.html*.

55. The World Bank Group and International Monetary Fund 2002 Annual Meetings, *http://lnweb18.worldbank.org/essd/essd.nsf/All/A808F4C3DFCD285885256C47005A9B01?OpenDocument*.

56. Jennifer Wilder, "The Power of Reading," *Oxfam Exchange* (Winter 2003), p. 11.

57. Staff of the World Bank, *Education: The World Bank Education Sector Strategy* (Washington, DC: The International Bank for Reconstruction/The World Bank, 1999).

58. Ibid., p. iii.

59. For a review of the influence of women's organizations on the World Bank, see the chapter on "The World Bank and Women's Movements" in Robert O'Brien, Anne Marie Goetz, Jan Aart Scholte, and Marc Williams, *Contesting Global Governance: Multilateral Economic Institutions and Global Social Movements* (Cambridge: Cambridge University Press, 2000), pp. 24–66.

60. "World Bank Partnerships on Gender Issues," *http://www.worldbank.org/gender/partnerships/index.htm*.

61. Karen Mason, et al., *Integrating Gender into the World Bank's Work: A Strategy for Action* (Washington, DC: The World Bank, 2002), p. xi.

62. Ibid. p. 2.

63. "Bangladesh: Educating Girls," *http://web.worldbank.org/WBSITE/EXERNAL/NEWS/0,,contentMDK:20052243~menuPK:67443~pagePK:36694~piPK:36693~theSitePK:4607,00.html*.

64. Karen Mason, et al., p. 1.

65. Ibid., p. 1.

66. Ibid., p. 4.

67. Ibid., p. 14.

68. Ibid., p. 5.

69. Ibid., p. 6.

70. Ibid., p. 9.

71. Ibid., p. 1.

72. See John Dewey, "School and Society," in *Dewey on Education* edited by Martin Dworkin (New York: Teachers College Press, 1959).

73. *Education: The World Bank Education Sector ...*, p. 1.

74. Ibid., p. 1.

75. Ibid., p. 2.

76. Ibid., p. 3.

77. Ibid., p. 6.
78. Ibid., p. 6.
79. Ibid., p. 8.
80. Ibid., p. 13.
81. Ibid., p. 15.
82. "OECD, Member Countries," *http://www.oecd.org/oecd/pages/home/ displaygeneral/0,3380,EN-countrylist-0-nodirectorate-no-no-159-0,00.html.*
83. *Education: The World Bank Education Sector* ..., p. 15.
84. "Commonwealth of Independent States," *http://www.cis.minsk.by/english/ invest1_engl/engl_hdr.htm.*
85. *Education: The World Bank Education Sector* ..., p. 15.
86. Ibid., p. 47.
87. Ibid., p. 72.
88. I have the permission of Amallia Orman to discuss her *Drawing Botswana: Development, Economics, and Education* (New York: Lang College, 2002).
89. "Summary of Regional Strategies: Bank-Supported Objectives," *Education: The World Bank Education Sector* ..., p. 73.
90. "Summary of Regional Strategies: Bank Means," *Education: The World Bank Education Sector* ..., p. 73.
91. Adriaan Verspoor, et al., *A Chance to Learn: Knowledge and Finance for Education in Sub-Saharan Africa* (Washington, DC: The International Bank for Reconstruction and Development/The World Bank, 2001), p. 21.
92. Ibid., p. 22.
93. Ibid., p. 21.
94. Ibid., pp. 22–23.
95. Ibid., p. 24.
96. Ibid., p. 23.
97. Ibid., p. 24.
98. Ibid., p. 25.
99. "Indigenous Knowledge Program: Goals," *httpwww.worldbank.org/afr/ik/ index.htm.*
100. "Indigenous Knowledge: Achievement as of December 2002," *http:// www.worldbank.org/afr/ik/achieve.htm.*
101. "Indigenous Knowledge Program for Development: Knowledge Pack Education," *http://www.worldbank.org/afr/ik/ikpacks/education.htm.*, p. 2.
102. Ibid., p. 3.
103. Ibid., p. 5.
104. LCSHD Education Team, *Educational Change in Latin America and the Caribbean: A World Bank Strategy Paper* (Washington DC: The World Bank, 2001), p. 41.
105. Laurence Wolff, Ernesto Schiefelbein, and Paulina Schiefelbein, *Primary Education in Latin America: The Unfinished Agenda* (Washington, DC: Inter-Development Bank, 2002), p. 12.
106. See Table 7 in *Educational Change in Latin America and the Caribbean* ..., p. 12.
107. Wolff, Schiefelbein, and Schiefelbein, p. 11.
108. Ibid., p. 11.
109. Robert C. Johnson, "A Revolutionary Education," *Education Week* (5 March 2003), p. 40.

110. *Educational Change in Latin America and the Caribbean* ..., p. 16.
111. U.S. Bureau of the Census, " Money Income in the United States: 2000," (Washington, DC: U.S. Printing Office, September 2001), p. 21.
112. Ibid., p. 15.
113. Ibid., p. 16.
114. See chapters 2 and 3 in Joel Spring, *American Education, Eleventh Edition* (New York: McGraw-Hill, 2004).
115. Ibid., p. 16.
116. Kin Bing Wu, et al., *Peruvian Education at a Crossroads: Challenges and Opportunities for the 21st Century* (Washington, DC: The World Bank, 2001), p. xi.
117. "STRATEGY TO INCLUDE INDIGENOUS COMMUNITIES IN THE RURAL EDUCATION PROJECT PERU: Rural Education and Teacher Development Project, May 2002," *Http://www-wds.Worldbank.Org/servlet/WDS_IBank_Servlet?pcont=details &eid=000094946_02061304435133*, p. 2.
118. Kin Bing Wu, et al., *Peruvian Education at a Crossroads* ..., p. 30.
119. Ibid., p. 61.
120. Ibid., p. 64.
121. See Joel Spring, *Deculturalization and the Struggle for Equality: A Brief History of the Education of Dominated Cultures in the United States, Third Edition* (New York: McGraw-Hill, 2001), pp. 17–35.
122. Kin Bing Wu, et al., *Peruvian Education at a Crossroads* ..., p. 64.
123. Ibid., p. 31.
124. "STRATEGY TO INCLUDE INDIGENOUS COMMUNITIES IN THE RURAL EDUCATION PROJECT PERU ..., p. 1.
125. Ibid., p. 1.
126. *Educational Change in Latin America and the Caribbean* ..., p. 18.
127. Ibid., p. 18.
128. Document of The World Bank, Report No: 24558, *PROJECT APPRAISAL DOCUMENT ON A PROPOSED LOAN IN THE AMOUNT OF US$42.0 MILLION TO THE DOMINICAN REPUBLIC FOR AN EARLY CHILDHOOD EDUCATION PROJECT* (Washington, DC: World Bank, July 31, 2002), p. 3.
129. Ibid., p. 2.
130. Education Sector Unit: East Asia and Pacific Region, *Education and Training in the East Pacific Region* (Washington, DC: World Bank, 1998), p. 12.
131. "Education in Indonesia: Impact of the Crisis," *http://www.worldbank.org/eapsocial/countries/indon/educ2.htm*.
132. Ibid.
133. "Education in the Philippines," *http://www.worldbank.org/eapsocial/countries/phil/educ1.htm*.
134. See "The African Virtual University ..." and the University's Web site *http://www.avu.org/*.
135. "The African Virtual University ...," p. 1.
136. Ibid., p. 2.
137. Ibid., p. 2.
138. Ibid., p. 2.
139. "Academic Programs," *http://www.avu.org/section/schedule/*.
140. "The African Virtual University ...," p. 3.

141. "EdInvest News-March 2003," *http://www.worldbank.org/edinvest*, p. 1.
142. Ibid., p. 1.
143. Ibid., p. 2.

CHAPTER 3

1. Joseph Wronka of Springfield College, USA, "Re: Culture of human," *From Global HRE List Moderators, hrelistmoderator@hrea.org, Date: Thur, 06 Mar 2003, To: hr-education@hrea.org*. The discussion of human rights culture took place between human rights educators in January and February of 2003 on the Listserv *hr-education@hrea.org*.
2. Margaret E. Keck and Kathryn Sikkink, *Activists Beyond Borders: Advocacy Networks in International Politics* (Ithaca: Cornell University Press, 1998), p. 11.
3. See Joel Spring, *The Universal Right to Education: Justification, Definition, and Guidelines* (Mahwah, New Jersey: Lawrence Erlbaum Associates, 2000) and *Globalization and Educational Rights* (Mahwah, New Jersey: Lawrence Erlbaum Associates, 2001).
4. "Report of the United Nations High Commissioner for Human Rights on the implementation of the Plan of Action for the United Nations Decade for Human Rights Education," *http://193.194.138.190/huridocda/huridoca.nsf/ (Symbol)/A.51.506.Add.1.En?OpenDocument*.
5. Ibid.
6. "About HREA," *http://www.hrea.org/abouthrea.html*.
7. Olive Moore, Youth for Human Rights, Ireland, "Re: Culture of human ...."
8. Ibid.
9. Maria Teresa Gutierrez of Argentina, "Re: Culture of human ...."
10. Greta Hoffman Nemiroof of Sisterhood is Global Institute, "Re: Culture of human ...."
11. Donna Habsha of the University of Windsor, Canada, "Re: Culture of human ...."
12. Bernie Weintraub of the Facing History and Ourselves, USA, "Re: Culture of human ...."
13. Ibid.X
14. Ibid.
15. Shulamith Koenig of the People's Movement for Human Rights Education, "Re: Culture of human ...."
16. Anna Pinto, Center for Organization, Research and Education, New Delhi, India, "Re: Culture of human ...."
17. Mike Pates of the American Bar Association, "Re: Culture of human ...."
18. I analyze the debate over the "universality" of the Universal Declaration of Human Rights in Spring, *The Universal Right to Education* ....
19. Canadian Human Rights Foundation, *Module: Building a Global Culture of Human Rights* (Montreal: Canadian Human Rights Foundation, 2002), p. 26.
20. Ibid., pp. 26–30.
21. Cristina Sganga, Amnesty International-Netherlands and Board member of the Human Rights Education Associates, "Re: Culture of human ...."
22. Ed O'Brien of Street Law, Inc., "Re: Culture of human ...."

23. Olive Moore of Youth for Human Rights, Ireland, "Re: Culture of human ...."

24. Gauri Bhopatkar of the Center for Empowerment, Pune, India, "Re: Culture of human ...."

25. Canadian Human Rights Foundation, *Module: Seeking Common Ground* (Montreal: Canadian Human Rights Foundation, 2002), p. 6.

26. Ibid., p. 15.

27. Ibid., p. 16.

28. Ibid., p. 16.

29. Ibid., p. 17.

30. Ibid., p. 20.

31. Horace Mann, "Twelfth Annual Report (1848)" in *The Republic and the School: Horace Mann on the Education of Free Men* edited by Lawrence Cremin (New York: Teachers College Press, 1957), p. 98.

32. Ibid., pp. 100–101.

33. Canadian Human Rights Foundation, *Module: The Global Human Rights Context* (Montreal: Canadian Human Rights Foundation, 2002), p. 10.

34. Ibid., p. 14.

35. Ibid., p. 16.

36. Ibid., p. 19.

37. Ibid., p. 23.

38. Ibid., p. 22.

39. Ibid., p. 25.

40. Keck and Sikkink, pp. 88–92.

41. For a review of Amnesty International's human rights education programs, see *http://www.amnesty-volunteer.org/usa/education/hrebro.html.*

42. *Human Rights Here & Now: Celebrating the Universal Declaration of Human Rights* (Minneapolis: Human Rights Educators' Network, Amnesty International USA, Human Rights Resource Center, 1998). The copy of the book I used is available online at *http://www.hrusa.org/hrh-and-n/* and it has unnumbered pages.

43. Fateh Assam, Program Officer for Human Rights, The Ford Foundation Office for the Middle East and North Africa, Cairo, Egypt, "Re: Culture of Human Rights," *hr-educaton@hrea.org* (29 January 2003).

44. *Human Rights Here & Now* ..., unnumbered pages.

45. Ibid.

46. Ibid.

47. Betty Reardon, *Educating for Human Dignity: Learning About Rights and Responsibilities: A K-12 Teaching Resource* (Philadelphia: University of Pennsylvania Press, 1995).

48. Ibid., pp. 189–191.

49. Ibid., p. 192.

50. Ibid., p. 192.

51. Ibid., p. 193.

52. Ibid., p. 194.

53. Ibid., p. 191.

54. Ibid., p. 191.

55. Ibid.

56. Ibid.
57. Ibid.
58. "Executive Order No. 27, Education to Maximize Respect for Human Rights," in Richard Pierre, *Educating for Human Rights: The Philippines and Beyond* (Quezon City, Philippines: University of the Philippines Press, 1996), p. 232.
59. "Memorandum Order No. 20 Education of Arresting and Investigating Personnel on Human Rights," in Ibid., p. 230.
60. "Article III (Bill of Rights) of the 1987 Philippine Constitution," in Ibid., pp. 228–229.
61. Ibid., p. 22.
62. "Human Rights Education Curriculum for the Police/Military," in Pierre, p. 245.
63. Ibid., p. 244.
64. Ibid., p. 248.
65. Ibid., pp 256–257.
66. Ibid., pp. 257–258.
67. For a discussion of the arguments leading up to the 1948 Declaration of Human Rights, see Keck and Sikkink, pp. 79–89, and Spring, *The Universal Right to Education* ..., pp. 1–18.
68. See *http://www.un.org/cyberschoolbus/qui.html*.
69. "What is this Project About?," *http://www.un.org/cyberschoolbus/humanrights/about/about.asp*.
70. Ibid.
71. Ibid.
72. "The Universal Declaration of Human Rights 1948" in *Basic Documents on Human Rights, Third Edition* edited by Ian Brownlie (Oxford: Clarendon Press, 1992), p. 23.
73. "Universal Declaration of Human Rights Plain Language Version," *http://www.un.org/cyberschoolbus/humanrights/resources/plain.asp*.
74. "The Interactive Declaration," *http://www.un.org/cyberschoolbus/humanrights/declaration/index.asp*.
75. "Human Rights in Action Part 1: Submission Form," *http://www.Un.org/cyberschoolbus/humanrights/activities/form1.asp*.
76. Ibid.
77. Ibid.
78. "Human Rights in Action Part 2: Submission Form," *http://www.un.org/cyberschoolbus/humanrights/activities/form2.asp*.
79. Ibid.
80. "Human Rights Questions and Answers," *http://www.un.org/cyberschoolbus/humanrights/qna/cynthia.asp*.
81. "Human Rights Questions and Answers," *http://www.un.org/cyberschoolbus/humanrights/qna/alston.asp*.
82. "Human Rights Questions and Answers," *http://www.un.org/cyberschoolbus/humanrights/qna/elsa.asp*.
83. Betty Reardon, *Comprehensive Peace Education: Educating for Global Responsibility* (New York: Teachers College Press, 1988), pp. 1–5.
84. Ibid., p. 3.

85. Quote in Ibid., p. 4.
86. "Purpose," *http://www.human.mie-u.ac.jp/~peace/Purpose.htm*.
87. Reardon, *Comprehensive Peace Education* ..., pp. 5–9.
88. Ibid., p. 46.
89. "About Us," *http://www.upeace.org/aboutus/mission.htm*.
90. Report of the United Nations High Commissioner for Human Rights on the Implementation of the Plan of Action ....
91. Betty Reardon, "Human Rights as Education for Peace," in *Human Rights Education for the Twenty-First Century* edited by George J. Andreopoulos and Richard Pierre Claude (Philadelphia: University of Pennsylvania Press, 1997), p. 22.
92. Ibid., p. 33.
93. "Peace Education," *http://www.un.org/cyberschoolbus/peace/content.htm*.
94. "Peace Education: Unit Three Critical Thinking and Active Non-Violence," *http:www.un.org/cyberschoolbus/peace/content3_1.htm*.
95. "Peace Education," *http:* ....
96. Ibid.
97. Ibid.
98. Ibid.
99. Ibid.
100. Ibid.
101. "Peace Education: Unit One Ecological Thinking and Respect for Life," *http:www.un.org/cyberschoolbus/peace/content3_1.htm*.
102. Ibid.
103. "Peace Education: Unit Two Tolerance and Respect for Dignity and Identity," *http:www.un.org/cyberschoolbus/peace/content3_1.htm*.
104. Ibid.
105. Ibid.
106. "Peace Education: Unit Three Critical Thinking ...."
107. Reardon, pp. 33–35.
108. Ibid., p. 34.
109. Ibid., p. 35.
110. "Peace Education: Unit Three Critical Thinking ...."
111. Ibid.
112. See Joel Spring, *The Universal Right to Education* ... and *Globalization and Educational Rights* ....
113. "SINGAPORE: Norishyam Mohamed Ali and Shaiful Edham Adam," *http://www.amnestyusa.org/urgent/nl0999.html*.

CHAPTER 4

1. For examples of writers who recognize the radicalism inherent in environmental education, see David Orr, *Earth in Mind: On Education, Environment, and the Human Prospect* (Washington, DC: Island Press, 1994); C. A. Bowers, *Education for Eco-Justice and Community* (Athens: University of Georgia Press, 2001); and Joy A. Palmer's historical overview of the movement in his *Environmental Education in the 21st Century: Theory, Practice, and Progress* (London: Routledge, 1998), pp. 3–82.

2. North American Association for Environmental Education, "Environmental Education Materials: Guidelines for Excellence," *http://naaee.org/npeee/ materials_guidelines/intro.html*.

3. Margaret E. Keck and Kathryn Sikkink, *Activists Beyond Borders: Advocacy Networks in International Politics* (Ithaca: Cornell University Press, 1998), pp. 10–11.

4. Lynton Keith Caldwell, *International Environmental Policy From the Twentieth to the Twenty-First Century, Third Edition* (Durham, North Carolina: Duke University Press, 1996), pp. 24–25.

5. Jacques Grinevald, "Introduction" to Vladimir I. Vernadsky's *The Biosphere* (New York: Copernicus, Springer-Verlag, 1997), p. 24.

6. Ibid., p. 31.

7. Vernadsky, p. 30.

8. Freeman Dyson, "What a World!," *The New York Review of Books* (15 May 2003), p. 4.

9. Vernadsky, p. 40.

10. As quoted in Caldwell, p. 26.

11. Ibid., p. 26.

12. Ibid., p. 26.

13. Quoted in Palmer, p. 5.

14. Ibid., p. 6.

15. Ibid., p. 7.

16. Caldwell, p. 48.

17. Second World Conservation Strategy Project, *Caring for the Earth: A Strategy for Sustainable Living* (Gland, Switzerland: The World Conservation Union/ United Nations Environment Programme/World Wide Fund For Nature, 1991), p. 77.

18. "Principle 10 of the Report of the United Nations Conference on Environment and Development: Rio Declaration on Environment and Development (12 August 1992), *http://www.un.org/documents/ga/conf151/ aconf15126-1annex1.htm* and Paul Pace, "From Belgrade to Bradford–20 Years of Environmental Education," in *A Sourcebook for Environmental Education: A Practical Review Based on the Belgrade Charter* edited by W. Leal Filho, Z. Murphy, and K. O'Loan (Pearl River, New York: Parthenon, 1996), p. 18.

19. Ibid., p. 19.

20. The Global People's Forum, "Civil Society Declaration," *http://www. worldsummit.org.za/*.

21. Ibid.

22. Ibid.

23. The Global People's Forum, "Programme of Action: A Sustainable World is Possible!, *http://www.worldsummit.org.za/*.

24. Peter Singer, *One World: The Ethics of Globalization* (New Haven: Yale University Press, 2002).

25. Ibid., pp. 1–2.

26. Ibid., p. 168.

27. Ibid., p. 157.

28. Ibid., p. 49.

29. Peter Singer, *Animal Liberation* (New York: HarperCollins, 2002), p. xx.

30. Singer, *Animal Liberation* ..., p. xxiv.
31. For a recent statement on animal rights, see Peter Singer, "Animal Liberation at 30," *The New York Review of Books* (15 May 2003), pp. 23–26.
32. Ibid., p. 5.
33. Ibid., p. 224.
34. Ibid., p. 233.
35. "Frequently Asked Questions," *http://www.peta-online.org/fp/faq.html*.
36. Ibid.
37. For a good summary of Deep Ecology ideas, see Christopher Manes, *Green Rage: Radical Environmentalism and the Unmaking of Civilization* (Boston: Little, Brown & Company, 1990), pp. 139–151.
38. Quoted by Manes, p. 146.
39. Ibid., p. 21.
40. "EF! is Different," *http://www.earthfirstjournal.org/efj/primer/different.html*.
41. "How It All Began," *http://www.earthday.net/about/history.stm*.
42. "Earth Day–Making A Difference," *http://www.earthday.net/about/difference.stm*.
43. Ibid.
44. UNESCO, *Educating for a Sustainable Future: A Transdisciplinary Vision for Concerted Action*, *http://www.unesco.org/education/tlsf/theme_a/mod01/uncom01t05s01.htm*, p. 23.
45. Palmer, p. 15.
46. Caldwell, pp. 242–244.
47. National Council for Science and the Environment, "Education for a Sustainable and Secure Future," *http://www.ncseonline.org/NCSEconference/2003conference/page.cfm?fid=2344*.
48. UNESCO, *Educating for a Sustainable Future* ..., p. 16.
49. "New Ideas in Pollution Regulation," *http://www.worldbank.org/nipr/index.htm*.
50. "The Earth Charter Consultation Process," *The Earth Charter Initiative*, *http://www.earthcharter.org/innerpg.cfm?id_page=108*.
51. "Introduction to the Earth Charter Initiative," *The Earth Charter Initiative*, *http://www.earthcharter.org/innerpg.cfm?id_menu=20*.
52. Moacir Gadotti, "Pedagogy of the Earth and Culture of Sustainability," (Sao Paulo, Brazil: Instituto Paulo Freire, Undated), p. 8.
53. "The Earth Charter," *The Earth Charter Initiative*, *http://www.earthcharter.org/files/charter/charter.pdf*, p. 1.
54. Ibid., p. 1.
55. " Indigenous Peoples' Caucus Statement at the World Summit on Sustainable Development: Johannesburg, South Africa, 4 September 2002," *http://www.tebtebba.org/tebtebba_files/wssd/wssdipsttmnt.html*.
56. Commission on Intellectual Property Rights, "Integrating Intellectual Property Rights and Development," (London: Commission on Intellectual Property Rights, 2002), p. 78.
57. Ibid., p. 78.
58. "Principle 22 of the Report of the United Nations Conference on Environment and Development: Rio Declaration on Environment and Development (12 August 1992)," *http://www.un.org/documents/ga/conf151/aconf15126-1annex1.htm*.

59. Indigenous Peoples International Summit on Sustainable Summit, "World Summit on Sustainable Development," *http://www.nciv.net/spaans/wssd/inheems.htm*.

60. Ibid.

61. Ibid.

62. "The Kimberley Declaration: International Peoples Summit on Sustainable Development, Khoi-San Territory, Kimberley, South Africa, 20–23 August 2002," *http://www.tebtebba.org/tebtebba_files/wssd/ipsummitdec.html*.

63. "Indigenous Peoples' Plan of Implementation on Sustainable Development, Johannesburg, South Africa," *http://www.tebtebba.org/tebtebba_files/wssd/ipsummitimplan.html*, p. 1.

64. Ibid., p. 1.

65. Ibid., p. 3.

66. Steven J. McCormick, "Sustaining Jobs, the Environment and Ourselves," *Nature Conservancy* (Spring 2003), p. 4.

67. Paul Gorman, "Awakenings," Ibid., p. 21.

68. Ibid., p. 22.

69. "Portraits of Faith," Ibid., p. 24.

70. Ibid., p. 26.

71. Ibid., p. 25.

72. I admit that I have found it very difficult to pinpoint the exact doctrines of New Agers. In visits to New Age bookstores, one can find a variety books and objects from Tarot Cards to Native American Dreamcatchers. A common theme appears to be a belief in the spiritual qualities of humans as a source of personal fulfillment. One source of information on New Age spirituality is the Religious Tolerance Web site, *http://www.religioustolerance.org/newage.htm*.

73. Ibid., p. 28.

74. Second World Conservation Strategy Project, *Caring for the Earth* ....

75. Ibid., p. 14.

76. Tove Skutnabb-Kangas, *Linguistic Genocide in Education or Worldwide Diversity and Human Rights* (Mahwah, New Jersey: Lawrence Erlbaum Associates, 2000).

77. *Caring for the Earth* ..., p. 14.

78. Ibid., p. 14.

79. Ibid., p. 14.

80. Ibid., p. 14.

81. Ibid., p. 14.

82. Ibid., p. 15.

83. Ibid., p. 15.

84. *Declaration of Thessaloniki, International Conference Environment and Society: Education and Public Awareness for Sustainability (Thessaloniki, 8-12 December 1997)*, (Paris: UNESCO, 1997), p. 1.

85. Ibid., p. 2.

86. UNESCO, *Educating for a Sustainable Future* ..., pp. 36–41.

87. Ibid., p. 40.

88. Ibid., p. 37.

89.   For a history of the education of consumerists, see Joel Spring, *Educating the Consumer-Citizen: A History of the Marriage of Schools, Advertising, and Media* (Mahwah, New Jersey: Lawrence Erlbaum Associates, 2003).

90.   Second World Conservation Strategy Project, *Caring for the Earth ...*, p. 52.

91.   Ibid., p. 52.

92.   UNESCO, *Educating for a Sustainable Future ...*, p. 34.

93.   Ibid., p. 33.

94.   Ibid., p. 34.

95.   Ibid., p. 34.

96.   Ibid., p. 33.

97.   Michael Hardt and Antonio Negri, *Empire* (Cambridge: Harvard University Press, 2000), p. 213.

98.   Martha Honey, *Ecotourism and Sustainable Development: Who Owns Paradise?* (Washington, DC: Island Press, 1999), p. 8.

99.   Ibid., pp. 3–31.

100.   Allison Humes, "The New World's New Groove," *Condé Nast Traveler* (August 2003), p. 95.

101.   Ibid., p. 129.

102.   "Ecotourism Explorer–Training and Education," *http://www.ecotourism.org/trainfr.html*, p. 3.

103.   "Statement on the United Nations International Year of Ecotourism Adopted by the Boards of Directors and Advisors of The International Ecotourism Society (TIES) January 6, 2001," *http://www.ecotourism.org/statement_on_un.html*.

104.   Ibid., p., 22.

105.   Ibid.

106.   "Québec Declaration on Ecotourism," *http://www.travelmole.com/cgi-bin/item.cgi?id=81853*.

107.   Ibid.

108.   Ibid.

109.   Ibid.

110.   "Frequently Asked Questions," *http://www.mamiraua.org.br/*.

111.   See Honey, pp. 32–55.

112.   Quoted by Honey, p. 35.

CHAPTER 5

1.   A four-part table of the World Wildlife Fund's emerging forms of education is given in William B. Stapp, Arjen E. J. Wals, and Sheri L. Stankorb, *Environmental Education forZ Empowerment: Action Research and Community Problem Solving* (Dubuque, Iowa: Kendall/Hunt Publishing Company, 1996), p. 6. This publication is copyrighted by the Global Rivers Environmental Education Network.

2.   EELink: A Project of the North American Association for Environmental Education, "Perspectives: Foundations of EE," *http://eelink.net/perspectives-foundationsofee.html*.

3.   E-mail from Richard Kahn to Joel Spring (29 July 2003).

4. Moacir Gadotti, "Pedagogy of the Earth and Culture of Sustainability," (Sao Paulo, Brazil: Instituto Paulo Freire, Undated), p. 5.
5. Ibid., p. 5.
6. Ibid., p. 10.
7. Ibid., p. 10.
8. David W. Orr, *Earth in Mind: On Education, Environment, and the Human Prospect* (Washington, DC: Island Press, 1994), p. 26.
9. Ibid., p. 29.
10. C. A. Bowers, *Educating for Eco-Justice and Community* (Athens: University of Georgia Press, 2001), p. 17.
11. C. A. Bowers, "Changing the Dominant Cultural Perspective in Education," in *Ecological Education in Action* edited by Gregory A. Smith and Dilafruz R. Williams (Albany: State University of New York Press, 1999), p. 162.
12. Orr, p. 32.
13. Ibid., 33.
14. Bowers, *Educating for Eco-Justice ...*, p. 13.
15. Ibid., 13.
16. Ibid., pp. 17–18.
17. Ibid., p. 9.
18. Bowers, "Changing the Dominant ...," p. 168.
19. C.A. Bowers, "Educational Implication of an Ecologically Centered View of Creativity," *Educational Theory on the Web: http://www.ed.uiuc.edu/EPS/ Educational-Theory*, p. 5.
20. Ibid., p. 7.
21. Bowers, "Changing the Dominant ...," p. 163.
22. Orr, p. 13.
23. Ibid., p. 13.
24. Ibid., p. 13.
25. Ibid., p. 32.
26. Bowers, *Educating for Eco-Justice ...*, p. 10.
27. Ibid., p. 11.
28. Bowers, "Changing the Dominant ...," p. 161.
29. Stephen Sterling, *Sustainable Education: Re-visioning Learning and Change* (Devon, United Kingdom: Green Books Ltd., 2001).
30. Ibid., p. 8.
31. See "Why Environmental Education: Belgrade Charter,"*http://www. nnrec.org/news/online/whyee.html* and Caldwell, p. 339.
32. Caldwell, p. 339.
33. Ibid., p. 339.
34. See Joy A. Palmer, *Environmental Education in the 21st Century: Theory Practice, Progress and Promise* (London: Routledge, 1998), p. 8.
35. "Why Environmental Education: Tbilisi Report," *http://www.nnrec.org/news/ online/whyee.html*.
36. Caldwell, p. 340.
37. Ibid., p. 340.
38. Ibid., p. 340.
39. Second World Conservation Strategy Project, *Caring for the Earth: A Strategy for Sustainable Living* (Gland, Switzerland: The World Conservation Union/

United Nations Environment Programme/World Wide Fund For Nature, 1991) and "Principle 10 of the Report of the United Nations Conference on Environment and Development: Rio Declaration on Environment and Development (12 August 1992)," *http://www.un.org/documents/ga/conf151/aconf15126-1annex1.htm*.

40. UNESCO, *Educating for a Sustainable Future: A Transdisciplinary Vision for Concerted Action*, *http://www.unesco.org/education/tlsf/theme_a/mod01/uncom01t05s01.htm*, p. 3.
41. Ibid., p. 24.
42. Ibid., p. 27.
43. Ibid., p. 27.
44. Ibid., p. 27.
45. Ibid., p. 27.
46. Ibid., p. 28.
47. Sterling, p. 22.
48. Ibid., p. 52.
49. Ibid., p. 53.
50. Ibid., p. 53.
51. Ibid., p. 56.
52. Ibid., p. 66.
53. Ibid., p. 67.
54. Singer, *Animal Liberation* ..., p. 215.
55. "Direct Action Gets the Goods," *http://ww.earthfirstjournal.org/efj/primer/DA.html*.
56. Edward Abbey, *The Monkeywrench Gang* (New York: Perennial, 2000).
57. "Monkeywrenching: What's up with that?," *http://www.earthfirstjournal.org/efj/primer/Monkeywrench.html*.
58. Dave Foreman and Bill Haywood, *ECODEFENSE: A Field Guide to Monkeywrenching* (Chico, California: Abbzug Press, 1993).
59. Quoted by Manes, p. 167.
60. Ibid., p. 170.
61. Ibid., p. 190.
62. Ingrid E. Newkirk, "Week 4: Veganize Your Cafeteria," (New York: Lantern Books, 2003).
63. Newkirk, "Week 11: Cut Out Dissection."
64. Newkirk, "Week 2: Make a Library Display."
65. Elizabeth Becker, "Animal Rights Group to Sue Fast-Food Chain," *The New York Times* (7 July 2003), p. A11.
66. Ibid.
67. William B. Stapp, Arjen E. J. Wals, and Sheri L Stankorb, *Environmental Education for Empowerment: Action Research and Community Problem Solving* (Dubuque, Iowa: Kendall/Hunt Publishing Company, 1996), p. 5.
68. Ibid., p. 49.
69. Ibid., p. 50.
70. Ibid., p. 31.
71. "A History of WWF," *http://www.panda.org/about_wwf/who_we_are/history*.
72. "CyberDodo," *http://www.panda.org/news_facts/education/virtual_wildlife/cyberdodo/index.cfm*.

73. "Episode 1: DODO Meets the Ant," *http://www.cyberdodo.com.*
74. "Episode 12: DODO and the Moles," Ibid.
75. "Episode 13, DODO's Lost Crop," Ibid.
76. "Episode 14, DODO's Liquid Profits," Ibid.
77. "Why Environmental Education: North American Association for Environmental Education," *http://www.nnrec.org/news/online/whyee.html.*
78. Ibid.
79. "Shop Online," *http://www.worldwildlife.org/default.Cfm?Sectionid= 136&newspaperid=11.*
80. "Earth Day Store," *http://www.earthday.net/store_frame.htm.*
81. "Mrs. Green's Natural Market," *http://www.livingnaturally.com/retailer/store-temlates/ shell_id_1.asp?storeID=7PDT21H24MS92L1E0G03N0ET9VG99J57.*
82. Amy Cortese, "They Care About the World (and They Shop, Too)," *The New York Times* (20 July 2003), Section 3, p. 4.
83. Caldwell, pp. 305–306.
84. "World Parks Congress," *http://www.iucn.org/themes/wcpa/wpc2003/.*
85. "Teacher's Corner," *http://www.parkscanada.gc.ca/edu/index_E.asp.*
86. You can check tour packages at *http://www.rockymountaineer.com/select_a_ vacation/canadian_gold_series/golden_circle.htm.*
87. I copied this statement directly from the guest book in my room at The Fairmont Banff Springs Hotel.
88. Quote given in brochure distributed by Fairmont Hotels and Resorts titled "Green Partnership: Together We Are Making A Difference."
89. Ibid.
90. Ibid.
91. Ibid.
92. "Overview," *http://www.audubonintl.org/aboutus/overview.htm.*
93. Ibid.
94. Quote given in brochure distributed by Fairmont Hotels and Resorts titled "Green Partnership: Together We Are Making A Difference."
95. "Education Services," *http://www.friendsofbanff.com/eduservice.htm.*
96. "Forest Connections: Food Web," *http://www.parkscanada.gc.ca/edu/TRC/ resource_d_e.asp?ID=4.*
97. Eduardo Martins, "Sustainability in Mamirauá: Construction of a New Vision for Humanity" in *Mamirauá* edited by Thiago De Mello (Tefé, Brazil: Sociedade Civil Mamirauá, 2002), p. 23.
98. Mello, *Mamirauá* ... and Matt Bannerman, *Mamirauá: A Guide to the Natural History of the Amazon Flooded Forest* (Tefé, Brazil: Instituto de Desenvolvimento Sustentável Mamirauá, undated).
99. Martins, p. 22.
100. Ibid., p. 23.
101. Bannerman, p. 138.
102. See Bowers, *Educating for Eco-Justice and Community* ....

CHAPTER 6

1. Samuel P. Huntington, *The Clash of Civilizations and the Remaking of World Order* (New York: Simon & Schuster, 1996).

2. United Nations Development Programme, *Human Development Report 2003: Millennium Development Goals: A Compact Among Nations to End Poverty* (New York: Oxford University Press, 2003), p. 2 and Jeff Madrick, "Grim Facts on Global Poverty," *The New York Times on the Web* (7 August 2003).

3. United Nations Development Programme ..., p. 2.

4. Ibid., p. 237.

5. Ibid., p. 240.

6. Ibid., pp. 239–240.

7. Ibid., p. 237.

8. Ibid., p. 240.

9. Ibid., p. 237.

10. Quoted by Pierre Janton in *Esperanto: Language, Literature, and Community* (Albany: State University of New York, 1993), p. 24.

11. Janton has made a timeline of some of these efforts dating from the 19th century on pages 19–21. Earlier efforts are discussed on pages 1–18.

12. Ibid., p. 29.

13. Ibid., p. 29.

14. Ibid., p. 29.

15. Ibid., p. 30.

16. Ibid., p. 33.

17. Ibid., pp. 113–122.

18. For studies on the rise of English as a global language, see Robert Phillipson, *Linguistic Imperialism* (Oxford: Oxford University Press, 1992); David Crystal, *English as a Global Language* (Cambridge: Cambridge University Press, 1997); and Braj B. Kachru, *The Alchemy of English: The Spread, Functions , and Models of Non-Native Englishes* (Urbana: University of Illinois Press, 1990).

19. Huntington, p. 60.

20. Ibid., p. 61.

21. See Kachru on the development and differences in Englishes.

22. Huntington, p. 62.

23. See Phillipson regarding the continuing cultural values embodied in English as a world language.

24. For a discussion of the insularity of Chinese society, see Ibid., pp. 20–57.

25. See Katherine Zoepf, "Princeton Stands in for Beijing: Studies of China adapt to SARS, *The New York Times on the Web* (10 August 2003).

26. Tove Skutnabb-Kangas, *Linguistic Genocide in Education or Worldwide Diversity and Human Rights?* (Mahwah, New Jersey: Lawrence Erlbaum Associates, 2000).

27. Huntington, pp. 65–66.

28. Ibid., pp. 22–23.

29. Ibid., p. 66.

30. Ibid., pp. 84–85.

31. Ibid., pp. 26–27, 84–85.

32. Ibid., p. 85.

33. Project for the New American Century, *http://www.Newamericancentury.org/statementofprinciples.htm*.

34. United States Agency for International Development (USAID), "Press Release April 17, 2003," *USAID Press Office, http://www.usaid.gov*.

35. Huntington, pp. 20–21.

36. Michael Hardt and Antonio Negri, *Empire* (Cambridge: Harvard University Press, 2000), p. 213.

37. *The Sayings of Muhammad* selected and translated from Arabic by Neal Robinson (Hopewell, New Jersey: Ecco Press, 1991), pp. 24–25.

38. James Legge, *Confucius: Confucian Analects, The Great Learning & The Doctrine of the Mean: Chinese; Translation with Exegetical Notes and Dictionary of all Characters* (New York: Dover Publications, Inc., 1971), p. 73.

39. Joel Spring, *The Universal Right to Education: Justification, Definition, and Guidelines* (Mahwah, New Jersey: Lawrence Erlbaum Associates, 2000) and *Globalization and Educational Rights: An Intercivilizational Analysis* (Mahwah, New Jersey: Lawrence Erlbaum Associates, 2001).

40. Spring, *Universal Right to Education* …, pp. 158–159.

41. Ibid., p.159.

42. Spring, *Globalization and Educational Rights* …, p. 162.

43. Spring, *Universal Right to Education* …, pp. 159–160.

Author Index

Subject Index